INDONESIAN MARTIAL ARTS
Pencak Silat Through My Eyes

by
Pendekar Herman Suwanda

P.O. Box 491788, Los Angeles, CA 90049

Disclaimer

Please note that the author and publisher of this book are NOT RESPONSIBLE in any manner whatsoever for any injury that may result from practicing the techniques and/or following the instructions given within. Since the physical activities described herein may be too strenuous in nature for some readers to engage in safely, it is essential that a physician be consulted prior to training.

Published in 2006 by Empire Books.

Copyright © 2003 by Yani Suwanda
Edited by Antonio Somera & Mark V. Wiley

All rights reserved. No part of this publication may be reproduced or utilized in any form or by any means, electronic or mechanical, including photocopying, recording, or by any information storage and retrieval system, without prior written permission from Empire Books.

Library of Congress Number: 2006009383
ISBN-10: 1-933901-03-9
ISBN-13: 978-1-933901-03-9

Library of Congress Cataloging-in-Publication Data

Suwanda, Herman, 1952-
Pentjak silat : through my eyes / by Herman Suwanda. -- 1st ed.
p. cm.
Includes index.
ISBN 1-933901-03-9 (pbk. : alk. paper)
1. Pencak silat. 2. Suwanda, Herman, 1952- I. Title.
GV1114.75.S89 2006
613.6'6--dc22

Empire Books
P.O. Box 49178. Los Angeles, CA 90049
(818) 767-9000

06 05 04 03 02 01 00 99 98 97 1 3 5 7 9 10 8 6 4 2

Printed in the United States of America

Dedication

This book I would like to dedicate to my father. I wish that my father would have able to see how much Pencak Silat Mande Muda has grown in the world and not just in Indonesia. I do believe he is watching me and in the way I have been teaching and spreading our art. I believe that each decision of my life my father has given me his guidance so I can better spread our family teachings. I also acknowledge my teachers and my ancestors of the Sundanese people they have given me the straight to create and teach.

Who would thing that I would be able to spread the art the way I have been doing. Traveling all across the United States and Europe meeting many good people and martial artists. My focus is to make the Indonesian Martial Arts a popular and a well-known art. To teach the art to all of those that are willing to learn, this is what my Father wanted me to do, keep teaching the arts and educate the public about the Indonesian Martial Art along with the rich culture and history.

I remember that when I was 10 years old he would say to me, "Son you will need to master our family art because this is going to be the path to your journey in the future".

He was right. I am so happy that he pushed me to keep learning the art day and night. I am also happy that he had the guidance to send me to many different teachers so I can learn the many different systems of Indonesian Martial Arts. My training with my teachers not only taught me the physical,

mental and spiritual aspects but it gave me the understanding of the ceremonies and rituals of their different villages. I remember walking through the jungle trying to get to the many different villages so I can be in the ceremonies of Pencak Silat.

These old experiences became a guideline for me in the modern world and gave me the knowledge to teach the many styles of Pencak Silat across the United States and Europe. Teaching, explaining demonstrating the techniques so everyone can see that Mande Muda is an effective art that would grow interest around the world. Thank you Bapak, now the time has come for me to show the public about our family culture and the Sundanese martial arts.

I would also like to dedicate this book to my loving wife Shannon Suwanda. You have helped me so much and have motivated me to finish this book. I thank you for being my strength for so many projects supporting me every step of the way and helping me to teach our family art. Thank you Dear Shannon.

Thank you to my beautiful daughter Yani Wulandari Suwanda, for understanding the way of our life style and relationship. Thank you for your understanding that you're Father is never home so we can live like any other normal family. I know sometimes you will not see me for a long period of time, but always remember my love is always with you and I will always be there for you, just close your eyes and think of me

I also dedicate this book to my sisters Betty, Rita, Ike and Ida, to my brothers Hery, Bambang and Diky. Thank you for helping me with our material and putting up with your older brother. You all have been keeping our family together and believing in me to make our Silat family strong and will continue to live in Indonesia and around the world.

Once again I am doing my best for all of my Mande Muda family thank you for making our family art grow around the world and please keep going, spreading the art in a positive way so that everyone will know more about West Java Pencak Silat and about our rich culture of Indonesia.

Thank you,
Herman Suwanda

Acknowledgements

Special thanks of acknowledgements to all of my father's teachers and to all of my teachers. Because your knowledge has taught to me to be a good Pencak Silat man and all of you have helped me to understand how our Pencak should be including your help to influence our Mande Muda making it a library of the Sundanese fighting arts. From the time I started with my father we wanted to make a school as the Mecca of fighting arts from West Java, this is why we are always trying to continue to learn in addition why we have continued to document as many Pendekar's including their styles and systems. I feel it is so very important that we document the way they use their techniques and including the way they move, the place and village they are from. Now the time has come for me to share to the public what the real Pencak Silat that comes from the many different areas. For this reason I give special thanks to you my teachers and my father's teachers.

To all my teachers and to my fathers 11 teachers.

1. Pendekar, Mang Aman, Pencak Silat Galih Pakuan, Style Cikalong, Nampon, Syahbandar, Ujun Ujungan, sampiyong.
2. Pendekar, Bapak Suherman, Pencak Silat Budi Kencana, Style Ckialong, Syahbandar, Cimande, Kari, Madi, Sera, Teteg, Benjang.
3. Pendekar Bah Uplik Style Cimande.
4. Pendekar Mang Miftah, Style Cimande Warungkiara.
5. Pendekar Aki Udep, Styel Cimande Tutugan.
6. Pendekar Ki Ende, Sytle Cimande, Kaum kulon, Sukabumi.
7. Pendekar Ma Onah, Style Cimande Sukabumi.
8. Aki Iyat Ruhiyat.
9. Kang Karma, Ujung Berung, Style 20 Ulin Bedog.
10. Pendekar Bapak H. Kosasih, Tarikkolot, Cimande.
11. Pendekar Bapak Ma'mun, Tarikkolot, Cimande.

Special thank you to my father's teacher, because all of you are Mande Muda.

1. Pendekar Bapak Kardi, Place, Kampung Limbangan, West Java.
2. Pendekar Bapak Uus Sonjaya. Place: Cijagra, Bandung, West Java.
3. Pendekar Bapak Darman, ke Cilentah Bandung, West Java.
4. Pendekar Bapak Haji Soleh. Place: Situ Wangi, Cililin, and West Java.
5. Pendekar Aki Ta'ip di Cikawao. Place: Bandung, West Java
6. Pendekar Bapak Aman, Cihaurgelis, Place: Bandung, West Java.
7. Pendekar Abah Upi. Place: Nyomplong Sukabumi, West Java.
8. Pendekar Ki Udep. Place: Tutugan, West Java.
9. Pendekar Aki Tohir. Place: Pakuan Parung Kuda, Sukabumi.
10. Pendekar ki Ende, Place: Kaum kulon, Sukabumi.

Acknowledgements

11. Pendekar Abah Hasyim, Place: Cibatu, Ujung Kulon, Banten.
12. Pendekar Mang Onin. Place Gunung Batu, Bogor, West Java.
13. Pendekar Uyut Emping, Place: Cimande Tarikkolot, West Java.
14. Pendekar Abah Yaman. Place Cimande Tarikkolot, West Java.
15. Pendekar Mang Sahla, Cimande Tarikkolot.
16. Pendekar Mang Ema, Cimande Tarikkolot.
17. Pendekar Bapak Haji Enur, Cimande Tarikkolot.
18. Pendekar Bapak Hiji Miftah, Cimande Tarikkolot.
19. Pendekar Bapak Haji Kosasih, Cimande Tarikkolot.
20. Pendekar Bapak R Ema Bratakusuma, Bandung.
21. Pendekar Bapak Suherman, Pencak Silat Budi Kencana Pusat.

Everybody in this list is my father's teachers and also my teachers in the 1960's. I am glad to have had the gift of growing up around all of these great people. Even as a child I would watch, learn and practice with these great people that I have wonderful memories of them all. Especially the training with my father and my mother along with all these great teachers this was some of the greatest times of my life.

I just would like to say thank you for all your work in helping to develop me as a Penca person to look and feel what you all wanted me to do has paid off.

Now I can share with all my students around the world the art you have given me. I am just the manager carrying the art to spread and teach what I have learned from all of you and do it the right way.

With tears in my eyes everyone will learn "Through My Eyes" the story of Pencak Silat Mande Muda in this book.

Contents

Foreword by Dan Inosanto viii
Foreword by Antonio Somera ix
Introduction xiv
Costumes, Rituals and Traditions xxi

Part 1: Sejarah, Indonesia (chronology)

Chapter 1: Beginning to 1500 AD
The Old Kingdoms and The Coming of Islam 3
Chapter 2: 1500 AD to 1670 AD
Great Kings and Trade Empires 19
Chapter 3: 1670 AD to 1800
Court Intigues and The Dutch 43
Chapter 4: 1800 AD to 1830 AD
Chaos and Resistance 57
Chapter 5: 1830 AD to 1910 AD
Imperialism and Modernization 69
Chapter 6: 1910 AD to 1940 AD
New Nationalism 87
Chapter 7: 1940 AD to 1945 AD
The Second World War 93
Chapter 8: 1945 AD to 1950 AD
The War for Independence 109

Part 2: Mande Muda History and Teachings

Chapter 9: Brief History of Pencak Silat . . . .
Chapter 10: History of Mande Muda . . . .
Chapter 11: Mande Muda Teachers And Association . . . .
Chapter 12: The Mande Muda Academy . . . .
Chapter 13: The 25 Styles of Mande Muda . . . .

Part 3: Foundations of The Art

Chapter 14: Official Uniform and Salutations . . . .
Chapter 15: Warm Up Exercises . . . .
Chapter 16: Hand Movements and Strikes . . . .
Chapter 17: Foot And Leg Movements and Strikes . . . .
Chapter 18: Body Positions . . . .
Chapter 19: Forms and Training . . . .

Part 4: Interviews with Herman Suwanda
Chapter 20: Harimau Old and New
by Antonio Somera . . . .
Chapter 21: Sabetan The Unexpected Slice
by Antonio Somera . . . .

Part 5: Reflections of a Pendekar
Chapter 22: My Teacher and Friend
by Jim Wimmer . . . .
Chapter 23: What I Remember
by Steve Tarani . . . .

Part 6: Epilogue
Epilogue *by Antonio E. Somera* . . . .

Part 7: Photographs Collages
Glossary of Terms. . . . .

Foreword

Pak Herman Suwanda is one of the most knowledgeable and gifted martial art instructors in the Indonesian martial art of Pencak Silat.

Pencak Silat Mande Muda was the system founded by Pak Herman's father, Uyuh Suwanda. It is a system comprise of 25 styles of Silat. Pak Herman became the head of the family system when his father passed away, and dedicated his life to the promotion and perpetration of this art. With his gift for organization and teaching, he popularized this art throughout the world.

My wife, Paula and I were fortunate to be students of Pak Herman's since the early 1980's. We received our instructorship under him in 1991. I have never met an instructor who was so giving of his massive treasury of knowledge. Yet with all his talent and ability, Pak Herman remained a humble, honest and sincere man. I wish that there were more people like him, not only in the martial arts, but also in the world.

My wife Paula and I shall miss him, not only as our instructor, but also as our dear, dear friend.

This book should shed some insight into this vast system, and his tribute to the man who dedicated his life to preserve and promote Pencak Silat Mande Muda.

Dan Inosanto

Foreword

It is an honor and privilege for me to write this foreword in regards to Pendekar Herman Suwanda and his book "Through My Eye's".

During the early 1980's Pendekar Herman Suwanda made his journey to American from the remote villages and jungles of Indonesia. Just like so many immigrants before him that had a dream to make his life and the life of his family better including the people of his village and country.

His dreams to teach and educate people on his system of Pencak Silat an Indonesian marital art that would eventually become a reality. Only until his arrival to American would the public learn more about Indonesia and its rich martial art culture. Pendekar Herman would open the door to the world about Pencak Silat and be one of the worlds leading authorities on many different systems of Indonesian fighting martial arts. At one time many people did not know of such an art and only a very few new of this fasinating Indonesian art of Pencak Silat.

Pendekar Herman or "Pak" had a long and hard road ahead of him with all the obstacles and barriers placed in his path. But Pak Herman being such an incredible and unique person that he was, he would introduce the world to his family system of Pencak Silat Mande Muda.

This book is an eye opening reality into the personal true to life story of one family system of Pencak Silat. It will give you the historical and basic fundamentals needed to learn more about the person Pak Herman and his family system.

During my private training with Pak Herman and Ibu Shannon, my wife Sally and I were able to share very special and rare times with them. We would travel to their apartment to train or they would come to Stockton and just spend time together with very good friends to share our experiences while we traveled and met so many different people. During the times we would share our experience together we would, laugh, talk, eat, train and laugh again and just have fun just like normal couples that had a mutual love and respect for each other. We all became very close and dear friends, Sally and I often looked forward to each week to visit with Pak and Ibu.

Pak Herman had the true "Eye of the Tiger", but also had the heart of a lion. He was a man that had the ability to talk and communicate with thousands of people with his broken English and the physical ability to wrap you up like a pretzel along the means to manipulate your body into many different compromising positions. For myself he will always remind me of his keen and clever senses of humor that made us all laugh, his loving heart and his ability to be your friend and teacher. He will always serve as a perfect roll model.

My wife Sally and I thank God that we had an opportunity to be a part of Shannon and Pak's life. Our memories will live on, as so will his art of Pencak Silat Mande Muda through the eyes of all his students and friends.

This book is a tribute to Pak Herman and his family system of Pencak Silat Mande Muda and should be a part of any martial artist's liberty including those that would like to learn more about the intriguing and mystical art of Pencak Silat Mande Muda.

To borrow a quote from my dear friend Paul Marrero,

"To know Pencak Silat Mande Muda is to know Pak Herman".

God has blessed us all that have known Pak Herman and Ibu Shannon and for those that will only know Pak and Ibu Shannon "Through Our Eye's".

Antonio E. Somera

Introduction

The questions have come from many of my friends in Indonesia and my students all over the world, asking me when am I going to write a book about Pencak Silat. Well it is not that easy. It has taken me a long time to write this book because of all my traveling and training. But now it is done, I hope that this book will educate more people who love and continue to practice Pencak Silat all over the world. I am hoping after you read this book you will understand more about Pencak Silat and about the culture and history of Sunda, West Java. The way we thing is to see things and understand things about our own ethnic group. As this person who was born and grew up in Sunda we had to go through many different ceremonies and rituals. We would listen to the stories from our parents and grandparents and many other older people. Many of the children in Sunda would follow the rule of the family, society and the rule of the government. Of course being a 2nd generation after World War II

we were the country that was trying to rebuild including our government. We had to figure out how to take care of our own people after the Dutch and Japanese had left our country.

1. West Java. Jawa Barat
2. Center Java (Jawa Tengah)
3. East Java (Jawa Timur)

In West Java we speak Sundanese and in Center Java along with East Java they speak Javanese. The language is totally disappearing; we don't understand our own people. But the good thing is that we have Bahasa Indonesian as our national language so we can communicate.

I am only writing about what I know really well, the way I see it, the way I think of the pasted and the way of the future of Pencak Silat that comes from my own people. That is why the title of this book is: Pencak Silat Through My Eyes.

I don't put extra and I don't take away from it. It is as it is.

After you read this book I hope you will understand the Indonesian art of Pencak Silat and when you come to my school in Indonesia we will visit many other schools and travel to many different places so you will be able to experience the culture of my people. We will have so much fun, I will personally take you on many different field trips and visit West Java, don't worry you will not get lost and the people will not get upset with you because you are from another land.

The culture of my people is disappearing, the language we speak the language of our body is also going away. Everyone's terminology in Pencak Silat is taken from the language structure of Indonesia and also in my case we will be talking from the Sundanese language and terminology

I believe that being around many of my father's instructors and also being with many of

Introduction

my instructors who would also include many of my friends many of the people that are old and young I feel we have very good relationships. These relationships are very good for the growth of Pencak Silat all over West Java. I see the way they are doing things and I see the way the many different way the many different teachers structure there silat. This will help us all to structure and use the same terminology in order to make all groups better to understand one another. I have visited the many teachers and sat with them for hours learning and discussing the way of their terms of life. Now that I am older I am so happy that my father made me travel and study Pencak Silat because it has taught me so much of our culture. Because of this I have made so many friends in which it has made it easy to train along with opening many doors for me to visit the many different pendekars that they have excepted me as there student or son and friend

Now I am so glad that my friends and students have pushed me to learn more about the Indonesian martial arts. I am so very happy that my wife has always listened to me and has been very helpful along with supportive of our many different projects. Shannon has given me the energy to create and finish this book; she has given me the love and power that has given me the faith in believing I can complete this book. My dream would be to continue and to "keep going" the education of Indonesian martial arts to all that are willing to share in this rich cultural art.

Who will know the future and what it will bring to us. But we must remain strong and focused on the positive way of life. It may become what we want and dream but also become come what we are not looking for, something we will not want or desirer.

When I was young and growing up in Indonesia I would have never dreamed of leaving or going to other countries. I was a pencak silat person that was growing up with many problems, many bad situations, I had to grow up as a martial artist in Indonesia with no life no future.

But look at me now traveling the world spreading the art the way my father wanted me to and the way my people wanted. I had promised to my father and to all of my teachers that I would keep spreading the art in the right way so when other people would go to Indonesia they would see and understand what I have been teaching. The way I teach to the public in general is the way we teach and train in Indonesia, this way it will not confuse the any of the students.

As the eldest son of a pencak silat family I need to take the responsibility to share in what my culture and family has taught me. As the eldest son my family has believed that I need to teach the best pencak silat to all of those that would like to learn. It has been so hard being the oldest son, my family has sacrifice so much to teach and guide me to become the person I am today.

Our family was so poor that many times when I was growing up there would be no food to eat for many days. We would all cry because we were so hungry. I could remember the faces of my brothers and sisters looking at me and asking me "why don't we have anything to eat"? I could not answer them

I was too young to understand. It was like a knife that was going through my heart and I can remember the warm tear in my eyes. One day we were so hungry that I left the house trying to find food. So I started to walk, I did not know what direction I was going I just started to walk. As I continued to walk it started to rain. For a moment the hunger would go away but soon would return.

You should have seen me back then I was so skinny. I wasn't even trying to loose weight. There was just not enough food. Life is funny... now I have money so I can buy food. I need to watch what I eat now because I can get really fat really easy, oh my God I need to lose weight. Maybe this is why I try to help as many people as I can back home in Indonesia. I try to feed as many people as I can, send as many children to school so they can get a good education. When I don't have money I need food and when I have money I am trying to not eat too much food. Oh well I guess that's life.

This book as a pencak silat teacher I am traveling from Indonesia to America and Europe trying to spread the art of

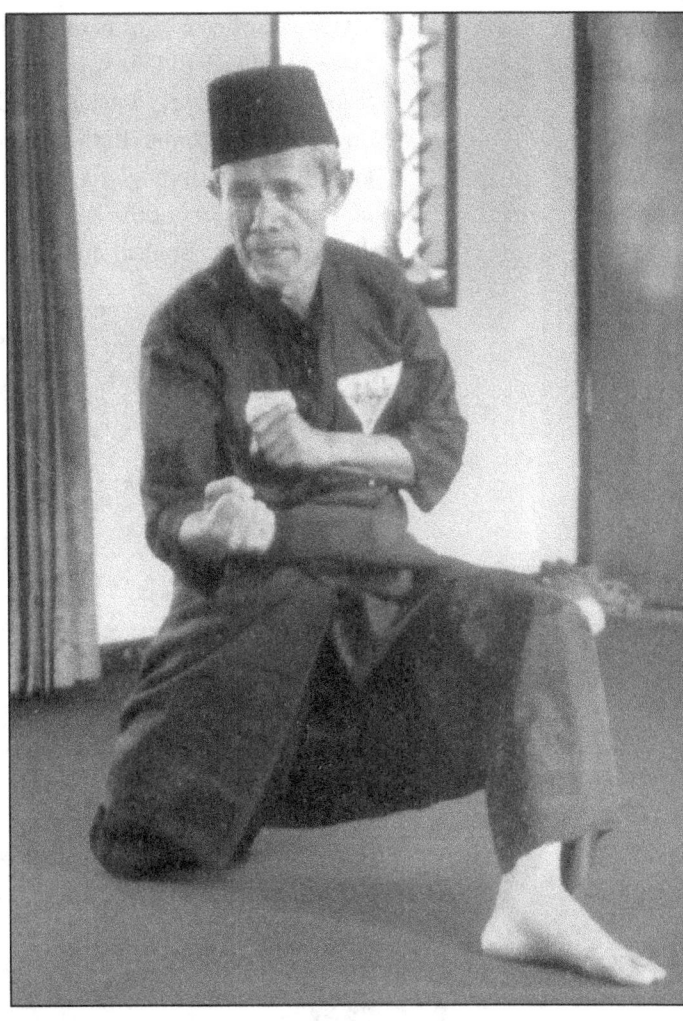

pencak silat and to educate the public on what I know. When I came to America in the early 1980's I first struggled not knowing the language not knowing the culture of America and especially not knowing what the western people would like to see and learn from a teacher like me.

As a pencak silat teacher there was no way I could make a living there was no way to help support my family in Indonesia.

I think that you should know how hard it was for my family and I and to learn of my background. This is so you will not think that I was a big success in America and that I was a over night success as a teacher of silat that was staying in America, eating the right food and traveling around the world spreading pencak silat, Good life eeeh?

I just want to say thank you God for you have given me the tools to support my family and myself and to help so many others with food and education.

Anyway when I got here to America I was so excited, this is the time and place to spread the art and what I am good at, wrong!!! It's not that easy teaching martial arts outside of Indonesia. It is so hard dealing with the people on how to expect you. I am the person whose life comes from a poor family. I know what the ringing of a telephone, dealing with America toilet and tissue, no to mention about the law and rules I know nothing about. On top of that I don't know any English and how to communicate to run and teach a class.

Introduction

Believe it or not the only word I know was " I Love You". I said to myself, God please help me to face living in America and help me to continue to teach pencak silat even only if I had a few students, I don't know anything else. I just needed to stay a little longer so I can learn the language and understand the American culture.

You know back then people did not even know what pencak silat really is? Many of them did not even know there was a place called Indonesia. Oh my! Still there was a long way in my journey to complete. Will I make it or will I end up back in Indonesia dealing with my pasted life of being poor with no future and no food and no respect from my people.

I can remember back home in Indonesia during the 60s and 70s, I was so embarrassed as a silat person it was like living on the dark side of society and feeling like being a criminal. This was because if you were around pencak silat weather you were a student or teacher of the martial arts everyone would think that you would end up in jail or dead. I can remember that when our family would visit other families in Indonesia they would ask my father, what does your son do for a living? He would say, he teaches pencak silat; this would cause them to look down at my family or me. I would have a difficult time trying to get along with other people.

But now it is not like that anymore. I feel that I have done a respectful job in teaching the art of our forefathers. I know that the people of Bandung West Java are happy for my family and me. This is because we are doing something good for our village. We are helping to build a better future for our families by educating the world about pencak silat. I truly hope that you will enjoy this book. It is not a complete review of how all pencak silat systems are in Indonesia but a short and small look at how our family trains in pencak silat "Through My Eyes". Thanks silat.

Pendekar Herman Suwanda

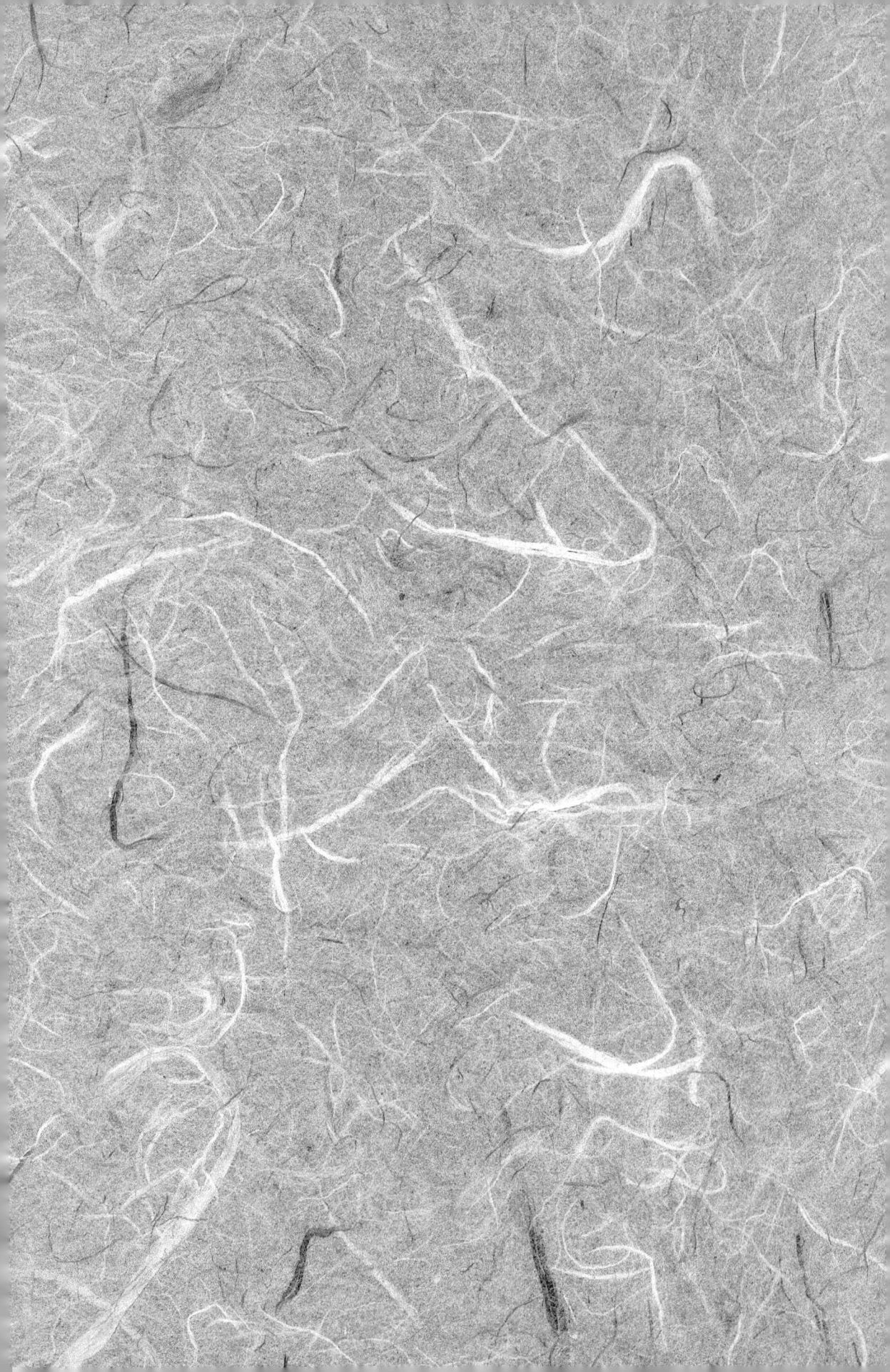

Costumes

Rituals

and

Traditions

Sundanese Traditional Dress Costume

This is the traditional dress costume of the people of from Sunda West Java. This type of dress ware is found in almost anywhere in Indonesia, only a few things that may be different from one ethic group to another. Some areas are more fancy that others and some are more colorful even more may have more gold woven into or on the material.

In Sunda this type of dress ware can be for formal occasions such as weddings.

Costumes Rituals and Traditions

Kebaya

The traditional dress ware is a modern Kebaya. The style of the kebaya is very powerful. In order enhance the look more gold can be worn and will include the traditional hairstyle of these young woman.

Ramayana

Hindu influence and Buddhist Muslim along with the local culture will mix and become what Indonesia is today. This is a costume from the episode of Ramayana in the story of Hindu. Until today you still can see the performance of the classical dance in Indonesia and gamelan used to as the background music. The performance of Wayang kulit (Shadow Puppet) and Wayang golek play all night long telling the story about Ramayana & Mahabrata. This kind of performance is still around spreading the history and culture in order for us to understand the background of our country.

Wayang Golek Puppets

This is the Wayang Golek puppet that comes from West Java. The story and character is the same as Wayang Kulit (Shadow puppets). Playing all night long many people in the village really look forward to this kind of performance, so exciding and fun to watch it is also nice to listen to the message the puppets will bring. This is the Gatotkaca, the hero from Mahabarta.

Ceremonies and Rituals

Ceremonies and rituals are a big part of Indonesian culture and history. These types of ceremonies and rituals also distinguish or identify them from the many different ethnic groups in Indonesia.

Costumes Rituals and Traditions

Innocences of many of the different ethnic groups still are alive and well in many parts of Indonesia.

Shannon Suwanda (Fig. 8)

Rita and Ika Suwanda

Herlan Herlambang Suwanda

Costumes Rituals and Traditions

Pendekar Guru Besar Bapak Uyuh Suwanda

Ibu Mimi Suwanda

Padepokan

Pendekar Guru Besar Herman Suwanda

Pencak Silat Mande Muda International

Pencak Silat Association

PPSI

Ikatan Pencak Silat Indonesia IPSI

Persekutuan Pencak Silat Antarabangsa International Pencak Silat Federation

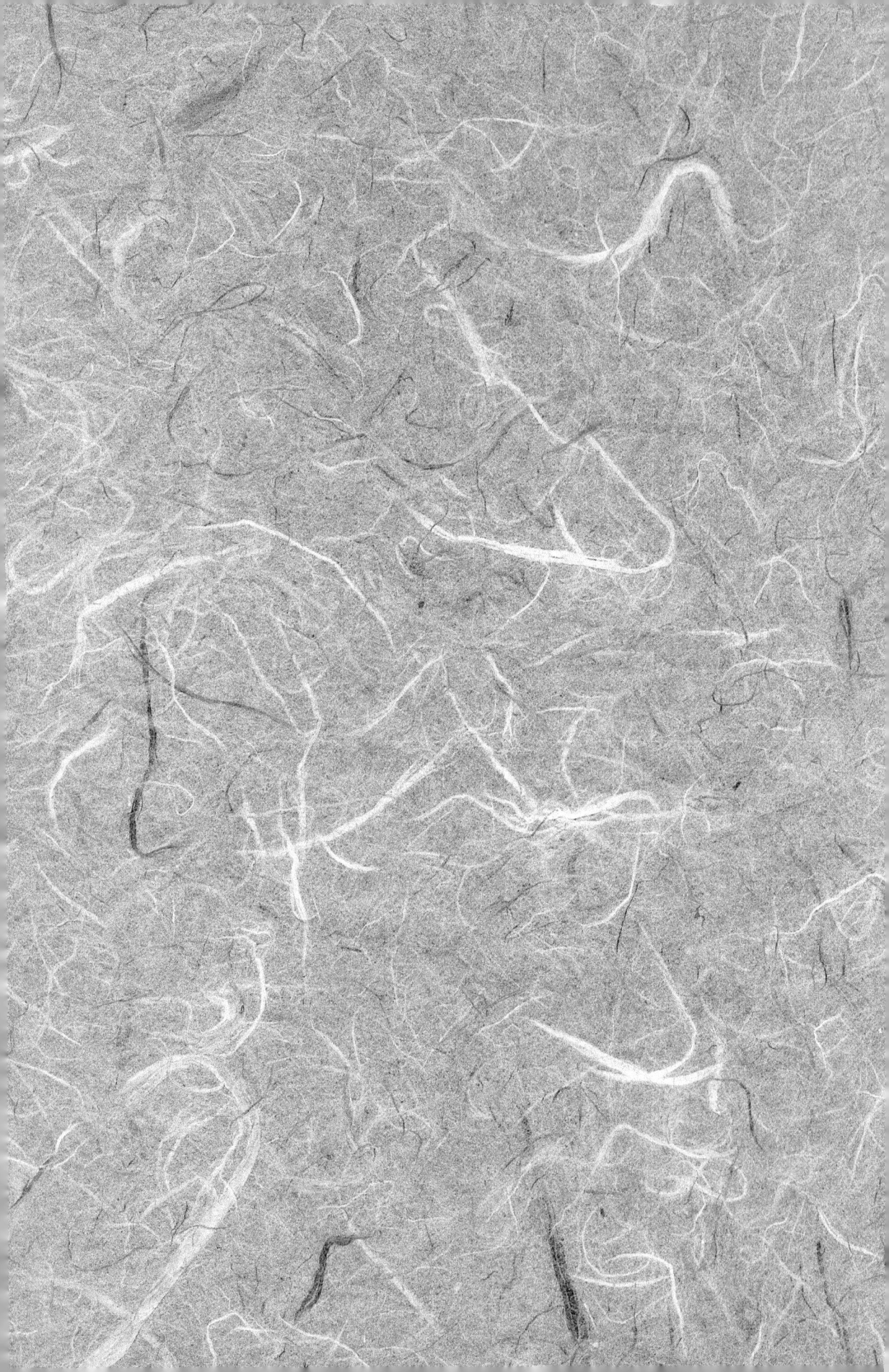

Part I
Sejarah, Indonesia
(chronology)

2

Chapter 1:

Beginning to 1500

The Old Kingdoms and the Coming of Islam

About 100	"Dvipantara" or "Jawa Dwipa" is reported by Indian scholars to be in Java and Sumatra
	Prince Aji Saka introduces writing system to Java based on scripts of southern India
	Mulavarman Kingdom rules from Kutai on Kalimantan
	"Langgasuka" Kingdom founded around Kedah in Malaya.
About 400	Taruma Kingdom flourishes in West Java
About 425	Buddhism reaches Sumatra. (Fig. 1)

Hinduism, one of Indonesia's five religions.

Early civilization in Java and Sumatra was heavily influenced by India. Today's cultures in Indonesia, and even the language,

still show influences from the Sanskrit language and literature.

(The first thousand years or so of this timeline are not well documented. Dates are approximate.)

In these early days, many new plants were introduced into Indonesia, including pepper and teak.

The Srivijaya and Sailendra kings were Buddhist, but later they would be replaced by Hindu kings again.

Today, both Hinduism and Buddhism are officially recognized in Indonesia.

About 500	Beginning of Srivijaya Kingdom near Palembang, Sumatra
About 600	Settlers from India arrive in the area of Prambanan in Central Java
About 650	Taruma Kingdom in West Java is taken by Srivijaya
About 670	Chinese traveler I Ching visits Palembang, the capital of Srivijaya
	Hindu temples are built in the high Dieng plateau of Central Java
686	Srivijaya sends expedition again Kingdom in Java
About 770	Sailendra King Vishnu begins building Borobudur
	Beginning of building activity on the plan of Prambanan
About 790	Sailendra Kingdom attacks and defeats Chenla (today Cambodia); rules over Chenla for about 12 years
About 825	Sailendra King Samaratunga, grandson of Vishnu, finishes Borobudur (Fig. 2)
	By now, Srivijaya had also conquered Kedah, on the Malay peninsula

Buddhism, one of Indonesia's five religions

The Sailendra king remembered that their ancestors came from what is now Thailand or Cambodia. (Fig. 3)

Sailendra King Samaratunga, grandson of Vishnu, finishes Borobudur.

About 835 Patapan of Sanjaya takes Sailendra's throne; replaces Buddhism on Java with Hinduism.

King Balitung rules in central Java.

About 850 Balaputra, claimant to Sailendra's throne, takes power in Srivijaya.

New Sanjaya King Daksa in central Java begins building Hindu temples at Prambanan. (Fig. 4)

Borobudur Borobudur is a huge Buddhist monument covering

a volcanic hill a few miles between present day Magelang and Yogyakarta. It is in level representing the stages to enlightenment. The large central stupa is empty. The many beautiful relief sculptures may have been used to educate young monks.

By this time, the Buddhist culture had spread as far east as Lombok.

929	Sanjaya King Mpu Sindok moves court from Mataram to East Java (near Jombang).

	Sri Isana Tunggawijaya, daughter of Mpu Sindok, succeeds Mpu Sindok as ruler in East Java.
About 975	King Udayana of Bali, father of Airlangga, is born.
990	Srivijaya is attacked by Mataram.
1006	Srivijaya attacks and destroys Mataram capital.
1017	Rajendra Chola, king of Coromandel in India, attacks Srivijaya.
1019	Airlangga takes rule in eastern Java, founds Kahuripan Kingdom, makes peace with Srivijaya, and protects both Hindus and Buddhists. He extends his rule over central Java, eastern Java, and Bali.
1025	Rajendra Chola of southern India takes Malay peninsula from Srivijaya for twenty years.

A major eruption of Mount Merapi in 928 or 929 may have been the reason that the king of Mataram and many of his subjects moved east.

Airlangga is remembered in today's Indonesia as a model of religious tolerance.

Around this time, Tumasik was a small kingdom on the site of today's Singapore. It may have been influenced by the newcomers from southern India.

Also around this time, the Panai kingdom was flourishing in the Batak area of northern Sumatra.

1045	Airlangga divides Kahuripan into two kingdoms, Janggala (around today's Surabaya) and Kediri, for his two sons.
1068	Vira Rajendra, king of Coromandel, conquers Kedah from Srivijaya.
1135	King Joyoboyo takes rule in Kediri until 1157.
1122	Ken Angrok, local ruler of Tumapel, takes both Janggala and Kediri; founds Singhasari kingdom.

Joyoboyo is remembered for a prophecy that Indonesia would be ruled by a white race for a long time, then a yellow race for a short time, then be independent.

Putri Dedes was the wife of Ken Angrok. She was the daughter of a Buddhist priest who was stolen away by the governor of Tumapel on Java. Ken Angrok himself stole Putri Dedes away from her first husband to be his wife, but she was already pregnant, and her son (later King Anusapati) was actually the son of the governor, Tunggul Ametung. Eventually, Ken Angrok conspired to have Tunggul Ametung killed so that he could become ruler of Tumapel.

Tumapel paid tribute to Kediri until Ken Angrok became powerful enough to conquer Kediri for himself in 1222. The last ruler of Kediri, Kertajaya, was considered cruel and overbearing.

Putri Dedes was long remembered as the mother of the royal line of Singhasari, and later Majapahit, Mataram, Yogya and Solo.

1227	Ken Angrok dies and is succeeded by Anusapati.
1247	Anusapati dies after a peaceful 20-year reign. Tohjaya, son of Ken Angrok by a concubine, becomes king of Singhasari.

1250	Tohjaya is killed in a rebellion and replaced as King Wisnuwardhana, son of Anusapati.
1268	King Wisnuwardhana of Singhasari dies and is succeeded by Kertanegara. Kertanegara promotes a mixture of Hinduism and Buddhism.
1275	Kertanegara conquers Jambi.
1281	Muslims from Jambi send embassy to Kublai Khan.
1284	Kertanegara takes Bali for Singhasari. By now, Jambi was an independent kingdom on Sumatra. Tradition says that the kings of Singhasari during this period were all murdered by their successors, as part of the feud arising from Ken Angrok stealing away Putri Dedes. (Fig. 5)
1289	Kublai Khan sends messengers to Singhasari to demand tribute; Kertanegara slashes their faces and sends them home.
1290	Kertanegara conquers Srivijaya.
1292	Marco Polo visits Sumatra and Java. Kublai Khan prepares invasion fleet of 1000 ships to take Java. Kertanegara killed in court rebellion; son-in-law Vijaya retreats and founds new court at Majapahit (today Trowulan), with the help of Arya Wiraraja, local ruler of Madura. Bali breaks away from Singhasari under Pejeng king at Ubud.
November	Mongol fleet leaves for Java; lands at Tuban.
1293	Vijaya forms alliance with Mongol forces against remainder of Singhasari in Kediri, led by Jayakatwang.
March	Combined force of Mongol/ Chinese soldiers and Majapahit takes Kediri. Majapahit was one of the few countries of that time to defeat a Mongol invasion, along with Japan and Egypt. However, the Mongol fleet was hit by a typhoon along the way and was refused permission to land in Champa (today's Vietnam) to take on supplies. By the time the fleet reached Tuban, the army was sickened and weak.

	Vijaya returned to Trowulan, then attacks. Mongols retreat and leave Java.
November	Vijaya is enthroned as king Kertanegara Jayawardhana of new Majapahit.
1295	Pasai in Sumatra converts to Islam.

Beginning to 1500: The Old Kingdoms and the Coming of Islam

1309	Jayanegara becomes King of Majapahit.
1328	Jayanegara is assassinated, possibly with the help of Gajah Mada. Tribhuwana Wijayatungga Dewi, daughter of Vijaya, is titular head until 1350.
1331	Gajah Madah becomes patih, or chief minister of Majapahit; rules as regent.
1333	Kingdom of Pajajaran is founded as a tributary of Majapahit, with a capital near today's Bogor.
1334	Hayam Wuruk is born to Tribhuwana Wijayatungga Dewi, heir to line of Majapahit.
1343	Force under Gajah Madah defeats the Pejeng King of Bali, Daiem Bedaulu, and takes Bali for Majapahit.
	Vijaya married all four daughters of the former King Kertanegara.
	With Gajah Madah as chief minister, the kingdom of Majapahit gained control or collected tribute from most of what is now Indonesia. He is remembered for the "Palapa Oath," saying that he would refuse to eat spices in his food (palapa) until all the islands around were united under one rule. Today in Yogyakarta, the university is named for him.
1344	Arab traveler and writer Ibn Battuta visits Pasai on Sumatra.
1347	Adityavarman, king of Melayu (Malaya), rules Minangkabau for Majapahit.
1350	Rajasanegara becomes King of Majapahit.
	Majapahit conquers Islamic kingdom of Pasai on Sumatra.
1364	Gajah Madah passes away.
	Hayam Wuruk becomes King of Majapahit.
	Majapahit sends navy again to Palembang.
1389	Hayam Wuruk passes away, beginning of decline of Majapahit.
1400	Aceh converts to Islam.

1401	War of succession begins in Majapahit, lasting four years. The power of Majapahit begins to lessen.
1402	Melaka founded by Parameshwara, rebel prince of Palembang.
1404	Parameshwara sends an embassy to Beijing; receives promise of protection from China.
	About this time, Majapahit held influence over Jambi as well. (Fig. 6)
	About this time, the kings of Gelgel began to rule as "Dewa agung", or chief king, in Bali.
1405	Chinese Admiral Cheng Ho visits Semarang.
1409	Cheng Ho visits Melaka.
1411	Parameshwara visits Beijing on a state visit.
1414	Parameshwara converts to Islam, takes name Iskandar Syah. Melaka is now an Islamic Sultanate.
1427	Queen Suhita inherits the Majapahit kingdom from Wkramawardhana.
1445	Hindu revolt in Melaka again Islam is suppressed. Thai attack on Melaka is driven back.
1447	Kertawijaya, brother of Suhita, becomes King of Majapahit. He converts to Islam on the advice of his wife, Darawati, a princess of Champa (in what is now Vietnam).
	Sunan Ampel, nephew of Kertawijaya, works to spread Islam around Surabaya.
	Islam, one of Indonesia's five religions.
	The Islamic religion had been common among traders in Sumatra and Java for some time. The Singhasari and Majapahit kingdoms probably had a few Muslims involved in their courts. Large-scale conversions to Islam began when local kings adopted the new religion. Aceh and Melaka were among the first. Most of Java did not become Muslim until the early 1500s.
	(Today, over 85% of Indonesians are Muslim.)

Beginning to 1500: The Old Kingdoms and the Coming of Islam

Sunan Ampel was the first notable member of the Nine Walis or Walisongo, an Islamic teacher who worked to spread Islam around Java in the late 1400s and early 1500s.

1451	King Kertawijaya is murdered and replaced by Rajasawardhana, who hinders the spread of Islam in Majapahit.

1456	Thai attack on Melaka by sea is driven back.
	Bhre Wengker becomes king of Majapahit after three years of chaos.
1459	Raja Abdulla of Melaka conquers Kedah and Pahang from the Thais.
1466	Suraprabhawa becomes king of Majapahit.
1468	Court rebellion in Majapahit: Bhre Kertabhumi drives Suraprabhawa out of his court at Tumapel. Suraprabhawa moves his seat to Daha, near Kediri.
1475	Ternate and Tidore convert to Islam.
1478	Daha region under Girindrawardhana, a great grandson of Kertawijaya, revolts. Majapahit kingdom falls into chaos. Bhre Kertabhumi, King of Majapahit at Tumapel, flees to Demak. Girindrawardhana sets himself up as ruler of Majapahit.
	Islamic kingdom of Demak founded by Raden Patah (or Fattah), a prince of Majapahit (son of King Kertawijaya by a Chinese wife). Masjid founded at Demak.

Around this time, Palembang converted to Islam.

Around this time, many Hindus from Majapahit left Java for Bali.

By the 1490s, the Portuguese had sailed around the southern tip of Africa and had landed in India.

Islamic Sultanate founded at Cirebon, formerly a possession of the Pajajaran King Siliwangi.

1486 Zainal Abidin becomes Sultan of Ternate (until 1500).

Court of Majapahit moves to Kediri. (Fig. 7)

Chapter 2:

1500 to 1670

Great Kings and Trade Empires

1500	Palembang converts to Islam.
1505	Trenggono, grandson of Raden Patah, becomes prince of Demak.
1509	Portuguese visits Melaka for the first time.
	Local power on Java around 1500 included:
	Demak. The chief power on Java in the early 1500s. Nearby Jepara participated in many naval expeditions.
	Surabaya. Some powers that later came under include Gresik, home of Sunan Giri and Pasuruan.
	Banten. A Hindu power under Pajajaran until the arrival of Sunan Gunungjati.
	The goal of the Portuguese was to take control of trade. Later trade empires would include Gowa, Banten, and the Dutch VOC or East India Company. The original goal of all of them was money before political power, but they did not always stick to their original goal. (Fig. 1)
1511 April	Portuguese Admiral Albuquerque sets sail from Goa to Melaka.
December	Albuquerque sends three ships under da Breu from Melaka to explore eastward.
1512	Da Breu expedition travels to Madura, Bali, Lombok, Aru and Banda. Two ships wrecked at Banda; da Breu returns to Melaka; Francisco Serrao repairs ship and continues to Ambon, Ternate and Tidore. Serrao offers support to Ternate in a dispute with Tidore - his men build a Portuguese post at Ternate.

1513	A force from Jepara and Palembang attacks the Portuguese in Melaka, but is repulsed.
	Portuguese send an envoy to King of Pajajaran. Portuguese are allowed to build a fort a Sunda Kelapa (now Jakarta).
	Portuguese make contact with King Udara, son of Girindrawardhana and ruler over the remnant of Majapahit.
	Udara attacks Demak with the help of the King of Klungkung on Bali. Majapahit forces are driven back, but Sunan Ngudung falls into battle. Many more supporters of Majapahit flee to Bali.
1514	Ali Mughayat Syah is the first Sultan of Aceh.
1515	First Portuguese visit Timor.
	Serrao writes to Magellan (who formerly served under Albuquerque, but pledged allegiance to Spain after being refused a promotion) telling Magellan about the riches of the Indies.

Power on Sumatra included:

Aceh, the first major Islamic power in what is now Indonesia.

Palembang, where sultans still ruled long after the fall of Srivijaya.

On Bali, the King of Gelgel (near today's Klungkung) was the most powerful king in the 1500s.

1518	Sultan Mahmud of Melaka takes power at Johore.
	Raden Patah passes away; Yunus becomes Sultan of Demak.
1520	Aceh begins taking northeast cost of Sumatra.
	Balinese attack on Lombok.
1521	Yunus leads fleet from Demak and Cirebon against the Portuguese in Melaka. Yunus is killed in battle. Trenggono becomes Sultan of Demak.
	Portuguese take Pasai in Sumatra; Gunungjati leaves Pasai for Mecca.
	Last ship of Magellan expedition around the world sails between Lembata and Pantar islands in Nusa Tenggara.
1522	Banten, still Hindu, asks for Portuguese help against Muslim Demak.
	Survivors of Magellan's expedition around the world visit Timor.
	Portuguese build fort at Hitu on Ambon
1523	Gunungjati returns from Mecca, settles at Demak and marries sister of Sultan Trenggono.
1524	Gunungjati and son Hasanudin do both covert and overt missionary work in West Java to weaken the kingdom of Pajajaran and it's alliance with the Portuguese. Local ruler of Banten, formerly dependent on Pajajaran, converts to Islam and joins Demak's side.
1526	Portuguese build first fort on Timor.
1527	Demak conquers Kediri, Hindu remnant of Majapahit state; Sultans of Demak claim to be successors to Majapahit claims;

Sunan Kudus take part.

Demak takes Tuban.

Demak takes Sunda Kelapa; renames it Jayakarta (credit is given to a "Fatahillah" or after the Portuguese mispronunciation, "Falatehan" - but this might be a name given to Sunan Gunungjati). Pajajaran Kingdom is pushed away from the sea.

Kingdom of Palakaran on Madura, based at Arosbaya (now Bangkalan), converts to Islam under Kyai Pratanu.

Expeditions from Spain and Mexico try to drive the Portuguese from Malaku.

1529 Demak conquers Madium.

Kings of Spain and Portugal agree that Malaku should belong to Portugal, and the Philippines should belong to Spain.

1530 Salahuddin is Sultan of Aceh.

Surabaya and Pasuruan submit to Demak. Demak takes Balambangan, the last Hindu state in easternmost Java.

The Sultanate of Johore was attacked by the Portuguese all through the 1520s.

Sultan Trenggono is remembered as a ruler who did much to spread Islam throughout East and Central Java.

Only 18 men survived Magellan's expedition, but they returned to Spain with about a ton of cloves, enough to make them wealthy for life. (Fig. 2)

About this time, much of Java began to convert to Islam, including Banten, Mataram and Central Java, and Surabaya.

Gowa begins expanding from Makassar.

New Sultanate found in Riau.

1536 Major Portuguese attack on Johore.

Antonio da Galvao becomes governor of Portuguese post at Ternate; founds Portuguese post at Ambon.

1537 Acehnese attack on Melaka fails. Salahuddin of Aceh is replaced by Alaudin Riayat Syah I.

1539	Aceh attacks the Bataks to their south.
1540	Portuguese in contact with Gowa.
1545	Demak conquers Malang.
	Gowa builds fort at Ujung Pandang.
1546	Trenggono of Demak dies and is succeeded by Prawata. His son-in-law, Joko Tingkir, expands power from Pajang (near present Sukoharjo).
	St. Francis Xavier travels to Morotai, Ambon, and Ternate.
	Catholicism (Katolik) is one of Indonesia's five religions.
	Around this time, Portuguese missionaries began to spread the catholic religion in Indonesia, especially in the east. Today, Catholicism is one of Indonesia's recognized religions.
1547	Aceh attacks Melaka.

1550	Portuguese begin building forts on Flores.
1551	Johore attacks Portuguese Melaka with help from Jepara.
	Force from Ternate takes control of Sultanate of Jailolo on Halmahera with Portuguese help.
1552	Hasanuddin breaks away from Demak and founds Sultanate of Banten, then takes Lambung for the new Sultanate.
	Aceh sends embassy to the Ottoman Sultan in Istanbul.
1558	Leiliato leads a force from Ternate to attack the Portuguese at Hitu.
	Ki Ageng Pemanahan receives Mataram district from Joko Tinggir, ruling at Pajang.
1559	Portuguese missionaries land at Timor.
	Khairun becomes Sultan of Ternate.
1561	Sultan Prawata of Demak passes away.
1565	Aceh sacks Johore.
	Sultan Khairun was friendly to St. Francis Xavier, and known to be a reasonable man, but the Portuguese threw him in prison and tried to poison him when he would not yield lands to them.
1568	Unsuccessful attack by Aceh on Portuguese Melaka.
1570	Aceh attacks Johore again, but fails.
	Portuguese murder Sultan Khairun of Ternate. Babullah becomes Sultan (until 1583).
	Maulana Yusup becomes Sultan of Banten.
1571	Alaudin Riayet Shah dies; disorder in Aceh until 1607.
1574	Japara leads unsuccessful attack on Melaka.
1575	Sultan Babullah expels Portuguese from Ternate. Portuguese build fort on Tidore instead.
	Portuguese build fort at the present site of the city of Ambon.

1577	Ki Ageng Pemanahan founds Kota Gede (near today's Yogya).
1579	Banten takes the remaining part of Pajajaran; converts it to Islam.
	November - Sir Francis Drake of England, after raiding Spanish ships and ports in America, arrives at Ternate. Sultan Babullah, who also hated the Spanish, pledges friendship to England.
1580	Maulana Muhammad becomes Sultan of Banten.
	Portugal falls under Spanish crown; Portuguese colonial enterprises are disregarded.
	Drake visits Sulawesi and Java on the way back to England.
1581	About this time, Ki Ageng Pemanahan takes over Mataram district (had been promised to him by Joko Tingkir, who delayed until Sunan Kalijaga of the Nine Walis pressed him), changes name to Ki Gedhe Mataram.
1584	Sutawijaya succeeds his father, Ki Gedhe Mataram, as local ruler of Mataram, ruling from Kota Gede.
1585	Sultan of Aceh sends letter to Elizabeth I of England.
1587	Sutawijaya defeats Pajang and Joko Tingkir dies; lineage passes to Sutawijaya. Mount Merapi erupts.
	Portuguese attack Johore.
	Sir Thomas Cavendish of England visits Java.
1588	Sutawijaya changes name to Senopati; takes Pajang and Demal.
	From Senopati one can easily trace the lineage of today's Sultan of Yogya and Susuhunan of Surakarta. Traditionally, the line is traced back all the way to the kings of the Majapahit.
1590	Original village of Medan founded.
1591	Senopati takes Madiun, then Kediri.
	Sir James Lancaster of England reaches Aceh and Penang, but his mission is a failure.

1595	April 2: Dutch expedition under De Houtman leaves for Indies.
	Suriansyah found Sultanate of Banjar on Kalimantan (later Banjarmasin).
1596	June: De Houtman expedition reaches Banten. Sultan of Banten, along with the Portuguese stationed in Banten, shell the Dutch ships off north coast of Java.
1597	Some members of the De Houtman expedition settle on Bali; refuse to leave.
	Remnants of De Houtman expedition (89 of an original 248 sailors) return to Holland with spices.
	Senopati attacks Banten, but is driven back.
	After this point, the power in central Java was definitely the Mataram district, around today's Yogyakarta and Surakarta, rather than around Demak.
	The Netherlands had been under Spanish rule, and Dutch sailors had been on Portuguese and Spanish voyages around the world. By the 1590s, the Dutch were ready to make money for themselves.
1598	Twenty-two Dutch expeditions set out for the east; States-General suggests that competing companies should merge. De Houtman's second expedition includes John Davis, an English spy. Van Noort sets off to sail around the southern tip of America to the Indies.
1599	Dutch expedition under Van Neck reaches Maluku.
	De Houtman is killed in conflict with Sultan of Aceh.
	Dutch churches begin calls for missionary work in the Indies.
1600	Dutch expeditioners make alliance with Hitu against Portuguese in Ambon.
	Makassar converts to Islam.
	Van Noort expedition attacks Spanish at Guam.
December 31	Elizabeth I of England charters East India Company.

1601	Senopati succeeded by Krapyak in Mataram.
	English set up fort at Banda.
1602 March 20	Dutch companies combine to form **Vereenigde Oost-Indische Compagnie** (VOC); led by Heeren XVII representing different regions of the Netherlands.
	In spite of its problems and dangers, the De Houtman voyages were so profitable that dozens of new voyages were planned to follow its path.
	States-General gives VOC power to raise armies, build forts, negotiate treaties and wage war in Asia.
	VOC establishes post at Gresik.
	Portuguese send naval expedition from Melaka to combat Dutch.
	Sir James Lancaster leads East India Company expedition, reaches Aceh, builds trading post at Banten.
	Dutch ships win skirmish with Portuguese off Banten.
1603	Official VOC trading post founded at Banten.
1604	English East India Company expedition under Sir Henry Middleton visits Ternate, Tidore, Ambon and Banda.
1605	Portuguese at Ambon surrender to ships under VOC.
	King of Gowa converts to Islam; other kings of the area refuse invitation to convert. Gowa attacks neighbors and converts them to Islam.
	VOC sends expeditions to Banda, Irian Jaya, and northern Australia.
1606	Spanish take Ternate and Tidore. VOC make unsuccessful attack on Portuguese Melaka.
	The Dutch East India Company was given most of the powers of a sovereign state, partly because communication between the Netherlands and Asia was so slow that colonial activities simply could not be directed from Amsterdam.

	(Until 1800 in this time-line, Dutch activities are marked with a VOC for East India Company.)
1607	Iskandar Muda is Sultan of Aceh.
1610	Krapyak of Mataram starts period of heavy attacks on Surabaya.
	Post of Governor-General is created for VOC in Asia, advised by Raad van Indie (Council of the Indies).
1611	English begin setting up many posts in the Indies, including at Makassar, Jepara, Aceh and Jambi.
	Dutch set up post at Jayakerta.
1613	Iskandar Muda of Aceh defeats Johore, carries away Sultan of Johore and VOC representatives.
	Mataram forces burn down Gresik; Krakyak asks VOC in Maluku for help against Surabaya.
	VOC sets up post in Jepara.
	VOC sets up first post on Timor.
	Krapyak succeeded by Sultan Agung.
1614	Johore throws out Aceh forces, creates alliance with Palembang, Jambi, and other Sultanates against Aceh.
	Aceh wins naval battle against Portuguese at Bintan.
	Aceh under Iskandar Muda and his successor, Iskandar Thani, was a center of Islamic scholarship and debate.
	Agung attacks Surabayan territories.
	VOC sends ambassador to Agung.
	Bandung founded.
1615	VOC closes post at Gowa, hostilities drag on for years.
	First Dutch Reformed church in the east founded at Ambon.
	English build warehouse at Jayakerta.
1616	VOC military expedition against Banda.

1617	Aceh takes Pahang.
	Agung defeats Surabaya at Pasuruan, defeats Surabayan expedition to his rear; Pajang moves inhabitants to Mataram.
1618	December: Sultan of Banten encourages English to drive Dutch out of Jayakerta.
	Agung bans sale of rice to VOC. Agung's governor of Jepara attacks VOC post there. Dutch burn down much of Jepara in retaliation.
	Sultan Agung was the greatest ruler of Mataram. At one point, all of Java, except for Blanten and Batavia, was under his rule.
	Protestantism (Kristen), one of Indonesia's five religions.
	The Dutch introduces the fifth of Indonesia's recognized religions: Protestant Christianity. Beside the missionary work on Java, there were soon many "Orang Kristen" around Manado on Sulawesi, in Ambon, and around Kupang on Timor and nearly Roti.
	The VOC, however, had very little interest in spreading religion.
1619 **January**	English force Dutch to surrender at Jayakerta, but Banten forces take over from English in surprise move. The English and Pangeran of Jayakerta retreat.
March	Dutch rename post at Jayakerta to Batavia (today's Jakarta).
	Jan Pietezoon Coen becomes Governor-General of VOC.
May	Coen passes through Jepara, burns down city again, including English post; Coen arrives at Jayakerta and burns it down, leaving only Dutch post of Batavia remaining, to become VOC headquarters.
	Agung takes Tuban from Surabaya, destroying the city.
1620	VOC under Coen almost exterminates population of Banda to prevent smuggling. Survivors settle on small island near Seram.
	Aceh takes Kedah.

Gowa extends influence on Sumbawa.

Rahmatullah becomes Sultan of Banjar on Kalimantan.

Agung was not pleased with the Dutch taking Jayakerta, since he had intended to take it himself.

Jan Pieterszoon Coen

The most aggressive Governor-General of the VOC.

In 1615-1616, the Schouten expedition became the first to sail around Cape Horn at the southern tip of South America, then made the first visit to Europeans to many south Pacific islands. When they arrived in Batavia (Jakarta), Coen had them jailed for violating the VOC's monopoly, and confiscated their ships.

(Years later, in 1722, the Dutch explorer Roggeveen would run into the same trouble after discovering Easter Island.)

British found trading post at Ambon.

1622	Mataram and VOC make overtures to each other.
1623	VOC agents in Ambon arrest, torture and execute English agents on charges of conspiracy.
	Aceh sacks Johore.
	Carstenz expedition for VOC explores southern coast of Irianjaya.
	Coen returns to the Netherlands. Carpentier is new Governor-General of the VOC.
1624	Aceh takes Nias.
	Sultan Agung takes Madura.
	Raden Praseno, a grandson of Pratanu, is named Pangeran Cakraningrat I by Agung.
1625	Agung dams Brantas River to cut off water supply from Surabaya, which finally surrenders.
	Cirebon is ally of Agung.
	Epidemics and ruin of war spread through Java.

	Abul Fath becomes Sultan of Banten.
1627	Coen returns from the Netherlands to serve as Governor-General of the VOC again.
	In 1625, the first "hongi" raids took place in Maluku. These were attacks, usually by local allies of the VOC, against anyone who was growing cloves without authorization of the VOC.
1628	Agung sends army against VOC in Batavia; dams Ciliwung River in attempt to deny fresh water to the VOC. He fails to oust the Dutch. Commanders of the Mataram army are executed for failure.
	Last of English leave Banda.
1629	Agung attacks Batavia again. He is defeated, although Coen dies during siege.
	Iskandar Muda sends navy of Aceh against Portuguese Melaka, but the Aceh navy is destroyed.
	Introduction of sugar cultivation in Banten.
1631	Agung suppresses rebellion at Sumedang.
1633	Agung raids east Java; the Hindu kingdom of Balambangan asks for VOC help and is refused. Balambangan then asks the King of Gelgel in Bali for help.
	War between VOC and Banten.
1634	Dutch arrest Kakiali, leader of Hitu in Maluku, on charges of smuggling.
	This was the "mercantilist" age of trade empires. There were many powers that wanted to create trade empires: the Dutch through the VOC, the English, Banten, and Gowa were among them. There was no such thing as "free trade" under these empires. The VOC especially wanted total control of trade, and any selling to anyone outside the VOC was considered smuggling.
1635	Agung tries to take Balambangan, but is defeated by Balinese forces.
1636	Iskandar Thani becomes Sultan of Aceh, supports Islamic learning.

Agung begins conquest of easternmost Java.

Agung, realizing that he cannot defeat the Dutch, make overtures toward VOC.

Van Diemen becomes Governor-General of VOC.

1637	VOC attacks Ternate.
	VOC releases Kakiali, who pledges friendship to VOC, but make anti-Dutch alliances between Hitu, Ternate, and Gowa.
	Local Muslims overcome Portuguese fortress at Ende on Flores.
	Agung finally takes Balambangan in easternmost Java.
1640	Sultanate of Bima founded on Sumbawa.
	Portugal regains independent crown from Spain.
	Around this time, the VOC started pushing the Portuguese out of many of their posts in Nusa Tenggara.
1641	Taj ul Alam becomes Sultana of Aceh, starts period of female rulers; Johore and Aceh settle differences.
	VOC takes Melaka from Portuguese.
	Kakiali and Hitu attack VOC on Ambon.
1642	VOC gets monopoly on trade with Palembang by treaty.
	Hidayatullah becomes Sultan of Banjar on Kalimantan.
	Tasman explores coast of Irian Jaya for VOC on voyage back from New Zealand.
1643	VOC has Kakiali murdered, continues drive to take Hitu.
1645	Agung begins building royal tombs at Imogiri (near today's Yogya).
	Mandarsyah becomes Sultan of Ternate with VOC help.
1646	Sultan Agung dies, and is succeeded by Susuhunan Amangkurat I. Mataram controls all Java, more or less except

	Banten and Batavia. Relations between Amangkurat I and the VOC are good in the beginning.
1647	Amangkurat I moves court to Plered near Karta; fights Balinese in easternmost Java.
	The VOC takeover of Melaka was the real end of Portuguese importance in the region. But after losing Melaka, some Portuguese started trading with Gowa and Sulawesi.
	After Taj ul-Alam became ruler of Aceh, the centralized power in Aceh lessened, regional ruler gained more power, and Aceh's tributaries began to show their independence.
1648	Cakraningrat II takes power in Madura, under Mataram.
1650	VOC intervenes in uprising against Sultan Mandarsyah of Ternate, sparking civil war.
	Amangkurat I orders Cirebon to attack Banten.
	Musta in Billah becomes Sultan of Banjar on Kalimantan.
1651	VOC reopens post at Jepara; Amangkurat I begins interfering with coastal trade.
	Sultan Ageng begins rule at Banten (not to be confused with Sultan Agung of Mataram).
	VOC takes Kupang on Timor.
1652	VOC takes Sultan Mandarsyah of Ternate to Batavia, makes him sign agreement not to grow cloves, starts military moves against opposing faction in Ternate.
1655	Amangkurat I orders that no boats of any kind shall set sail from his ports.
1656	VOC deports population of Hoamoal near Ternate to Ambon.
1657	Amangkurat I attack Banten again.
1658	VOC sets up post at Manado.
	War between VOC and Palembang.
1659	VOC forces burn down Palembang and reestablishes the VOC post.

	Amangkurat I has several family members murdered, including the mother of future Amangkurat II.
	VOC builds fort in the Aru Islands, but soon abandons it.
1660	VOC attack Gowa, destroys Portuguese ships in harbor, and forces peace treaty on Sultan Hasannuddin of Gowa.
	Arung Palakka of Bone rebels against Gowa.
	Buleleng begins drive to become power on Bali; King of Klungkung remains as "dewa Agung" or chief king.
	Amangkurat I closes ports again; VOC leaves Jepara.
1661	Court rebellion against Amangkurat I.
	Banten takes diamond-bearing area of Landak on Kalimantan.
1663	Spanish abandon post at Tidore.
	VOC allows Arung Palakka and followers to settle at Batavia.

	Banten begins direct trade with Manila.
1667	VOC and Arung Palakka fight nearly a year to take Gowa, enforce 1660 treaty.
	Tidore submits to VOC.
	The future Amangkurat II begins seeking VOC help against his father.
	English give up claims to Banda in exchange for Manhattan Island in America.
1669	Sultan Hasanuddin of Gowa passes away; continuing trouble against the VOC in Gowa finally ends.
	By the end of the 1600s, Banten was trading directly with China, Japan, Thailand, India and Arabia. Sultan Ageng of Banten was a strong opponent of the VOC monopoly who insisted on promoting trade with other European, Arab and Asian traders as he pleased. (Fig. 3)

Chapter 3

1670 to 1800

Court Intrigues and The Dutch

1671	Trunojoyo unites Madura under his control, drives out Mataram forces.
1672	Gunung Merapi erupts in Mataram.
1674	Famine in Mataram.
	Bugis under Arung Palakka attack Toraja.
	Makassarese unhappy with Arung Palakka settle in east Java.
1675	Rebellion in Mataram.
	Makassarese exiles attack ports on north coast of Java. Trunojoyo of Madura takes Surabaya. Rebels appeal to Islamic sentiments.
	(Note: Throughout this page, VOC stands for Vereeniggde Oostindische Compagnie, or the Dutch East India Company. The VOC had been granted many of the powers of a sovereign state by the government of the Netherlands.) (Fig. 1)
1676	Trunojoyo defeats Mataram army at Gogodog.
1677	Arung Palakka becomes King of Bone (until 1696).
February	VOC promises help to Amangkurat I.
May	VOC pushes Trunojoyo out of Surabaya, but Trunojoyo moves on to loot the court of Mataram at Plered. Both loyal and rebellious members of the family of Amangkurat I flee. Trunojoyo takes the royal treasure and retreats to Kediri.
	Banten forces occupy Cirebon and the Priangan.
July	Amangkurat I dies; Amangkurat II seeks VOC help.

	Balinese from Karangasem drive Makassarese off of Lombok.
	VOC occupies Sangir Islands.
1678	Amangkurat II, without money to pay his debts to the VOC, promises to give up Semarang, his claims to the Priangan, and fees from coastal ports until debts are paid.
	VOC and Amangkurat II march on Kediri and destroy Trunojoyo.
	Inayatullah becomes Sultan of Banjar on Kalimantan.
	Throughout this period, the rulers of Mataram borrowed money from the VOC, which turned out to be a bad deal for both. The rulers of Mataram lost power and sovereignty, but the debts to the VOC were never fully repaid, and the VOC lost money year after year.
1679	Trunojoyo captured and executed.
	VOC and Arung Palakka drive Makassarese out of East Java.
	Banten retreats from Cirebon and Priangan.

	VOC make treaty with Minahasans at Manado.
1680	VOC forces attack rebel areas in Mataram.
	Pangeran Puger continues to run court at Plered against Amangkurat II. Amangkurat II founds new court at Kartasura, and then drives Puger out of Plered.
	Banten declares war on VOC. Sultan Ageng is replaced in coup by his son, Sultan Haji, who seeks help from the VOC.
	VOC forces invade Madura, supposedly on behalf of Mataram. Cakraningrat II, uncle of Trunojoyo, takes power in West Madura. VOC retains control of East Madura.
1681	Pangeran Puger builds new force and retakes center of Mataram, but not Kartasura. VOC forces push him back and defeat him.
	VOC intervenes in Roti, puts allies in power.
	Karangasem begins trying to take Lombok.
1682	Sultan Ageng's supporters retake Banten against his son. VOC reacts by taking Banten. VOC expels English and other European traders from Banten, and begins to control Cirebon, the Priangan, and Lampung. Syekh Waliyullah, Islamic scholar and enemy of the Dutch, is exiled to the VOC post in Ceylon.
1684	Surapati, a former slave and outlaw now employed as a VOC soldier, attacks a VOC column, escapes, and is given refuge by anti-VOC members out the court of Mataram at Kartasura.
1685	English found post at Bengkulu.
	VOC forces treaty on Sultan of Riau.
	Sa'dillah becomes Sultan of Banjar.
1686	VOC sends an embassy to the Mataram court at Kartasura. AMANGKURAT II stages a fake attack on Surapati's residence, then turns to cut down VOC representatives and soldiers. The remaining VOC presence at court leaves for Jepara.
	Surapati leaves Kartasura for Pasuruan; begins building new kingdom.
	Amangkurat II sends secret letter to Johore, Minangkabau,

	English East India Company, even Siam - trying to find help against the VOC.
1689	Plot against VOC in Batavia fails; rebels flee to Kartasura.
1690	Amangkurat II attacks Surapati, but fails.
1696	Arung Palkka, King of Bone, passes away.
1697	Surapati takes area around Madium.
1700	Tahlilillah becomes Sultan of Banjar.
1710	Three years of confusion in VOC over post of Governor-General.
	Sultan of Banjarmasin tries to eject British post by force, but fails.
1702	Amangkurat II sends secret representative to VOC, hoping for help in the face of court intrigues.
1703	Amangkurat II dies, Amangkurat III faces opposition from Pangeran Puger.
1704	Puger leaves the court of Mataram at Kartasura for Semarang, seeking VOC help. Puger gets support from Cakraningrat II of Madura. VOC accepts Puger as Susuhunan Pakubuwono I; their army takes Demak, other coastal areas.
1705	Pakubuwono I makes deal with VOC; Mataram debts to VOC are wiped out, East Madura goes to VOC control, Semarang is officially a VOC city after years of occupation, Cirebon is officially a VOC protectorate, Javanese sailors must stick to their home water.
	Army of Pakubuwono I with VOC help takes the court of Mataram at Kartasura. Amangkurat III flees to Surapati with the pusaka (emblems of heirlooms of the house of Mataram). Four years of warfare begin.
1706	Surapati is killed, but the war on Java continues.
	Muhammad Mansur Jayo Ing Lago becomes Sultan of Palembang.
1707	VOC and Pakubuwono I of Mataram takes Pasuran; Amangkurat III flees to Malang.

	Cakraningrat II flees power in West Madura.
	Banjarmasin finally throws out the British.
1708	Amangkurat III surrenders and is sent into exile by the Dutch.
1710	Dewa Agung (High king) on Bali moves court from Gelgel to Klungkung.
1714	British begin building port Marlborough at Bengkulu.
1717	King of Mengwi becomes most powerful king on Bali.
	Surabaya rebels against Mataram with help from Bali.
1718	VOC takes Surabaya from rebels. Some rebellions continue in East Java.
	Cakraningrat III of Madura is killed by VOC soldiers while traveling to talks; Cakraningrat IV takes power.
1719	Amangkurat IV takes rule in Mataram. Court rebellion breaks out almost immediately; rebel princes flee eastward. Several more years of war continue.
1722	Plot to overthrow VOC in Batavia is foiled.
1723	Rebel princes and Surapati's descendants in East Java are subdued by VOC forces.
	VOC begins compulsory coffee production in Priangan.
1724	Badaruddin becomes Sultan of Palembang.
1726	Pakubuwono II takes power in Mataram.
	Bugis prince Arung Singkang takes Pasir and Kutai in Kalimantan.
1728	Court intrigues in Kartasura result in Pangeran Mangkunegara being sent into exile by Dutch.
1729	King of Roti becomes a Christian.
1733	Arung Singkang attacks Banjarmasin.
	Mengwi defeats forces in Buleleng on Bali.

	Pakubuwono II agrees to heavier debt service payments to VOC; has minister Danureja sent into Dutch exile.
1735	Plague in Batavia.
	Official VOC archives in Batavia are founded.
1738	VOC tells Pakubuwono II to exile Pangeran Purbaya.
1739	Arung Singkang attacks Bone and Makassar, but VOC drives him back.
1740	Anti-Chinese riots break out in Batavia. 10,000 ore more Chinese are killed. Chinese district is burned down.
	Karangasem on Bali takes Lombok.
1741	Escaping Chinese from Batavia attack Semarang and Rembang; VOC leaves Demak.
	Pakubuwono II changes sides, send force to attack VOC at Semarang, destroys VOC garrison at Kartasura.
	Cakraningrat IV declares allegiance with VOC, starts taking East Java.
	Rival Governor-Generals in Batavia; Valckenier arrests Van Imhoff and sends him back to Europe, Heeren XVII in the Netherlands names Van Imhoff Gov-Gen, Valckenier eventually arrested and jailed.
1742	Negotiations begin between VOC and Pakubuwono II as VOC and Cakraningrat IV spread their power; popular rebellion under Sunan Kuning against VOC and Mataram takes hold in countryside, and then takes Kartasura.
	Cakraningrat IV retakes Kartasura from rebels; VOC is suspicious, orders Pakubuwono II put back on the throne.
1743	Rebellion continues under Pangeran Mangkubumi, Pangeran Singasari, and Pangeran Mas Said.
	Pakubuwono II gives VOC Surabaya, Rembang, Jepara and claims to easternmost Java and West Madura. VOC receives a say in court appointments.
	Mixed Portuguese local attack VOC post at Kupang on Timor; VOC solidifies control of western part of Timor.

1745
February 17 Pakubuwono II moves into the Kraton Surakarta.

Cakraningrat IV wages war with the VOC and retakes much of Madura and East Java. HE is eventually defeated by VOC, caught and exiled. Cakraningrat V takes title in East Madura.

Gov-Gen Van Imhoff founds Buitenzorg (today's Bogor).

Tamjidillah becomes Sultan of Banjar.

1746 Pangeran Mangkubumi, disgusted with capitulations to the VOC, announces full-scale rebellion. He is joined by Pangeran Mas Said.

August 26: First VOC post office opened in Jakarta.

1747 Bugis internal war begins over dissatisfaction with Arung Singkang.

1748 Mangkubumi's rebel forces attack Surakarta.

VOC sends Sultan of Banten into exile, makes his wife Ratu Sarifa regent, but takes direct control.

1749 December: Pakubuwono II becomes sick, signs treaty giving full sovereignty in all Mataram to VOC. (Treaty is widely ignored.)

VOC declares Pakubuwono III as heir to throne. Mangkubumi claims title for himself, rules from Yogya.

Pakubuwono II dies.

1750 Pangeran Mas Said attacks Surakarta for Mangkubumi.

Rebellion in Banten against ratu Sarifa and VOC. Rebels threaten Batavia and Lampung.

1751 VOC forces destroy Banten rebellion; guerilla attacks continue against VOC plantations around Batavia.

1754 Mangkubumi considers negotiating with VOC, worries about possible disloyalty from Mas Said.

Arung Singkang abdicates from power, continues guerilla attacks.

1755	Mangkubumi changes title from Susuhunan to Sultan, takes name Hamengkubuwono I, is now Sultan Hamengkubuwono I. Treaty of Gijanti: Sultan Hamengkubuwono I gets VOC recognition of title and lands. Builds Kraton at Yogyakarta. Mas Said, now without allies, attacks VOC force.
1756	Mas Said attacks new court at Yogyakarta. Bugis attacks VOC at Melaka.
October 7	Hamengkubuwono I officially moves into Kraton Ngayogyakarta.
1757	Mas Said agrees to negotiations. Overt hostilities end; Mas Said becomes Pangeran Mangkunegara I with his court also at Surakarta. The Courts of Central Java as they were founded in the mid-1700s have continued down to the present days, a Susuhunan of Surakarta, and a Pangeran Mangkunegara. The Sultan of Yogya still has special powers within the Daerah Istimewa or Special Area of Yogyakarta; the others retain their palaces and titles, but no special power.
1758	VOC expedition to Malang against descendants of Surapati capture Pangeran Singasari, who dies in custody.
1759	French expedition steals clove plants from Ambon to break VOC monopoly.
1770	English Captain James Cook visits Batavia.
1771	Last of Surapati's line is captured by VOC forces in Malang. Malang now falls under VOC control. VOC forces work to push Balinese out of easternmost Java. Syarif Abdurrahman from Arabia found Pontianak, becomes first Sultan.
1773	Division of lands between Yogyakarta and Surakarta is formalized.
1776	Bahauddin becomes Sultan of Palembang.

1778	Tahmidillah becomes Sultan of Banjar.
	Gunung Api on Banda erupts.
1780	War between Netherlands and Britain; extra troops sent to Java.
	Plague in Batavia.
	Islamic reform movement grows in Minangkabau.
1784	Treaty of Paris open VOC controlled Indies to free trade.
	Sultan of Paris dies without successor; VOC takes complete control.
	Bugis attack VOC at Melaka.
1785	Future Hamengkubuwono II of Yogya builds fortifications around Kraton.
1786	British found Penang in Malaya.
1788	Pakubuwono III succeeded by Pakubuwono IV.
1790	Rumor spread that Pakubuwono IV is planning the massacre of Dutch in Java; takeover of Yogya and Mangkunegara court; forces from Yogya and VOC surround Surakarta; Pakubuwono IV orders his advisors to leave court, VOC sends them into exile.
1792	Hamengkubuwono I dies and is succeeded by Hamengkubuwono II.
	VOC declares that Mangkunegara title and possessions are hereditary.
1794	Heeren XVII dismissed for last time.
1796	Mangkunegara II inherits court, but much of treasury is stolen by VOC resident at Surakarta.
	British occupy Ambon.
1797	Nederlands Zendelinggenootschap or Dutch Missionary Society is founded.
	This was the beginning of heavy activity by Dutch Protestant

missionaries in Indonesia, not only to Java and Sumatra, but also to very remote areas, eventually even to Irian Java.

1798	Napoleonic Dutch government revokes charter of VOC, assumes debts and assets.

The VOC was losing money to corruption and political intrigues. By the end of the 1700s, it was fully bankrupt. On January 1, 1800, it ceased to exist.

The Sultan of Tidore sets up subsidiary Sultan of Jailolo on Halmahera.
(Fig. 2)

Chapter 4

1800 to 1830

Chaos and Resistance

1800	VOC formally dissolved on January 1; properties revert to Dutch government.
	During these times, the Netherlands was occupied by Napoleon's France.
1803	Padri movement takes strength in Minangkabau area, promotes more orthodox Islam.
	The "Padri" advocates on Sumatra were heavily influenced by the Wahhabiyah in Arabia, a fundamentalist movement founded by Ibnu Wahhab in the 1700s. The movements are still favored in Saudi Arabia today.
	Ambon returns from British occupation to the Dutch.
	Badruddin becomes Sultan of Palembang.
1805	Pangeran Diponegoro experiences prophetic visions.
1806	British Navy skirmishes with French and Dutch forces off Java.
1807	Rebellion against Dutch in Minahasa.
1808	Mangkunegara II organizes "Mangkunegara Legion" with Dutch financing.
	French-run government of the Netherlands sends Daendels as Gov-Gen.
	Daendels moves his residence to Buitenzorg (near Bogor).
	Herman Willem Daendels Daendels was a product of revolutionary Europe, but he was also a colonialist. Daendels did not like the Sultans and Princes of Java at all, but he himself was sent to rule in their

place. He thought he was ending oppression, but he was really bringing in a newer, heavier rule from Europe.

He faced problems from every side. The previous VOC government had lost huge amounts of money in its last years, and the British imposed a naval blockade that choked off much economic activity.

Pakubuwono V appeals Daendels; Hamengkubuwono II opposes him.

British decide to abandon Melaka; Stamford Raffles, then a clerk, writes urgent letter to India urging a reversal of the decision. The decision is reversed, and the British stay in Melaka.

Sulaiman becomes Sultan of Banjar.

1809	Daendels built a mountain route from Batavia to Cirebon (jalan Raya Post/Groote Postweg), orders town of Bandung to be relocated to the road (its current site). Pangeran Kornel, local ruler of Sumedang, refuses to cooperate due to the mistreatment of locals.
	While in Batavia, Daendels started a campaign to clean up the city's canal. lives of many laborers.
1810	May: British retake Ambon, Ternate and Tidore.
	Raden Rangga, brother-in-law of the Sultan, starts failed revolt against Dutch in Yogya; Daendels marches on Yogya, forces Hamengkubuwono II to abdicate in favor of young Hamengkubuwono III.
	Raffles visits Lord Minto, British Governor-General in India, in Calcutta, urging him to drive the French and Dutch from Java. Minto is convinced.
1811 **January**	Daendels imposes new treaties on Yogya and Surakarta, including end to rent payments by Dutch for north coastal areas.
	Hamengkubuwono III hands over Pangeran Natakusuma to Dutch on suspicion of being involved in 1810 rebellion.
May	Daendels is replaced by Jan Willem Janssens. (Daendels soon served under Napoleon on his failed Moscow campaign.)

August 26	British under Lord Minto take Batavia. The Dutch, having suffered heavy losses, retreat to Samarang.
September	Dutch surrender to British at Salatiga.
	Thomas Stamford Raffles appointed Lt-Governor of Java.
	Dutch residents at Palembang and company are killed, probably on orders of Sultan Badruddin; British have Badruddin dethroned and replaced by brother.

Sir Thomas Stamford Raffles
Raffles was known for his scientific interests as well as the work he did for the British East India Company; governing Java, governing the output at Bengkulu, Sumatra which was British at the time, and of course, for founding Singapore.

	Hamengkubuwono II retakes title in Yogya.
December	Raffles visits Yogya Kraton, generates much hostility.
	Pakubuwono V sends secret letter to Yogya offering assistance against the British, but hoping to make Yogya overextend themselves; British begin secret negotiations with Hamengkubuwono III; Natakusuma offers help to British.
1812	June British shell, take and loot Yogya; Pakubuwono V offers little help; Hamengkubuwono II replaced again by Hamengkubuwono III and sent into exile at Padang; Natakusuma becomes Pangeran Pakualam I, founds Pakualam House.
	Raffles had the same delusion as Daendels, that he was ending oppression, when in fact he was bringing in a tighter colonial rule. The nobility of Yogya considered the British to be horribly impolite.
	In Raffles' favor, it could be said that he liberalized the economy of Java with free market reforms that helped farmers. He abolished forced labor and the compulsory cultivation of crops. He also tried to stamp out the slave trade between Indonesia and foreigners. (Fig. 1)
October	British sign treaty with Sultan of Banjarmasin.
	British take Timor.
1813	Baharuddin becomes Sultan of Palembang.

1814

June — Lord Minto, British governor of India and Raffles' patron and promoter, dies. Charges of corruption are brought against Raffles, who is eventually found innocent.

August 13 — British agree on eventual return of possessions in the Indies to the Dutch.

British war with Balinese in Buleleng and Karangasem over

	the slave trade.
	Bone attacks British.
	British residents stationed in Banjarmasin and Pontianak.
	Hamengkubuwono IV takes rule in Yogya.
	British expedition reports on Borobudur and Prambanan to Europe for the first time.
1815	Much of Minangkabau nobility killed by Padri supporters; Padri begin to expand promotion of Islam into batak areas.
April–July	Mount Tambora on Sumbawa erupts: 12,000 are dead from eruption itself; later 50,000 die from related famine.
	The eruption of Mt. Tambora changed the climate worldwide; in the northern United States 1815, it was called the "year without a summer" and snow fell in July.
May	Raffles visits Borobudur.
1816	Bone attacks British again.
August 19	Dutch return to Batavia. Cornelis Elout continues Raffles' reform policies.
	Dutch unsuccessfully try to get rajas of Bali to accept Dutch authority.
1817	Madura consolidated into single kabupaten.
	Pattimura leads revolt against returning Dutch in Ambon; hanged in December.
	Botanical Gardens founded at Bogor.
1818	Raffles is sent to govern British fort at Bengkulu. Raffles makes several attempts to extend British influence in Sumatra.
	Dutch attack Palembang.
1819	Raffles founds Singapore.
	Dutch return to Padang.
	Najamuddin Pangeran Ratu becomes Sultan of Palembang.

1820	Pakubuwono V becomes Susuhunan of Solo.
	Dutch send expedition to the Aru Islands. (Fig. 2)
1821	Remaining Minangkabau nobles sign treaty, giving Minangkabau to Dutch in exchange for protection against the Padri. "Padri War" begins.
	Cholera appears in Java for the first time; rice harvest fails.
	Najamuddin Prabu Anom becomes Sultan of Palembang.
1822	Hamengkubuwono IV dies amid rumors of poisoning. Hamengkubuwono V is new Sultan.
	Mount Merapi erupts near Yogya.
1823	Dutch forces defeated by Padri at Lintau.
	Governor-General van der Capellen abolishes land leases in Central Java.
	Pakubuwono VI ascends in Solo.
	Kramo Jayo becomes Sultan of Palembang.
	Raffles, in poor health, returns to England.
1824	British and Dutch sign Treaty of London and divide the Indies between themselves. The Dutch claim Sumatra, Java, Maluku, Irian Jaya, and so on. The British claim Malaya and Singapore. Aceh is supposed to remain independent.
	Bone takes Dutch areas in south Sulawesi.
1825	Dutch and Gowa defeat Bone before Java War.
May	Diponegoro and court retainers clash in dispute over new road.
July	Dutch send troops to arrest Diponegoro, who declares rebellion. This was the beginning of the "Java War," which lasted until 1830.
	Adam al-Wasi' Billah becomes Sultan of Banjar.
	Diponegoro had support of many princes and bupati, rural farmers, and religious leaders, including Kyai Maja. The Yogya

Kraton did not side with him. Pakubuwono IV of Surakarta supported him quietly.

Line of succession in Palembang ends.

Dutch issue orders to arrest Raden Intan in Lampung. Raden Intan dies and is succeeded by Raden Imba Kusuma.

1826	Guerilla warfare widespread throughout central and eastern Java.
August	Dutch return Hamengkubuwono II from exile in Ambon, and reinstall him as Sultan of Yogya.
October	Diponegoro pushed back from Solo.
1827	Dutch reorganize forces, change to more flexible tactics, and take offensive against guerilla bands.
1828 April	Javanese successful against the Dutch.

Madura consolidated with Surabaya.

Smallpox epidemic in Bali.

Fort Du Bus founded by Dutch in Irian Jaya.

November Kyai Maja, spiritual advisor to Diponegoro, is taken prisoner by the Dutch after hand-to-hand combat.

1829
September Pangeran Mangkubumi (uncle of Diponegoro) surrenders, allowed to return to palace.

October Sentot surrenders; Dutch make him a Lieutenant Colonel.

1830
March Diponegoro agrees to negotiations in Magelang, is arrested, exiled to Manado, then to Ujung Padan (until 1855).

Pakubuwono IV suspected by Dutch, exiled to Ambon (until 1849). Pakubuwono VII becomes Susuhunan of Solo.

Prince Diponegoro
Pangeran or Prince Diponegoro is remembered as a great hero today. He had the mystic vision of a religious leader, the pedigree of the House of Yogya, and an affinity for the common people. Many streets and public institutions have been named for him.

Chapter 5

1830 to 1910

Imperialism and Modernization

1830	Johannes van den Bosch is named Governor-General, begins cultuurstelsel or "culture system."
	It was only after the Java War that the Dutch began to think about a real empire in the Indies. From 1830 to the end of the century, the Dutch began to drive a take complete control of the areas from Aceh to New Guinea, and to extract as much profit as possible from the valuable areas, such as Priangan area of West Java.
	First steamboat arrives in the Indies.
	Revenues from the Indies paid for as much as one-third of the Dutch government's budget in the mid-1800s.
	Dutch organize KNIL-the Royal Netherlands Indies Army.
	The government was called the Netherlands East Indies, or the Nederlands-Indie in Dutch, or Hindia Belanda in Indonesia today.
1831	Nederlands-Indie government manages a balanced budget.
	Under the "culture system," Javanese were required to grow a certain amount of crops for export - more coffee, sugar, spices and indigo, but less rice to feed the people.
1832	Dutch depose Sultan of Jailolo and take control of Halmahera.
1833	Sultan of Jambi asks for Dutch help against Palembang.
	Padri war heats up in Minangkabau; Dutch seal off coast; Sentot fights on Dutch side, but was probably not pro-Dutch in his heart. Dutch place Sentot under watch in Bengkulu (until 1955).

1834	Dutch force Jambi to recognize Dutch sovereignty. (Fig. 1)
1836	Dutch abandon Fort Du Bus on Irian.
	"Dvipantara" or "Jawa Dwipa" is reported by Indian scholars to be in Java and Sumatra
1837	Bonjol in Minangkabau falls to Dutch in Padri War, Tuanku Iman Bonjol surrenders and is sent into exile.
	Among the fighters against the Dutch in the Padri War were the "Harimau Nan Selapan" or "eight tigers", led by Jaji Miskin.
1838	Dutch victory at Daludalu ends Padri War in Minangkabau. Direct Dutch rule in Minangkabau is enforced (adat law and nobility appear pro-Dutch, Islamic leaders appear anti-Dutch).
	Dutch expedition against Flores.
	Bone renews Treaty of Bungaya.

	Dutch establish presence on Nias.
	Sulaiman inherits rule of Aceh, but Tuanku Ibrahim rules as guardian, ruling Aceh until 1870.
	Mataram kingdom on Lombok takes whole island, plus Karangasem on Bali.
1841	The rajas of Badung, Klungkung, Karangasem and Buleleng on Bali sign treaties recognizing Dutch sovereignty; rajas to keep internal power.
	James Brooke begins creating private empire for himself in Sarawak.
1842	Dutch withdraw from east coast of Sumatra north of Palembang due to British worries.
	The nobility in Surakarta is arrested under suspicion of inciting revolt.
1843	Rajas of Lombok accepts Dutch sovereignty.
	Famine in Cirebon.
1846	Dutch attack Buleleng; other rajas secretly support anti-Dutch forces.
	Dutch expedition against Flores.
	Typhoid epidemic in Java.
	Dutch open coal mines on Kalimantan.
	Revolt in Banten
1847	Dutch military expedition to Nias.
1848	Dutch attack Bali, then withdraw.
	New constitution in Netherlands: Dutch States-General has some control over colonial affairs. (Fig. 2)

Dutch Imperialism: 1815–1870
The Dutch fought two major wars in the 1820s. They still did not control many areas in their imagined sphere of influence, including Aceh, Bali, much of Sulawesi and Nusa Tenggara.

Figure 2

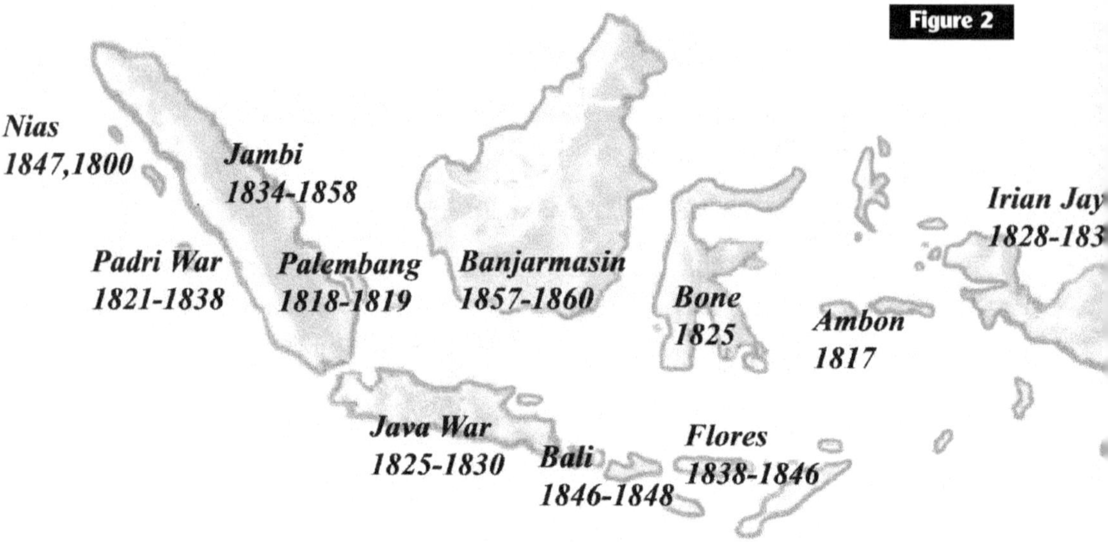

Nias 1847, 1800
Jambi 1834-1858
Irian Jaya 1828-183[?]
Padri War 1821-1838
Palembang 1818-1819
Banjarmasin 1857-1860
Bone 1825
Ambon 1817
Java War 1825-1830
Bali 1846-1848
Flores 1838-1846

Leaders among the Indonesians included:

Pattimura in Ambon in 1817

Pangeran Diponegoro in the Java War, 1825–1830

Imam Tuanku Bonjol in the Padri War in the 1830s

1849	Dutch reduce Buleleng, north Bali; raja of Lombok attacks and takes Karangasem.
	Dutch take full control in Palembang.
1850	Dutch begin missionary work among Bataks of north Sumatra.
	Famine in Central Java.
	Dutch purchase remaining Portuguese posts son Flores.
1851	"Dokter-Jawa" school founded in Gambir, Batavia.
1852	Aceh sends emissary to Napoleon III of France.
1853	Dutch begin administering north Bali.
	Mangkunegara IV takes his title in Surakarta.

1854	Netherlands government issues regulations for the government colonies; local rulers in the Indies are to continue to have traditional powers over their subjects, ruling on behalf of the Dutch.
	Aceh establishes authority over Langkat, Deli and Serdang on east coast of Sumatra ("pepper ports").
	Introduction of quinine cultivation to the Priangan.
1855	Hamengkubuwono VI becomes Sultan of Yogya.
	Dutch military expedition to Nias.
1857	Dutch intervene in succession to Sultanate of Banjarmasin, support Tamjidillah over more popular Hidayatullah.
1858	Dutch expedition against south Sulawesi. Ratu Taha Saifuddin of Jambi refuses treaty with Dutch, flees into jungle with pusaka (emblems of heirlooms of his house), fights until 1904.
	Dutch take Siak in north Sumatra by treaty; define boundary as including Langkat and Deli, infringing on Acehnese territory.
	Nederlands-Indie government running at a deficit due to military expenses.
	Pakubuwono VIII becomes Susuhunan of Solo.
1859	Banjarmasin War led by Pangeran Antasari; Dutch withdraw support for Tamjidillah, send him to Bogor.
	Portuguese recognize Dutch claim to Flores.
	Dutch government bans slavery in the Netherlands Indies.
1860	"Max Havelaar" published.
	Dutch open Savu.
	Dutch abolish Sultanate of Banjarmasin, enforce direct colonial rule.
	"Max Havelaar" exposed the abuses of Dutch colonial rule on Java, and put political pressure on the Netherlands government to make reforms in the colonies.

1861	Pakubuwono IX becomes Susuhunan of Solo.
1862	Hidayatullah surrenders in Banjarmasin, and is exiled to Java. Antasari dies of smallpox, guerilla war continues.
	Compulsory pepper cultivation ends.
1863	Dutch military expedition to Nias.
	British send gunboats to Langkat, other "pepper ports" on Sumatra.
1864	April 1: First Netherlands Indies postage stamp is issued.
	Dutch experiment with rubber cultivation in Java and Sumatra.
	Compulsory clove and nutmeg cultivation in Java and Sumatra.
	Dutch claim Mentawai Islands.
1865	Compulsory tea and cinnamon cultivation ends.
	Dutch introduce tobacco to Deli and northern Sumatra.
1866	Compulsory tobacco cultivation ends.
1867	Gunung Merapi erupts near Yogya; 1000 are killed.
1869	1/3 of Savu dead from smallpox.
	Aceh appeals to Ottoman Empire for protection.
	In 1869, the Suez Canal opened, which greatly reduced the travel time and effort between Europe and Asia by sea.
1870	Minahasa area comes under direct Dutch rule.
	Sultan Mahmud Syah rules Aceh until 1874.
	New Agrarian Law encourages privatization of agriculture, starts to dismantle many practices of the "culture system."
	Coffee blight in Java.
1871	Smallpox kills 18,000 in Bali.

November	Treaty of Sumatra between British and Dutch: Dutch give Gold Coast to British; Dutch may send contract labor from India to Dutch Guiana, Dutch get free hand in Sumatra, British and Dutch both have trade rights in Aceh. Effect of this treaty: no more foreign objection to Dutch taking Aceh.
1872	Batak War begins in north Sumatra, lasts until 1895.
1873	Emissary from Aceh holds talks with the American consul in Singapore, but USA help is rejected by Washington. The Dutch respond with war.
March	Dutch bombard Banda Aceh. The Dutch would waste over 30 years trying to take full control of Aceh, and would never fully succeed.
April	Dutch invade Banda Aceh, but are forced to withdraw.
November	Dutch invade Aceh again, suffer heavy losses to disease. The Dutch would waste over 30 years trying to take full control of Aceh, and would never fully succeed.
1874	Acehnese abandon Banda Aceh and retreat to the hills. Dutch announce that Sultanate of Aceh is ended. Sultan Mahmud Syah dies in jungle; Sultan Ibrahim Mansur Syah heads sultanate in hills until 1907. Teuku Umar leads the Acehnese forces. Dutch expedition to Flores. Dutch send an official to the Aru Islands.
1877	Hamengkubuwono VII becomes Sultan of Yogya. After this point, the Nederlands-Indie government operates at a loss.
1878	Compulsory sugar and coffee cultivation starts to be eliminated.
1879	R.A. Kartini born at Jepara. **Raden Adjeng Kartini** R.A. Kartini is remembered today for her collected letters, works of high literary quality. Far ahead of her time, Kartini was an early advocate both for Indonesia and for the interests of women everywhere.

1880	Rail line completed from Batavia to Bandung.
1881	Dutch falsely declare Aceh War to be over, but they control nothing outside their cities and forts.
1882	Bali and Lombok become single residency; rajas of south Bali are unhappy, but continue to fight among themselves.
	Aru and Tanimbar Islands come under Dutch administration.
	Tjokroaminoto born.
	Sugar blight hits Java.
	Dutch military expedition on Seram.
1883	Krakatau erupts: 36,000 are killed in West Java and Lampung.
	A.J. Zijlker gets approval from Dutch to start drilling for oil in Langkat, north Sumatra.
	Revolt in favor of Pangeran Suryengalaga fails in Yogya.
1887	Sultans of Madura have been reduced to bupati status.
	Economic depression in Java.
1888	Earthquake hits Bali.
	Dutch Resident in Surakarta takes control of the finances of the Mangkunegara house.
	Revolt in Banten led by Qadiriyya.
	On Java in this period, there were over 80 local rulers keeping the title of "Sultan", "Susuhunan" or "Bupati" ruling in theory, while the Dutch held the real power.
	North Borneo (Sabah) becomes a British protectorate.
1890	Zijlker founds company that would become Royal Dutch Shell.
	Dutch expedition against Flores.
1891	Mengwi in Bali taken over by Badung.
	Naqshbandiyya rebel in Lombok against Mataram-Balinese rule, Dutch intervene.

1893	Pakubuwono X becomes Susuhunan of Solo.
1894	Final Dutch intervention in Lombok is successful; nobility goes down in puputan; Karangasem becomes Dutch dependency.

A "puputan" was a suicide charge by Balinese nobility to defend their honor when all else was lost. The families of the court would put on ceremonial clothes, arm themselves with false weapons and walk directly into enemy gunfire.

"Batak War" ends.

Rebellion against Portuguese in East Timor. |
| 1895 | Jami'at Khair founded, organization dedicated to Arabic education. |
| 1896 | King Chulalongkorn of Thailand makes a state visit to the Netherlands Indies. |
| 1898 | Dutch begin exploring Irian Jaya.

Van Heutsz becomes Dutch governor of Aceh. His advisor Snouck Hurgronje introduces "Korte Verklaring", a short treaty recognizing Dutch rule, to replace older complicated agreements with local rulers; Dutch pursue alliance with uleebalangs against Islamic leaders.

Starting about this time, the Dutch began to encourage Islamic worship and practice, as long as politics were not involved. The goal was to channel Islamic enthusiasm away from politics and nationalism. |
| 1899 | R.A. Kartini begins letter-writing career.

Pesantren Tebuireng, a famous Islamic school, is founded at Jombang, East Java.

Teuku Umar, leader of the guerilla forces in Aceh, is killed during a Dutch ambush. (Fig. 3)

Dutch Imperialism: 1870–1910
During this period the Dutch tried to take complete control of all the areas they claimed. This was the era of "high imperialism", when powers such as British and France were facing competition from new colonial powers such as Germany and Italy, and most unclaimed parts of Africa, Asia and the Pacific |

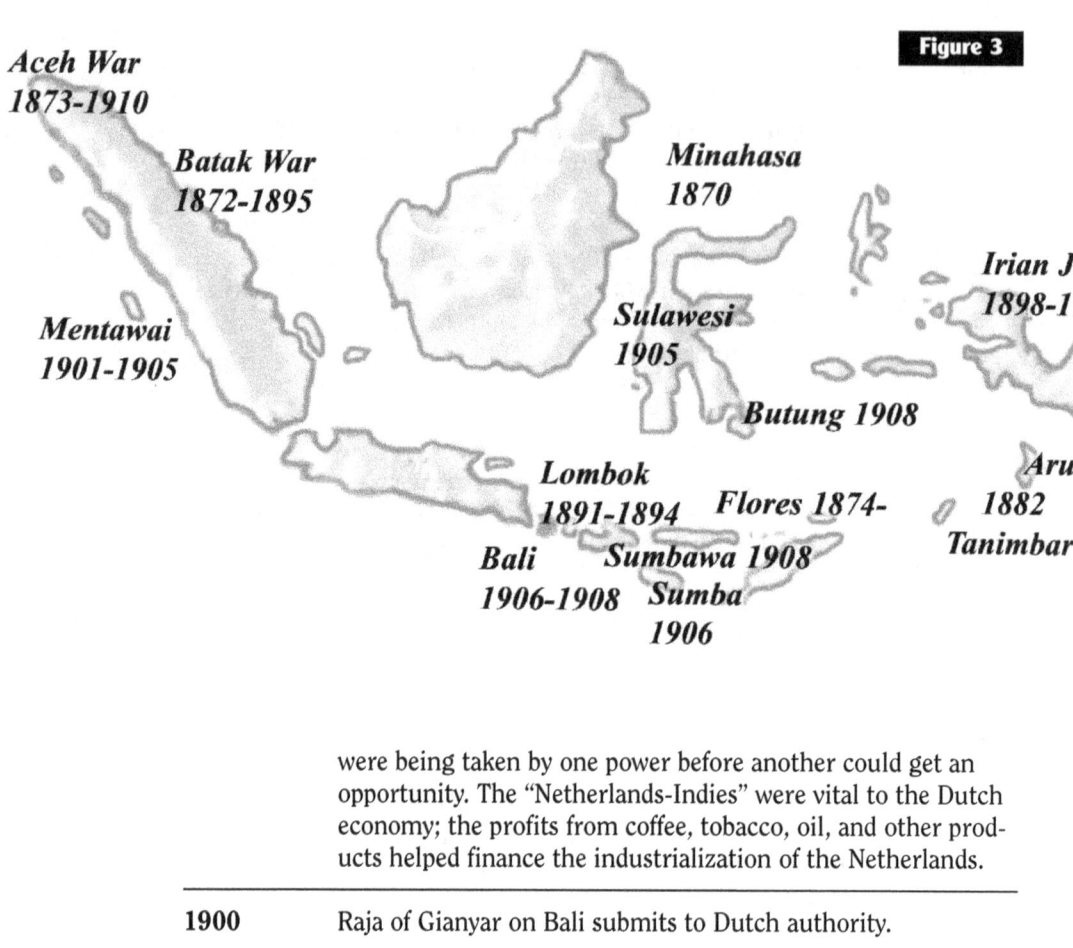

Figure 3

1900	Raja of Gianyar on Bali submits to Dutch authority.

were being taken by one power before another could get an opportunity. The "Netherlands-Indies" were vital to the Dutch economy; the profits from coffee, tobacco, oil, and other products helped finance the industrialization of the Netherlands.

1900   Raja of Gianyar on Bali submits to Dutch authority.

Upper schools at Bandung, Magelang and Probolinggo reorganized to train Javanese candidates for local civil service.

1901   Jambi placed under control of Dutch Resident of Palembang during succession question and related unrest.

By this time, the Dutch government was sending more money to support the Netherlands-Indies than it was collecting from the Indies in revenues. Most of the cash flow from the Indies to the Netherlands after 1900 was in the hands of private businesses.

Zijlker's Royal Dutch oil company expands to Kalimantan.

Dutch place garrison on Mentawai Islands.

Sukarno born.

	Queen Wilhelmina of the Netherlands announces "Ethical Policy" towards the Indies.
1902	Dutch end restrictions of the hajj (pilgrimage to Mecca).
1903	Sultan of Aceh, Tuanku Daud Syah, surrenders to Dutch, but keeps secret contact with guerillas.
	Dutch begin opening MULO schools for elementary education.
1904	Taha of Jambi killed by Dutch.
	Dutch military expedition takes control of Batak region of Sumatra.
1905	August Dutch forces land at Pare Pare. Major Dutch advance on Sulawesis; Bugis, Makasar, Toraja areas are taken for good.
	Acehnese resistance contacts Japanese consul in Singapore for help.
	Dutch occupy Mentawai Islands.
	First trade union founded by railway workers.
1906 September	Major Dutch advance on Bali; Dutch invade at Sanur; Dutch naval force shells Denpasar. Nobility of Badung commits puputan. King of Tabanan is captured by Dutch, but commits suicide. Klungkung falls in final puputan.
	Rubber production takes off in Sumatra with new plant varieties.
	Dutch take direct control of Sumba.
1907	Dutch military puts down rebellion in Flores, takes complete control.
	Unrest finally put down in Jambi.
	Aceh guerillas attack Dutch in Banda Aceh.
	King Sisingamangaraja of the Bataks revolts against the Dutch.
	Zijlker's Royal Dutch oil company merges with Shell Transport and Trading to become Royal Dutch Shell.

	Dutch send police to the Tanimbar Islands to stop intertribal conflict.
1908	Klungkung revolts against Dutch; nobility commits suicide by puputan to preserve their honor.
	Dutch intervene in local conflicts on Sumbawa, take tighter control.
	Butung comes under direct Dutch rule.
	Budi Utomo was a less political organization, primarily devoted to the promotion of Javanese culture. Its interest was limited to Javanese culture.
	VSTP (rail workers union) founded, accepts Indonesian members.
May 20	Budi Utomo is founded among upper-class Javanese students in Jakarta.
October	Budi Utomo holds congress in Yogya.
	Indische Vereeniging founded for Indonesian students in the Netherlands.
1909	Sarekat Dagang Islamiyah founded by Kyai Haji Samanhudi in Jakarta; Tjokroaminoto rises to leadership.
1910	Islamic resistance in Aceh decimated.
	Jami'at Khair replaced by Al-Irsyad (Jamiat Islam al Irsyad al Arabia), organization for Arab Muslims in Indonesia.
	Dutch expedition to Komodo reports on Komodo dragons to Europe for the first time.

Chapter 6

1910 to 1940

New Nationalism

Sejareh, Indonesia

1911	Abendanon publishes R.A. Kartini's letters with the title "Door Duisternis Tot Licht".
	Newspaper al-Munir begins publishing in Padang.
	Bubonic plague outbreak in Java.
1912	Sarekat Dagang Islamiyah changes name to Sarekat Islam.
	Kyai Haji Ahmad Dahlan founds Muhammadiyah in Yogya.
	The Muhammadiyah remains one of the large, respected Islamic organizations in Indonesia today. It has been known for its "modernist" Islamic viewpoint.
	Indische Partij founded by Setiabudi (Douwes Dekker), Dr. Cipto Mangunkusumo and Ki Hajar Dewantoro. All three are exiled within a year.
	Portuguese suppress revolt in East Timor.
1913	Kartini Fonds founded in Netherlands to support women's education on Java.
	Governor-General Idenburg recognizes Sarekat Islam as legal organization.
	Indische Partij banned; leaders go to Netherlands.
1914	Hollandsch-Inlandsche schools are reorganized, become schools for Indonesian well to do.

	Pasundan organization founded for Sundanese in western Java.
May 9	Sneevliet founds Indische Sociaal-Democratische Vereeniging, would become PKI (Indonesian Communist Party).
	In the beginning, the ISDV and PKI would have mostly Dutch members.
	War in Europe: Dutch government considers local militia for Indonesia.
	Great Colonial Exhibition in Semarang, attended by Pakubuwono X of Surakarta and entourage.
	Nias comes under complete Dutch control.
1915	Haji Agus Salim joins Sarekat Islam, promotes Islamic modernism. Soedirman born.
1916	Delegation with members from Budi Utomo, Sarekat Islam, etc. tours Netherlands.
December	States-General in the Netherlands passes bill to create Volksraad for the Netherlands Indies.
	Governor-General J.P. Count van Limburg Stirum until 1921.
	Young Sukarno attends school in Surabaya, lives with Tjokroaminoto.
	Mohammed Natsir, age 24, takes charge of new Persatuan Islam schools, writes that Islam must be the basis of the new Indonesia.
	Dutch require independent schools to get permission from the government to operate; factions unite against it.
1933	February: Mutiny of Dutch and Indonesian sailors on Dutch naval vessel Zeven Provincien.
	Dutch suppress independent schools and political leaders in Minangkabau.
August	Sukarno, Hatta, Sjahrir are arrested. Sukarno is exiled to Ende on Flores without a trial.

1934	Dutch begin protectionist drive to keep out less expensive Japanese products in favor of more expensive Dutch ones.
	Dutch pressure Pakempalan Kawula Ngayogyakarta to renounce overt political activity.
	Around this time, there was a political crackdown on fascists and communists in the Netherlands, along with the attacks on nationalists in Indonesia.
	Hatta and Sjahrir are arrested, sent to Boven Digul.
	Nahdlatul Ulama Young Wing, Ansor, is founded
	Cokroaminoto passes away.
1935	Budi Utomo AND Persatuan Bangsa Indonesia combine to form Partai Indonesia Raya or Parindra. Membership includes Thamrin; includes some pro-Japanese members. Calls for independence through cooperation with Dutch.
	Al-Ittihadiah (modernist Islamic association) founded at Medan.
	Nahdlatul Wathan, an organization for Islamic education, is founded on Lombok.
1936	Van Starkenborgh is named Governor-General; holds title at least until 1945. Hatta and Sjahrir are moved to Banda. Volksraad votes to support petition for autonomy for Indonesia within the constitution of the Netherlands.
1937	Gerakan Rakyat Indonesia founded: Gerindo, includes Yamin and Amir Sjarifuddin. Supports independence, but cooperates with Dutch against Japanese.
	Antara News Service founded.
September	MIAI founded: Majlis Islam A'laa Indonesia, umbrella group for cooperation between Muhammadiyah, NU, Persatuan Islam, and other groups.
1938	Sukarno, still under Dutch custody, is moved to Bengkulu.
	First outsiders reach Bliem Valley on Irian Jaya.
	Moscow tells PKI to stop anti-Dutch activities.

By the late 1930s, the Dutch were building up their defenses at Surabaya, Amboina, Cilacap and other bases, in apprehension of Japanese expansion in the area. Yet, the Dutch resisted arming Indonesians for defense purposes.

Persatuan Arab Indonesia formed from existing Arab Muslim organizations.

November 16: Netherlands government rejects the 1936 autonomy petition for Indonesia.

1939 Gabungan Politik Indonesia, or GAPI, is formed, an umbrella group of nationalist organizations. Large congress is held in Batavia, presents demand for full parliament.

Pakubuwono X of Surakarta passes away; Pakubuwono XI is new Susuhunan.

Pakubuwono X was a huge man, very much loved by the people of Surakarta, who predicted that after his rule there would be no more like him.

Hamengkubuwono IX becomes Sultan of Yogya.

Japanese occupy Spratly Islands.

May PUSA (Persatuan Ulama Seluruh Aceh) is founded by Muhammad Da'ud Beureu'eh to coordinate anti-Dutch activities in Aceh.

1940
February Dutch again reject autonomy.

May Netherlands falls to Germany, Dutch government flees to London.

Hinduism, one of Indonesia's five religions.

Chapter 7

1940 to 1945

The Second World War

1940
February — Dutch say autonomy for Indonesia is out of the question

May 10 — Germany invades the Netherlands.

May 15 — The Netherlands surrenders to Germany; Dutch government flees to London.

Even after the Netherlands had been taken over by Nazi Germany, the Dutch still held onto their colonies. For over a year and a half, the Netherlands East Indies government continued to rule over Indonesia, reporting to the Dutch government-in-exile. Efforts by Indonesian activists to organize self-rule were ignored.

June — Young Suharto enters military school at Gombang.

July — Indonesian exports to Japan stopped; Japanese assets frozen.

1941
January — Dutch arrest Thamrin, others; Thamrin dies in custody five days later.

June — Talks between Dutch and Japanese collapse. Netherlands Indies government places an embargo on exports to Japan, including oil.

July 25 — Japan announces a "protectorate" over Indochina.

July 30 — Dutch government in exile promises to hold conference on Indonesia after the war.

December — Australian troops occupy East Timor.

In August 1941, the Atlantic Charter was signed by the USA, Britain, and the governments-in-exile of many of the occupied

January 13 Japanese take Manado.

January 15 British General Wavell takes command of ABDACOM, the first Allied joint command (Australian, British, Dutch, American) in the war.

The Netherlands Indies government had few resources of its own. With the Netherlands under control and the home government in exile in London, defense of the area fell mostly to the British and the Americans. When the British lost Malaya and Singapore, and the Americans lost the Philippines, the defense of the Netherlands Indies became hopeless.

January 16 Acehnese agents return from Malaya with promises of Japanese support against the Dutch.

January 23 Japanese take Balikpapan.

Hinduism, one of Indonesia's five religions.

January 25 Japanese take Kendar on Sulawesi.

January 31 Japanese attack Ambon. Australian defenders suffer 90 percent casualties; Ambon is taken within 24 hours.

Japanese take Pontianak.

British troops evacuate Malaya for Singapore.

February 3 Japanese begin air raids on targets in Java.

February 4 Battle of Makassar Strait (naval battle between Kalimantan and Sulawesi); Japanese air and sea power forces Allies to withdraw to Cilacap. Japanese advance into Sulawesi.

February 8 Japanese begin main assault on Singapore.

February 10 Japanese take Ujung Pandang (Makassar).

February 15 Singapore falls; 130,000 troops under British command are taken as prisoners of war.

Japanese land paratroopers at Palembang, take oil industry.

February 19 Battle of Badung Strait (naval battle between Bali and Lombok); small Japanese force drives back Dutch and Australians. Japanese land on Bali. First Japanese air raid on Darwin, Australia.

nations of Europe, including the Netherlands. The Charter called for the "right of all peoples to choose the form of government under which they will live", among other things. In September of that same year, Dutch diplomats clarified that they did not think this applied to Indonesia.

December 8 Japanese invade Malaya, landing in southernmost Thailand and northern Malaya. Japanese begin attacking the Philippines. The Netherlands, among other nations, declares war on Japan.

December 10 British battleships Prince of Wales and Repulse are sunk within hours of each other off Malaya.

In 1941, the British and the Americans as well as the Dutch began to tighten restrictions on business with Japan, including embargoes on supplies that could be used to wage war. In response, Japan announced that it would try to organize the "Greater East Asian Co-Prosperity Sphere", a bloc that would supply raw materials to Japan and receive exports in return. The original idea stretched the bloc as far as India and New Zealand. The bloc would be controlled by the

Japanese military. Japanese propaganda also advanced the idea that Asian colonies of European powers should be free from Western control-but this implied that control of those colonies would fall to Japan by military force.

December 10 Anti-Dutch Acehnese make contact with Japanese forces. Malaya.

December 17 Australian-led force lands in East Timor. Portuguese dictator Salazar protests.

Japanese lands in Sarawak.

December 22 Main Japanese invasion force lands in the Philippines.

December 24 Japanese attack British forces at Kuching, Sarawak.

1942
January 2 Japanese take city of Manila.

January 3 Japanese take Sabah.

January 10 Japanese begin invasion of Indonesia in Kalimantan and Sulawesi.

January 11 Japanese take Tarakan.

The Dutch actually transferred Communists being held in prison camps in the Netherlands Indies, some of them since 1926, to prison camps in Australia when the Japanese arrived.

February 20 Japanese land on Timor.

February 23 Revolt against Dutch begins in Aceh and North Sumatra, with Japanese support.

Dutch transfer Sukarno to Padang; Sukarno slips away in chaos as Dutch evacuate.

Dutch evacuate Sjahrir and Hatta from Banda by air minutes before the Japanese begin bombing the island.

Japanese claim fall of Timor; Australian forces continue guerilla warfare.

February 27 to March 1 Battle of Java Sea; Japanese destroy much of the Dutch and Australian naval forces near Surabaya. American destroyers escape to Australia. Dutch Admiral Doorman is killed.

March 1 Battle of Sunda Strait: Japanese invasion force lands at Banten.

Japanese invasion force lands west of Surabaya.

Japanese air raid on Medan.

March 5 Japanese air strikes at Cilacap. Japanese enter Batavia.

March 7 Rangoon falls to Japanese.

March 8 Dutch in Java surrender outside Bandung.

Japanese take Surabaya.

March 11 Acehnese resistance engages in battles with retreating Dutch.

March 15 Japanese forces arrive in Aceh.

Oil fields at Tarakan: Indonesia's strategic natural resources made it a valuable prize during the Second World War. Oil fields and refineries were important to the Japanese war effort, and were frequent targets of Allied bombing raids.

Japanese ban all political activities and existing organizations. Volksraad is abolished. A ban is placed on merah-putih flags.

	Japanese 16th Army in charge of Java; 25th Army in Sumatra (headquarters at Bukittinggi); Navy controls eastern Indonesia (headquarters at Ujung Pandang).
April	Japanese try to organize "AAA" movement; start propaganda campaigns.
	ABDACOM is dissolved. British and Americans divide responsibilities of war: British will try to retake Malaya and Sumatra as well as Burma. Rest of the Pacific and Indonesia become the responsibility of the U.S. (working with Australia).
April 19	Japanese take Hollandia (now Jayapura).
July	Japanese assemble Sukarno, Hatta and Sjahrir in Jakarta.
	Outwardly cooperating with the Japanese was the only option Sukarno and Hatta really had. The ultimate goal, of course, was not to support Japan, but to win independence for Indonesia. Later, the returning Dutch would try to accuse Sukarno of being a Japanese collaborator in order to get British support against the new Indonesian republic.
	Sukarno, Hatta, Sjahrir meet privately; Sukarno to rally masses for independence, Hatta to handle diplomatic connections, Sjahrir to coordinate underground activities.
	Sjahrir, for his part, directed underground activities from his sister's house at Cipanas, near Bogor. Information was frequently and quietly shared between Sukarno, who could get information from Japanese inner circles, and Sjahrir.
	Sukarno accepts Japanese offer to be head of Indonesia government, but answerable to Japanese military.
August 29	Japanese begin transferring some forces from Sumatra and Java to the Solomon Islands.
September	Indonesian Muslims refuse to bow towards Japanese Emperor in Tokyo.
October	At the beginning, Japanese propaganda sounded like an improvement over Dutch rule. After the Japanese troops began stealing food and taking men for forced labor, the opinion of Indonesians turned against them.
	Against Indonesians, the Japanese military was mostly guilty of three things: **1. Forced labor**, in which many Indonesian men were taken

from their homes and sent as far as Burma to do construction and other hard labor in terrible conditions. Many thousands died or disappeared;

2. Forced requisitioning, in which Japanese soldiers took food, clothing, and other supplies from Indonesian families by force and without compensation. This led to much hunger and suffering during the war;

3. Forced slavery of women, in which Indonesian women were kept as "comfort women" for the amusement of Japanese soldiers.

In addition, the Japanese kept Dutch civilians in internment camps under poor conditions and treated military prisoners of war in Indonesia badly.

Japanese military advances in the Pacific stop; Japanese commanders told to organize pro-Japanese sentiments in occupied areas.

October 16 Japanese 16th Army sends garrisons to Lombok, Sumba and Timor.

War crimes in Indonesia were not nearly as serious as those committed in China or Korea during the same period, however. Some commanders, such as Gen. Imamura in Java, were publicly criticized in Tokyo newspapers for being too "soft." There were even Japanese officers who were sympathetic to the idea of Indonesian independence, and who went out of their way to support Indonesian political figures and organizations, right up to Sukarno himself.

November Revolt in Aceh put down by Japanese.

December 27 Japanese open first internment camp for Dutch women at Ambarawa.

1943
January Japanese arrest Amir Sjarifuddin, break up his resistance movement.

The case of Amir Sjarifuddin is an unusual one. He was a Communist, yet received funds from the Dutch government-in-exile to support his resistance movement against the Japanese.

Australian guerillas evacuate East Timor.

February 9 Japanese send extra troops to Tanimbar and Kai Islands, and Irian Jaya.

March 9	Japanese organize Putera (Pusat Tenaga Rakyat, a political auxiliary organization). Sukarno is named chairman.
	Japanese begin to organize local ilitary auxiliaries, including Heiho. By the end of the war in 1945, over two million Indonesians are in them.
July	Japanese arrest 1000 in South Kalimantan.
July 7	Japanese Prime Minister Tojo promises Indonesians limited self-government in a speech at Gambir, Jakarta.
August 13	U.S. bombers from Australia hit Balikpapan.
	Around this time, many Protestant ("Kristen") churches established Indonesian leaderships after Dutch churchmen and missionaries had been sent to Japanese internment camps. A side effect of the Japanese occupation was to make Protestant churches more Indonesian.
	Japanese begin to take over sugar estates in favor of Japanese sugar producers; European managers are sent to internment camps.
September	Revolts against Japanese put down in South and West Kalimantan.
	Orders go out to Japanese military to organize "Giyugun" (local armies).
October 3	Japanese organize PETA (Pembela Tanah Air).
	Japanese organize Masyumi (Majlis Syurah Muslimin Indonesia)
	Many notable figures were signed up for PETA, including Soedirman and Suharto. Independence activists saw military training not so much as support for Japan as preparation for possible independence. By mid-1945, there were 120,000 armed fighters in PETA. This group later formed the core of the new Indonesian Armed Forces (ABRI) after independence was proclaimed in 1945.
	Japanese begin to impose compulsory labor on villagers (romusha); many thousands die or disappear.
	Japanese impose rice requisitioning.

November 10 Sukarno, Hatta and Kyai Bagus Hadikusumo are flown to Tokyo to be decorated by the Emperor of Japan.

This was the first time that Sukarno had traveled abroad. Hatta, who had spent years in Europe, was less easily impressed.

December Barisan Hizbullah organized by Japanese; armed force of Muslim youths associated with Masyumi.

1944
January Putera replaced by Jawa Hokokai/Java Service Association. Sukarno is chairman.

April 19 Allies bomb Sabang in Aceh.

April 22 Allies retake Hollandia (now Jayapura).

May 9 Japanese commanders decide to abandon Irian Jaya.

May 17 Allied air raid on Surabaya.

May 27 U.S. force lands on Biak.

June 4 Japanese begin counterattack on Biak.

August 11 Allied air raid on Palembang.

A small Netherlands East Indies administration was et up in the eastern areas that Allied forces passed through in 44-45 on their way to the Philippines.

August 28–29 Ambon is mostly destroyed by Allied air raids.

September 7 Japanese General Koiso promises that Indonesia will be independent in the "very near future."

September 8 U.S. forced finally clear last Japanese from Biak.

September 15 Allies land on Morotai.

October Australian forces begin bombing Balikpapan.

December Barisan Hizbullah, an armed auxiliary to Masyumi, is organized by the Japanese.

Pakubuwono XII becomes Susuhunan of Surakarta.

1945
February 14 PETA soldiers at Blitar attack Japanese armory.

March 1	Badan Penyelidik Usaha Persiapan Kemerdekaan Indonesia (BPUPKI), a committee to prepare for Indonesia independence, is announced by the Japanese. Members include Sukarno, Hatta, Wahid Hasyim, many others, Chairman is Dr. Radjiman Wediodiningrat.
	In early discussions among the members of BPUPKI, it was assumed that the new Indonesia would not only include all the Netherlands Indies, but also Portuguese Timor, Sarawak, Sabah, and British Malaya.
April	Japanese Vice-Admiral Maeda, head of Naval Intelligence in Indonesia, sponsors speaking tour by Sukarno and Hatta to Ujung Padang.
April 30	Australian and Dutch forces land at Tarakan.
May	Supomo speaks to independence committee against individualism, in favor of national integration.
May 3	Acehnese guerillas overrun Japanese outpost at Pandrah, killing all Japanese forces with no losses of their own.
June	Maeda sponsors speaking tour by Sukarno and Hatta: Bali and Banjarmasin.
June 1	Sukarno describes "Pancasila" doctrine in speech to independence committee.
June 10	Australian forces land in Brunei.
	Dutch forces land in North Sumatra.
June 24	Allied forces land on Halmahera.
July	Japanese military meets in Singapore; plans to hand over Indonesia to Indonesians.
July 1	Australian forces take Balikpapan.
	U.S. bombers hit Watampone, other sites in Kalimantan and Sulawesi.
July 11	U.S. air raid on Sabang.

The Pancasila is the national doctrine of Indonesia, the ideals that society should try to live up to.

PANCASILA
The Pancasila idea was first described by Sukarno in a speech in June 1945. It is summed up in five principles:
(1) Kebangsaan (nationalism)
(2) Kemanusiaan (humanism or internationalism)
(3) Kerakyatan (representative government or democracy)
(4) Keadilan Sosial (social justice)
(5) Ketuhanan (monotheism)
…all based in gotong royong which is "community cooperation" or "working together."
In more recent years, Pancasila has been made part of the standard curriculum, and all organizations in Indonesia have been required to adopt Pancasila as their guiding ideology. This led to some quiet controversy in the 1980s, as some Muslims felt uncomfortable that they were possibly being asked to place Pancasila above their religion. Others felt that Pancasila was being redefined to mean loyalty to the person of then President Suharto.

Chapter 8

1945 to 1950

The War for Independence

1945

August 9 Sukarno, Hatta, and Radjiman Wediodiningrat are flown by the Japanese to Vietnam to meet with Marshal Terauchi. There they are informed of the collapse of Japanese forces, and that Japan will grant Indonesia independence on August 24.

August 14 Sukarno, Hatta, and Radjiman Wediodiningrat return to Jakarta, mistrustful of the Japanese promise.

August 15 Japan surrenders to the Allies. The Japanese army and navy still control Indonesia. Japan has agreed to return Indonesia to the Dutch.

August 16 Sukarno and Hatta are spirited away by youth leaders to Rengasdengklok at 3:00 a.m. They later return to Jakarta, meet with General Yamamoto, and spend the next night at Vice-Admiral Maeda Tadashi's residence. Sukarno and Hatta are told privately that Japan no longer has the power to make decisions regarding the future of Indonesia.

August 17 Sukarno reads the brief, succinct, and unilateral "Proklamasi"; the Declaration of Independence.

PETA forces, radical youths, and ordinary people in Jakarta organize defense of Sukarno's residence. Flyers are distributed proclaiming independence. Adam Malik sends out a short-wave announcement of the Proklamasi.

August 18 Piagam Jakarta (Jakarta Charter) mentioning Islam among the Pancasila principles is dropped from the preamble to the new constitution.

PROCLAMASI: the Declaration of Independence.
PROKLAMASI: Kami bangsa Indonesia dengan ini menjatakan Kemerdekaan Indonesia. Hal-hal jang mengenai pemindahan kekoeasaan dll. Diselenggarakan denga tjara saksama dan

dalem tempo jang sesingkat-singkatnja.Djakarta, hari 17 boelan 8 tahoen 1945Atas nama bangsa Indonesia. Soekarno/Hatta

The original constitution of 1945 is not very specific on many issues, and placed much power in the hands of the President. In 1950, a more comprehensive constitution was adopted that gave the most power to the Assembly, but this constitution was dropped in favor of a return to the 1945 constitution under Sukarno's orders in 1959.

In the opinion of the victorious Allied powers in 1945, Lord Mountbatten, the Allied supreme commander in southeast Asia, was in charge of Sumatra and Java. Australian forces were given responsibility for Kalimantan and eastern Indonesia.

August 22 Japanese announce their surrender publicly in Jakarta.

The New Republic: The constitution that had been drafted by the prepatory committee, and announced on the 18th, is adopted (UUD 45). Sukarno is declared President, Hatta is declared Vice-President. KNIP (Central Indonesian National Committee) is the temporary governing body until elections can be held. The new government is installed on August 31.

Former PETA and Heiho soldiers, Islamic forces try to organize themselves into a new fighting force.

Scattered violence breaks out between youths and Dutch former internees. Dutch soldiers who had been prisoners of war under the Japanese are put back into active service against the Republic.

Australian troops take surrender from Japanese navy. Australian military gives support to NICA (Netherlands Indies Civil Administration) to retain government control in eastern areas, Sulawesi, and Kalimantan.

October 5 ABRI founded.

October 8 Republican forces in Surabaya take Captain Huyer in custody.

British troops in Padang, Medan, Palembang.

Fighting escalates between Republican youths and foreigners. Dutch troops attack civilians.

ABRI forces skirmish with Dutch on Java, Sumatra and Bali.

1945 to 1950: The War for Independence

Japanese military police massacre Republican youths in Pekalongan.

Japanese troops push Republican out of Bandung; hand over city to British.

October 14 Republican youths begin five-day battle against Japanese troops in Semarang.

October 16 Sutan Sjahrir and Amir Sjarifuddin take over Central Indonesian National Committee (KNIP). Sjahrir is Prime Minister of the Republic. Sjahrir publishes pamphlet in support of democracy and social justice, and against feudalism, fascism and the remnants of Japanese fascist thought.

October 17 Van Mook sends telegram to Dutch government urging that negotiations with the Republic be rejected.

Sjahrir was more inclined to negotiate with the Dutch, Sjahrir was not only a Communist, but also a figure who had received covert support from the Dutch government-in-exile during the war.

October 18 Japanese troops secure Semarang; hand city over to British.

There was friction between Sjahrir as Minister of Defense, who was secretly Communist and may have had Dutch ties, and ABRI, which was dominated by officers who served in PETA under the Japanese and had Islamic sympathies.

October 22 Nahdlatul Ulama proclaims that a state of jihad exists against the Dutch, making participation obligatory for Muslims.

October 23 Under British pressure, Van Mook meets with Sukarno for informal talks. Neither side gives ground.

Van Mook was never quite happy that he had been named Lieutenant-Governor" instead of "Governor-General" of the Indies.

Japanese Admiral Shibata surrenders Surabaya to Dutch, but hands over his weapons to Republicans. Many Japanese troops are disarmed by Republican youths.

October 25 British 49th Indian Infantry arrives under General Mallaby.

October 27 British airplanes drop leaflets on Surabaya demanding surrender by Republican forces within 24 hours. British troops on the ground are nearly destroyed by Indonesian troops and

79

mobs of ordinary people.

October 29 Sukarno and Hatta arrive in Surabaya by plane. Sukarno and General Mallaby agree on a truce. Poor communications and general chaos prevent Sukarno from enforcing the truce.

Australian commander in South Sulawesi bans all political activity, organization of militias, etc. among the public under his control.

October 30 British Mayor General Hawthorn flies to Surabaya from Jakarta. Sukarno, Hatta, Mallaby and Hawthorn sign a cease-fire. Five hours later Mallaby is killed.

British bombard Surabaya as punishment, thousands left dead or homeless. British strafe civilian refugees on highway.

PKI created again.

November 3 Sukarno lifts ban on political parties.

November 9 Sukarno asks Sjahrir to form a Cabinet.

British 5th Indian Division lands at Surabaya.

November 10 (Heroes' Day/Hari Pahlawan) Indonesia counterattack in Surabaya. Fighting continues for three weeks. Six hundred Indian troops defect from the British and join the Indonesians.

Many of the British occupying troops in Indonesia in 1945 were actually from India. Nehru strongly protested the use of Indian troops against Indonesians; this was an important reason that the British withdrew.

Some Japanese troops battle ABRI forces on Java, Sumatra, and Bali.

Dutch abandon Aceh forever.

Japanese-favored leaders removed from NU and Muhammadiyah.

Kongres Ummat Islam Indonesia meets, remakes the originally Japanese-organized Masyumi as an Indonesian and Islamic political party.

November 23 British Foreign Secretary Bevin urges negotiations between the Dutch and the Republic.

December 12–15 Battle of Ambarawa.

December 15 Soedirman installed as Panglima Besar (supreme commander).

Allies evacuate remaining Japanese from Aceh; a few Japanese remain to help Republic.

In the areas that were controlled by the new Republic of Indonesia, ABRI forces carried out their mission to repatriate Japanese soldiers, Allied prisoners of war, and former internees.

"Social War" breaks out in Aceh: the traditional aristocracy loses in a bloody conflict with Islamic leaders.

Sjahrir, Sjahrifuddin and their followers form Partai Sosialis.

Dutch forces begin to replace Australians as occupying power in eastern areas.

1946
January PNI reestablished.

Persatuan Perjuangan (Union of Struggle) formed by Tan Melaka to oppose Sjahrir government and negotiations. Soedirman speaks against negotiations and Sjahrir.

"Barisan Banteng" radicals kidnap Pakubuwono XII of Surakarta.

At the beginning of 1946, Dutch forces in Indonesia numbered about 20,000.

Republic of Indonesia government leaves Jakarta for Yogya.

Gajah Mada University founded in Yogya; Sultan offers front portion of Kraton to house it.

Dutch forces occupy Bangka and Belitung.

Indonesia issue raised in U.N. for the first time.

February 10 Van Mook sends proposal to Sjahrir for "democratic partnership" between the Netherlands and Indonesia, but which still does not provide for real independence.

March "Social War" breaks out in Batak areas of Sumatra.

Tan Malaka and Persatuan Perjuangan increase criticism of

	Sjahrir.
March 12	Sjahrir publicly replies to Van Mook's offer of February, demanding immediate recognition of Indonesia's sovereignty without delay.
	Sjahrir secretly agrees with Dutch to negotiate for Republican control of Java, Madura and Sumatra only, in a political union with the Netherlands, Curacao and Surinam.
April	King of Bone and Republican government arrested by Dutch in Sulawesi.
	Dutch replace British in Bandung. "Bandung Lautan Api": Indonesians burn down city rather than surrender it to the Dutch.
	Barisan Banteng rules Surakarta in defiance of Sjahrir government.
April 14	Dutch and Indonesian representatives begin talks at Hoge Veluwe in the Netherlands. The talks are unsuccessful.
May	Violence between Toba and Karo Bataks in Sumatra.
	Nasution takes command of Siliwangi division of ABRI.
	Soedirman gives speech with Sukarno present: Government must work for the principles of the Constitution (UUD 45) and independence.
June	Government revokes privileges of Pakubuwono and Mangkunegara houses in Surakarta, under pressure from Soedirman.
June 27	Army units under General Sudarsono open the jail in Surakarta and release Tan Malaka and his followers. Sjahrir is arrested in Surakarta while on an overnight stay in the same night, and is taken to the Kraton (Sultan's Palace) with other notable figures. General Sudarsono's troops occupy Yogya.
	Surakarta declares martial law and demands Sjahrir's release. Troops loyal to Sukarno advance on Surakarta from Surabaya; the loyal Siliwangi division sends troops to Yogya.
	Adam Malik, young radical, others are arrested.
July	Allies officially turn over all of Indonesia, except Java and Sumatra, to Dutch.

July 2 General Sudarsono and Mohamed Yamin visit Sukarno in person, and demand that Sjahrir be replaced by Tan Malaka. Sjahrir, supposedly still a captive, surprises everyone by walking into the room. Sukarno orders that Sudarsono and Yamin be arrested.

The Philippines became independent from the United States on July 4, 1946.

July 3 "July 3rd Affair": army units release Adam Malik from jail and demand that Soedirman be put in charge of security. Sukarno takes control of the situation.

Sjahrir reorganizes government to include Natsir, Sjarifuddin, the Sultan of Yogya, Haji Agus Salim, and Djuanda.

July 15 Van Mook calls conference at Malino, Sulawesi, to plan for new Dutch-sponsored state in eastern Indonesia.

September Talks are reopened between the Sjahrir government and the Dutch at Linggajati, near Cirebon.

October 14 Prelim military truce signed at Linggajati.

November 15 Linggajati agreement: Dutch recognize Republic of Indonesia authority in Java, Sumatra and Madura. Both sides agree to form United States of Indonesia with Netherlands crown as a symbolic head.

November 20 Battle of Marga; resistance on Bali led by Ngurah Rai is defeated by Dutch force.

November 29 Last British troops leave Indonesia.

Dutch Capt. Raymond Westerling begins campaign in South Sulawesi against Republican youths. Westerling and his men commit many war crimes against citizens, including atrocities against children and hospital patients.

December 18 Dutch create state of East Indonesia/Negara Indonesia Timur at conference in Denpasar, Bali. Sjahrir protests.

The Dutch delayed signing the Linggajati agreement for months. Many of their actions over the following six months appeared to be aimed at undermining it.

"Left Wing/Sayap Kiri" coalition packs KNIP with pro-Linggajati members.

1947	
February	Sukarno and Hatta threaten to resign if Linggajati is not ratified.
March 25	Netherlands government finally ratifies Linggajati agreement.
	Dutch create state of West Kalimantan with Sultan of Pontianak at head; Sjahrir protests.
June	Dutch complain that Indonesia is stopping shipments of rice to Dutch-controlled areas.
June 26	Dutch forces mobilize for an invasion of Madura, and eventually Java. William Foote, a USA diplomat, intervenes and offers to mediate between Dutch and Indonesians. The invasion is postponed.
June 27	Amir Sjarifuddin and the "Left Wing" withdraw support of Sjahrir. Sjahrir leaves the government and becomes Indonesia's representative at the United Nations. Amir Sjarifuddin becomes Prime Minister.
July 8	Amir Sjarifuddin government makes conciliatory offer to Dutch: Republic of Indonesia will stop seeking international recognition; Netherlands officials can take government positions in the Republic.
July 20	First Dutch "police action": Dutch troops occupy West Java, East Java, Madura, Semarang, Medan, Palembang, Padang, bomb many cities.
	At the start of the first Dutch "police action," there were 92,000 Dutch forces in Indonesia.
July 30	Young students blow up bridge at Bumiayu, preventing Dutch forces from taking Purwokerto.
	USA and British unhappy, India, Australia, Soviet Union support the Republic of Indonesia in the U.N. Refugees pour into Central Java. Australia boycotts Dutch shipping.
August 1	U.N. Security Council calls for ceasefire in Indonesia.
August 4	ceasefire agreed to by Dutch and Sukarno, but is ignored in the field. Dutch declare "Van Mook line" at the edge of their military advances in Java and Sumatra.
October	Dutch military tries to consolidate control of areas within the

"Van Mook line." Dutch take control of all of Madura.

December   Dutch create state of East Sumatra.

December 8   Dutch and Indonesian representatives meet on board the U.S.S. Renville, a U.S. Navy transport stationed in the Philippines, which was moved to Jakarta harbor for the talks.

1948
January 17   Renville agreement under U.N. auspices draws ceasefire line favorable to Dutch.

The Renville agreement called for a truce along the so-called "Van Mook line." The original draft did not even mention the Republic. Amendments were added that included mention of the Republic of Indonesia after the United States applied pressure on the Dutch, and it was only then that the Indonesians agreed.

"Dvipantara" or "Jawa Dwipa" is reported by Indian scholars to be in Java and Sumatra

PNI, Masyumi, and Tan Malaka oppose the Renville agreement.

Amir Sjarifuddin resigns as Prime Minister.

Sukarno appoints Hatta to head emergency cabinet answerable to President.

February   Sjahrir forms PSI, supports Sukarno.

Dutch create state of Madura, state of "Pasundan" in West Java.

The Dutch blockaded the areas under control of the Republic of Indonesia around this time, causing shortages of food and medicine.

"Left Wing" under Amir Sjarifuddin renames itself People's Democratic Front. Sjarifuddin criticizes Renville agreement.

Col. Nasution leads Siliwangi division out of West Java to Central Java.

March   Van Mook creates provisional government for federated Indonesia.

By this time, Van Mook saw that Indonesia would not remain a colony of the Netherlands forever.

	His actions became not so much efforts to keep the Netherlands Indies, as ways to manage a slow transition to self-rule.
May	Kartosuwirjo proclaims himself Imman of Negara Islam Indonesia, or "Darul Islam." Islamic state rebelling against both Dutch and the Republic.
July 8	Representatives of 13 Dutch-controlled states created by Van Mook convene at Bandung, to begin process of created United States of Indonesia.
August 11	Musso, former PKI leader from the 1920s, arrives in Yogya after spending twelve years in the Soviet Union. Sjarifuddin announces that he has been an underground member of PKI. PKI sponsors strikes and demonstrations.
	Hatta, with little money to pay troops, begins demobilizing some ABRI units.
September	Dutch create state of South Sumatra.
	PKI gains recruits from PDF; new Politburo includes Aidit, Lukman and Njoto.
	Republican Government releases Tan Malaka from custody as counter to PKI influence.
September 5	Musso gives speech advocating that Indonesia align itself with the Soviet Union.
	The "Madiun incident" was the second time the PKI made an unsuccessful, poorly planned revolt. The first was against the Dutch in 1926-1927; the last was in 1965.
September 17	Siliwangi Division drives PKI out of Surakarta; PKI retreats to Madiun.
September 18	PKI attempts coup in Madiun, kills pro-government officers there.
September 19	PKI figures Yogya arrested; Sukarno denounces Madiun coup; Musso replies that he will fight; popular opinion sides with Sukarno.
September 30	Siliwangi Division recaptures Madiun. PKI abandons Madiun, pursued by army. Aidit and Lukman leave for China.
October	Pro-government Tan Malaka followers create Murba Party. Tan

Malaka is arrested again.

October 11 Van Mook resigns as Lt. Governor of the Indies.

October 31 Musso killed while attempting to escape arrest.

November Dutch create state of East Java.

December 1 Amir Sjarifuddin captured.

December 11 Dutch inform U.N. representatives that further talks with the Republic are "futile."

December 18 Dutch officials tell representatives of the United States and the Republic of Indonesia in Jakarta that they are canceling the Renville agreement. The news does not reach Yogya, as the Dutch have already cut the phone lines there.

December 19 Second Dutch "police action" begins at 5:30 a.m. without warning. Yogya falls to the Dutch.

Civil government of republic, including Sukarno, Hatta, and Sjahrir allows itself to be captured, hoping to outrage world opinion; Sukarno and Sjahrir are taken into Dutch custody, and eventually flown to Bangka. Sultan Hamengkubuwono IX of Yogya remains in his palace, and does not leave during the entire Dutch occupation.

Dutch occupy Bukittinggi. Emergency government for Indonesia is declared (PRDI) at Payakumbuh nearby.

Tan Malaka escapes again during the confusion.

December 20 Army executes Sjarifuddin, withdraws from Yogya.

All of Indonesia except Aceh in Dutch control; guerilla warfare heats up; Soedirman leads guerilla war from sickbed.

Panglima Besar Soedirman

Soedirman is warmly remembered today as perhaps the greatest hero of the revolution. Towards the end of the fighting, he fell ill and directed troops from his sickbed.

Many American newspapers publish editorials against the Dutch.

December 22 Nasution declares military government for Java.

U.N. is outraged at Dutch; Dutch attack while U.N. observers are at Kaliurang.

19 Asian countries boycott Dutch.

Dutch-chosen members of east Indonesia state government vote to condemn the "police action."

United States suspends postwar aid to the Netherlands (Marshall Plan money) that is budged for military use in Indonesia.

December 24 U.N. Security Council calls for end to hostilities.

December 31 Dutch accept U.N. call for ceasefire in Java.

1949
January 5 Dutch accept U.N. call for ceasefire in Sumatra.

Sultan Hamengkubuwono IX of Yogya refuses Dutch offer to head new Javanese state, resigns as head of Yogya government, aids Republic guerilla fighters.

There was significant guerilla activity against the Dutch during this period.

January 28 U.N. Security Council demands release of the Republic government, and independence for Indonesia by July 1, 1950.

February 7 Resolution is introduced in United States Senate to stop all Marshall Plan aid to the Netherlands. Resolution is defeated on March 8.

March 1 Guerillas retake Yogya for six hours under Suharto.

March 31 U.S. Secretary of State Dean Acheson privately tells Dutch that their Marshall Plan aid is still in jeopardy.

April 6 United States Senate passes resolution to stop Marshall Plan aid to the Netherlands, but only if the U.N. Security Council votes sanctions against the Netherlands.

April 16 Tan Malaka is captured and executed by an ABRI commander after a Dutch contingent attacks the town where he was staying.

April 22 Dutch announce that they will return the Republican government to Yogya if the guerilla war stops.

May	Sukarno and Hatta remain in custody on Bangka.
May 7	Dutch agree to restore Republic of Indonesia government, and to hold talks according to the U.N. Security Council resolution of January 28.
	General Spoor, commander of the Dutch in Indonesia, resigns. He dies of a heart attack on May 25.
June 24	Dutch troops begin evacuating Yogya.
June 29	ABRI troops enter Yogya.
August	Republic troops retake Surakarta.
August 11	Ceasefire on Java.
August 15	Ceasefire on Sumatra.
	Hamengkubuwono IX of Yogya coordinates handovers from Dutch to Republic.
	Dutch begin releasing 12,000 prisoners.
August 23	Round Table Conference begins in the Hague. Hatta head delegation for the Republic of Indonesia, Sultan of Pontianak heads delegation from the Dutch-created states.
November 2	The Hague Agreement is the result of the Round Table Conference: "Republik Indonesia Serikat" would have the crown of the Netherlands as a symbolic head, Sukarno as President, and Hatta as Vice-President. It consists of 15 Dutch-created states plus the original Republic. Sovereignty is to be transferred by December 30. Dutch investments are protected, and the new government is responsible for the billion-dollar Netherlands Indies government debt. The Dutch keep Irian Jaya.
December 19	Universitas Gadjah Mada founded at Yogya.
December 27	Dutch formally transfer sovereignty to Republic of Indonesia.
December 28	Sukarno returned to Jakarta.
	The Dutch finally signed their defeat at this table, preserved still in the Kraton Yogyakarta.

1950
January 23	Dutch Captain Westerling attempts assassination and coup in

	Bandung; some members of Dutch-created Pasundan government are involved.
January 27	Pasundan government dissolves itself.
January 29	Soedirman dies.
February	Westerling sneaks out of country.
March	Most Dutch-created states have dissolved themselves and joined Republic.
April	Sultan of Pontianak arrested for connections with Westerling plot. RUSI takes over West Kalimantan state.
	Republic and pro-Dutch forces clash at Ujung Padang; East Indonesia government is shaken.
April 25	Republic of South Maluku proclaimed at Ambon.
May	East Indonesia decides to dissolve itself into the Republic of Indonesia.
July	Republic of Indonesia troops begin putting down Republic of South Maluku.
	As many as 300,000 Dutch citizens left Indonesia for the Netherlands around 1950.
	Dutch disband Netherlands Indies armed forces (KNIL).
August 17	New constitution; the new Republic of Indonesia is made out of the original (now expanded) republic, East Sumatra and East Indonesia. There is no more RUSI. Jakarta is the capital of the Republic.
1951	Pendekar Guru Besar Bapak Uyuh Suwanda opens his first Pencak Silat Mande Muda school in his own home. (Fig. 1)

As you can see from the beginning of the history, the name of Java, or we say Jawa, the original word was Dvipantara.

Reported by Indian scholars to be in Java and Sumatra.

And Prince Aji Saka introduces writing system to Java based on scripts of southern India.

Until today's cultures in Indonesia, and even the language, still show influences from the Sanskrit language and literature.

Indonesia is interesting place of many with mixed culture, with all the many cultures living together hand-to-hand, together under Pancasila, the Indonesian rule.

The five religions recognized by the governor are:
1. Islam
2. Kristen
3. Hindu
4. Buddhism
5. Muslim

I'm as the person born and growing up in Indonesia, I have to go through many different belifs and culture. As a child it did not matter where we live but that it is the culture and belief we follow, when I was born most babies take on many ceremony and the reason is to make sure that the children grows up to be adult.

Even in one kingdom power is always the point of journey, as humans always want to recognize that they will survive and will protect there own territory from the in and out of attacks from others. The power of the king from each island becoming so strong because they believe in there own power and spirit that they have there own structure way to take care of people, the way life is and the way life is suppose be.

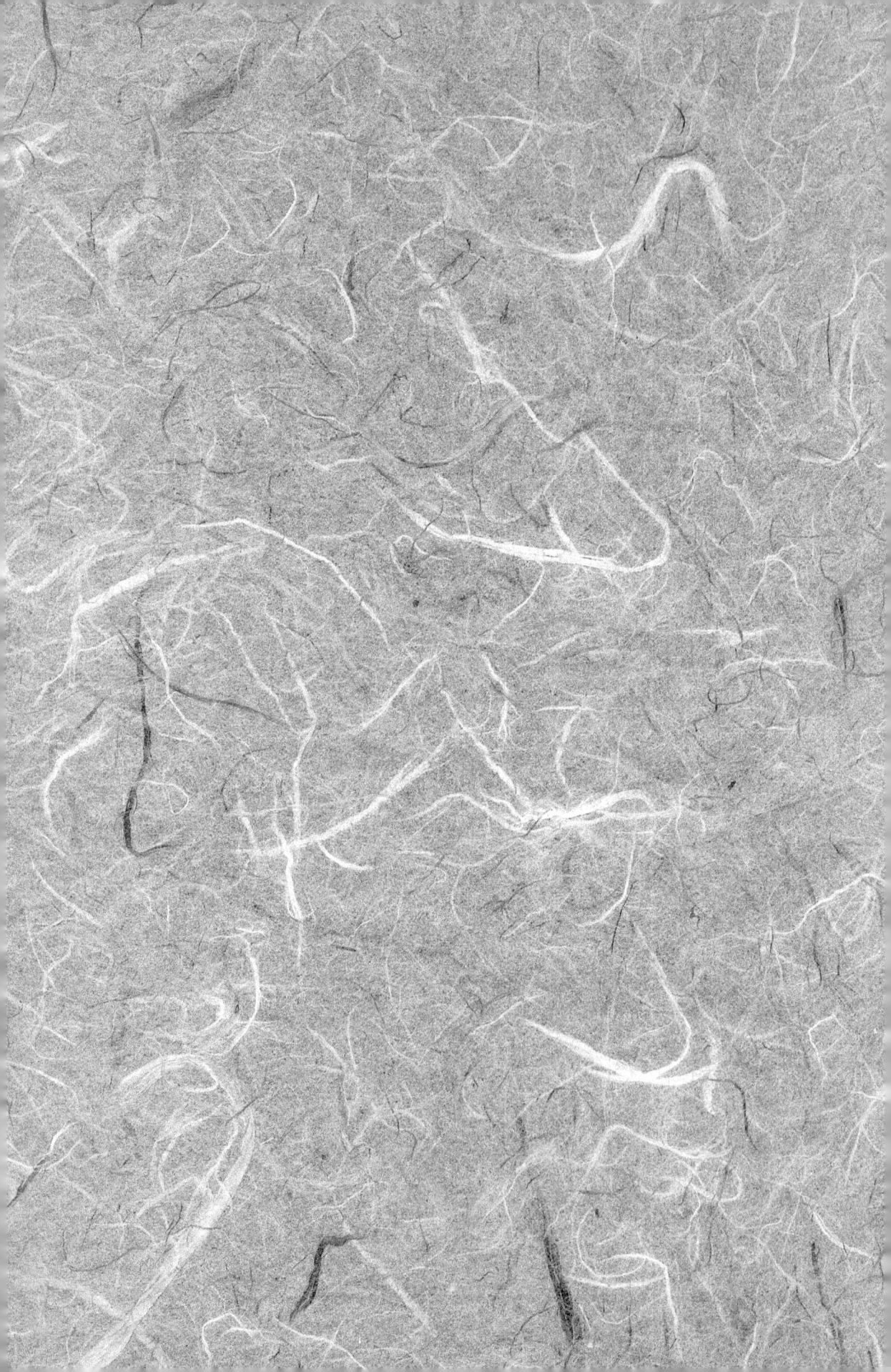

Part II

Mande Muda History and Teachings

Chapter 9

Brief History of Pencak Silat

Pencak Silat (Fig. 1) is a martial art that originated in Indonesia. Indonesia is an archipelago made up of more than 1,300 islands, 360 spoken languages, and a population of approximately 200 million people. With over 1,800 different styles of Pencak Silat found throughout the islands, you can imagine why no two styles of Pencak Silat look exactly alike. Each style depicts its area of origin and ethnic group with its own characteristics. (Fig. 2)

West Java

The beautiful rice fields, tea plantations and rubber tree crops found in West Java (Fig.3) are a result of the rich fertile earth that surrounds the volcanoes and make the area beautiful and colorful in scenery, culture and arts. The *West Javanese people*, otherwise know as the *Sunda* people, are easy going and happy in their rich environment.

The word *pencak* is originally from Java and refers to the *martial arts* of that area. Pencak without the inclusion of the letter 'k' (i.e., *penca*) is the original spelling found in the

Sunda language. Pencak with the k, comes from Bahasa Indonesia, the national language of the country and refers to the movements or beauty of the martial arts. The word *Silat* refers to *fighting*, and is in common use in the areas of Sumatra, southern Philippines, Malaysia, Singapore, Brunei and other areas in South East Asia.

In West Java, the application of Pencak is called *Maenpo*, which means, "to do *Pencak*." In the past the word Maenpo was used when challenging someone to a fight to the death. In Sudanese, Maen literally means, *"to play,"* and *Po* means, *"to forget."* Thus, the translation of Maenpo is *"forget to play."* This terminology is rarely used today.

In Indonesia, Pencak Silat was originally a secretive art taught only to family and members of the village. Today, however, there is a modern version of Pencak Silat that caters to the public. It is taught in the school systems, from elementary school to college and universities levels.

In West Java, from the 1940s through the 1970s, one could routinely see Pencak Silat performed in village ceremonies (Fig. 4). It was also commonly seen at weddings, celebrations of the rice harvest, and circumcisions. It was especially important to perform Pencak Silat at circumcisions because it is believed that when a boy is circumcised he becomes a man-it is a rite of passage. In Indonesia, Pencak Silat is viewed as a reflection of manhood and also helps divert a boy's concentration from the pain of the procedure. This ceremony can still be found in some villages, but it is rarely performed in the big cities.

The various names of the Pencak Silat styles come from various sources, such as the name of the village it originated in, or the name of the founder or creator of the system. Most villages in West Java start with the prefix "Ci." *Ci means pointing to a particular village* or *Chi, which can mean water*. This is

why many of the rivers start with Ci, as well as names of Pencak Silat styles. While there are many styles found in West Java, the three major styles are Cimande, Cikalong, and Syahbandar.

Cimande

Cimande (Fig. 5) is the *name of a village, a river, and a style of Pencak Silat* found in West Java (Fig. 6). Cimande has simple jurus (training forms) and applications. The Cimande style is found in three different villages: Cimande Tarik Kolot, Cimande Tengah, and Cimande Girang. Tanah Sareal is the area where Bah Kahir founded the style and is also buried. Bah is a title that

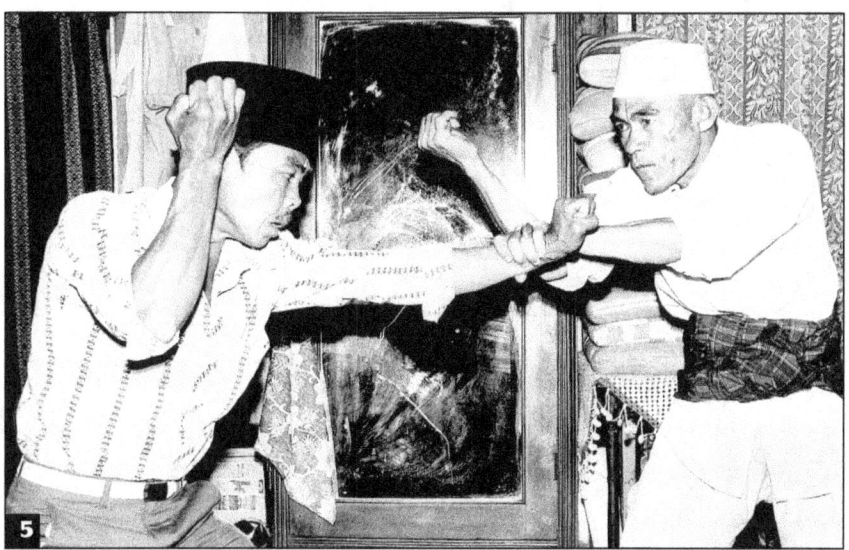

comes from Abah, meaning grandfather. Eyang and Mama are also titles that hold the same meaning. The founder of the style is referred to by one of these titles; which title one uses depends on the origin of the person speaking his name. Selup is a trademark movement of Cimande and anyone who studies this system will know this movement (Fig. 7).

 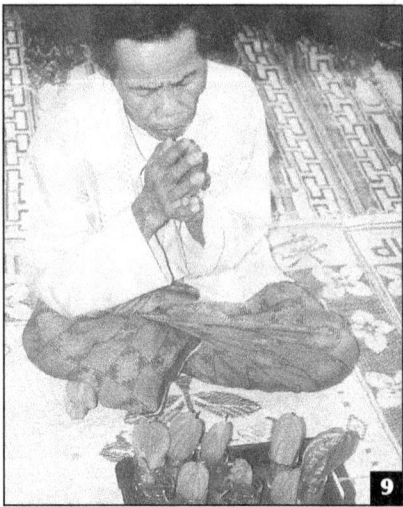

Cimande has a reputation throughout Indonesia for healing bruised or broken bones. Practitioners of the style use a special oil called balur for the purpose of healing the bones. *Balur* is often used after training to *heal injuries to the forearms* (Fig. 8). Cimande is highly respected for both its bone healing and its Pencak Silat. A special ceremony called Kecer Mata is performed in the Cimande system to initiate members. The leader of Cimande, Tarikkolot, prays during the ceremony while members are inducted (Fig. 9). During this time the initiates drop water (that has been blessed) into their eyes (Fig. 10). Following this, the new members are given a Talek (a set of by-laws to follow). To my knowledge, until now only members knew of this ceremony and the by-laws.

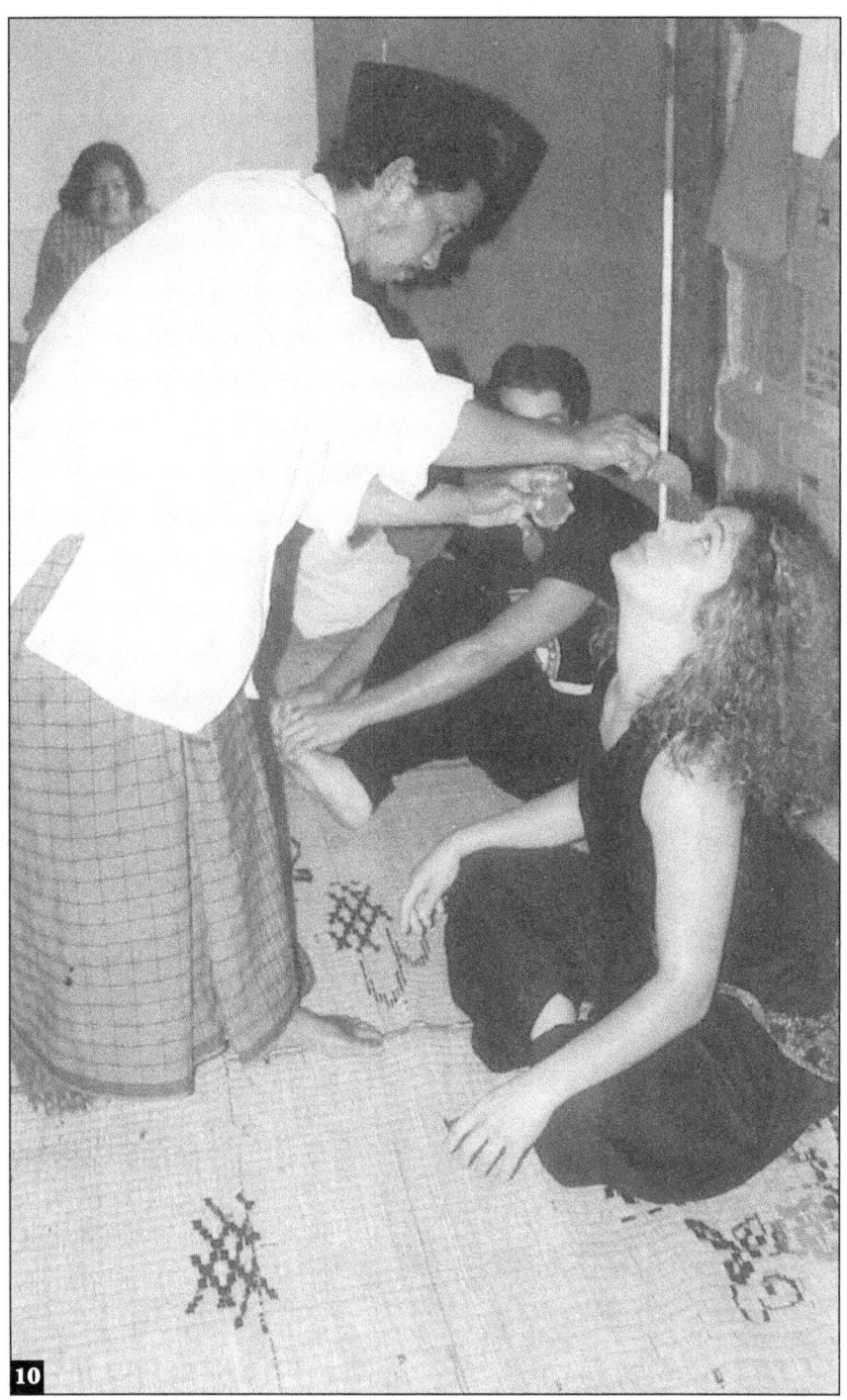

Cikalong

Cikalong (Fig 11) is both the name of a *village and a style of Pencak Silat*. Cikalong Pencak Silat practitioners move quickly and lightly, their methods are very effective in evading and taking down an opponent. The cikalong practitioner will use the outside of the body to perform the entries needed to defend him from any attack. This system is not related to an animal style.

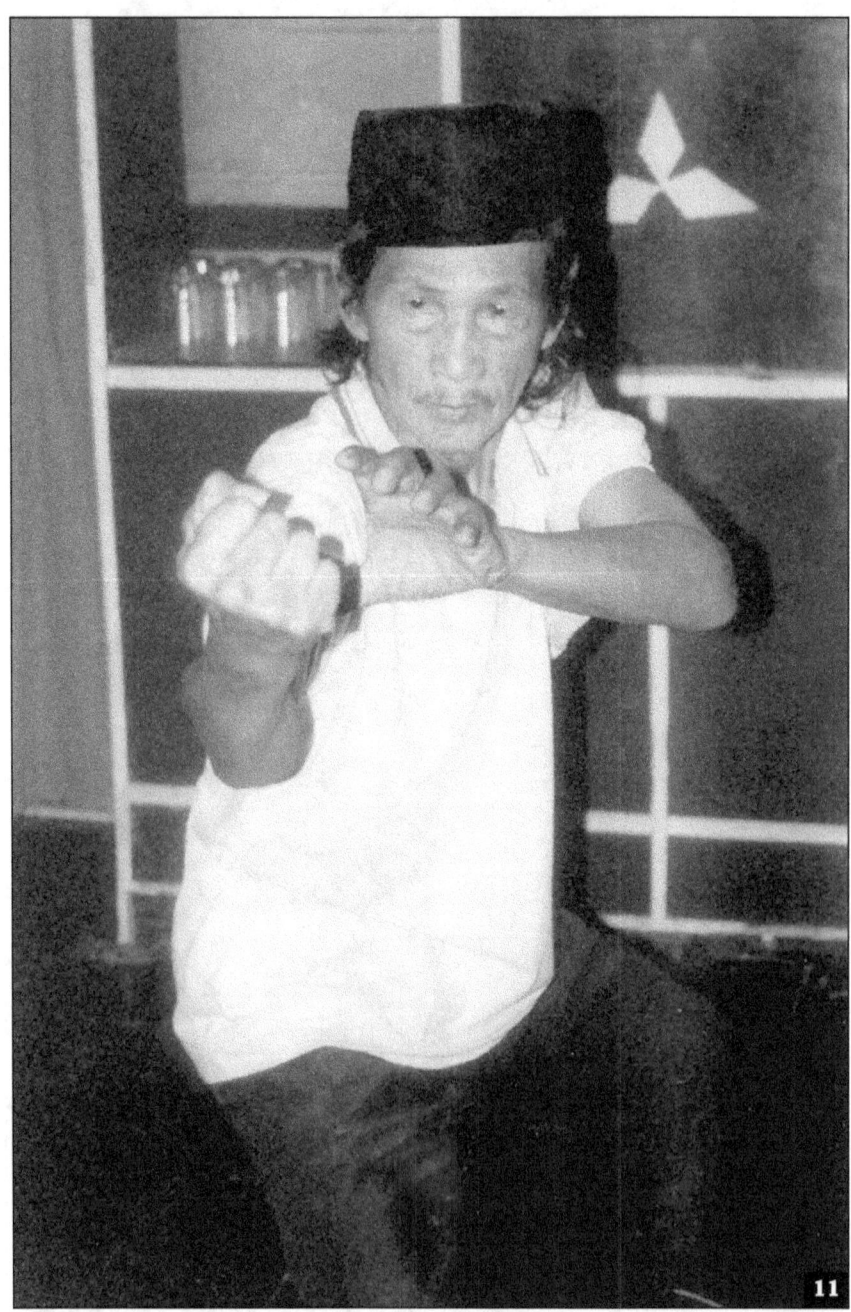

Syahbandar

The *Syahbandar* style (Fig. 12) is *named for its founder, Mama Syahbandar.* I believe he was originally from Sumatra but he traveled to West Java, where he studied Pencak Silat, and remained in West Java to teach the art. Syahbandar is known for its entries by using the center of the body to defend against any attack while using the feet only to move forward, backward, and side to side. These movements are normally done in a kuda-kuda (horse stance).

1

Chapter 10

History of Mande Muda

In 1951, my father Uyuh Suwanda founded the Pencak Silat Munde Muda system. This style of Pencak Silat has its roots in both ancient and traditional styles of Indonesian Silat. The first Pencak Silat Munde Muda school was formed in 1951, in Bandug, West Java, Indonesia (Fig. 1). Like the traditional Pencak Silat schools in Indonesia, the school's teachings were not available to the public. *Bapak* Uyuh studied 17 styles of Pencak Silat until he married my mother, Mimi Rumini, who came from and practiced the Indonesian system of Cimunde (Fig. 2). Together they taught Pencak Silat to their family and close friends. These became the first 18 styles found in the Pencak Silat Munde Muda system.

The word *Mande comes from the word Cimunde*. Bapak Uyuh used this name because he believed Cimunde was the original Pencak Silat of West Java.

2

103

He removed the prefix "Ci" because his system taught more than just Cimunde. The word *Muda means young or new*, thus Mande Muda is like a young child, always growing and looking for new Silat material and is open to all the arts.

Bapak Uyuh believed that each Silat technique could mean many things in combat, but also that there was not one technique that would always answer the many questions of attack. For that reason he studied many systems of Pencak Silat and this provided him with the many answers to the questions of combat. Eighteen styles combined to make one method of fighting, and this is what makes Pencak Silat Mande Muda unique and rich with knowledge, culture and family.

The main principle of Pencak Silat Mande Muda is to continue to grow as a practitioner. Only death can stop your growth and study in the art. Another principle is waiting. Bapak Uyuh believed it was better to answer the question of attack rather then to ask it. His definition of a question is that by asking a question you attack the person, if the person gives you a good answer you will be on the ground. A good answer will leave the attacker unable to ask another question.

Uyuh Suwanda

My father was strong in character and knew much about the traditional cultural beliefs of West Java. He implanted in his children his love of the traditional ways and his determination to preserve them. Therefore, he always said to us that Mande Muda must not die. When the leader of the family system dies, then another must take his place. *Pendekar Guru Besar Bapak* Uyuh Suwanda died in 1989, and Mande Muda is still alive because of the spirit and principles that he gave us. This spirit will continue to grow within all of us who practice and will continue practicing and promoting the Suwanda family art of Pencak Silat Mande Muda.(Fig. 3)

For many years it was my father's dream to build a school so our students didn't have to practice outdoors or in the living room where we lived. As you know, Pencak Silat is traditionally family oriented and would normally be taught to someone inside the family or neighbors that befriended the family. Practice might be carried out in the rice fields or under a bamboo tree where there was shade so the sun would not adversely affect the body during practicing.

For many years my family in Bandung taught in our living room, where, due to lack of space, only a few students could be taught at a time. My father's dream of building a school continued until the day he passed away. Since then, I have carried his dream in my heart but had to put it on hold, as it seemed impossible to accomplish. Meanwhile, little by little, I continued to spread the art around the world, traveling around the United States and Europe.

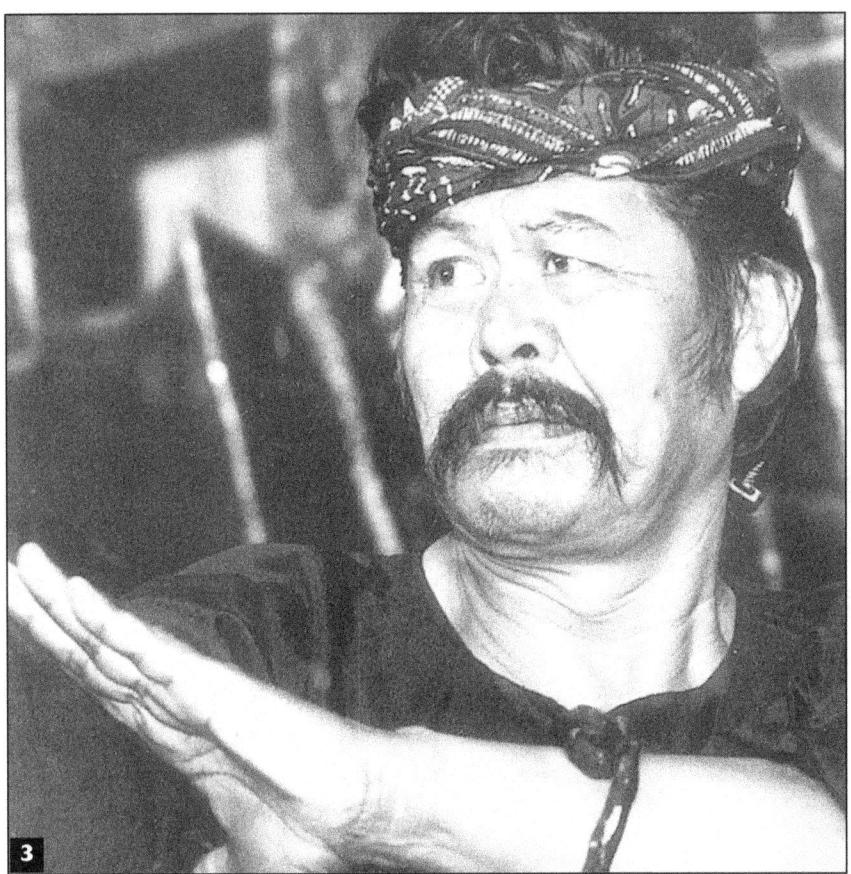

For years I had the idea of bringing many groups of Westerners to Indonesia so they could experience a special program that I put together-a Pencak Silat Mande Muda training camp in Bandung, Indonesia. This way I could do more to educate Westerners about our culture, not just with words, but also with action and new experience, with me as their guide, for them to see for themselves what Pencak Silat is really about.

Let me make this clear to all that there have been some former instructors of mine who claim to have had formal training under the guidance of my father's Pendekar, Guru Besar Bapak Uyuh Suwanda. This is not true! Even though I did bring some of my students to meet him during a brief visit, his sharing of one or two techniques does not constitute formal training or any title earned on their behalf.

If someone wishes to study Pencak Silat from me or any other West Java style teacher, it is important that they know about Indonesian culture in general and Sundanese culture in particular. In my opinion, this goes for anyone learning any art from outside of his or her own country and culture. They should travel to where the art originated and learn more about the people and culture behind it. These students will find that things are as I have

reported them to be and instead of relying on my words they can see for themselves. I'm not afraid to take them, because I have nothing to hide and I am happy that they can take this opportunity to learn more. I feel it is important for them to know more because I feel that I'm an ambassador of Pencak Silat and the Sundanese culture. It is my duty to share this information to all those who desire it.

Many people have taken me up on my offer and have gone to Indonesia with me. They have met many Pendekars, have gone to Cimande village, and so far I'm the only person that I know of providing such opportunities to share this culture. But still, I am not happy that we don't have a place to practice in my area. My father's school is still around (this is in our living room), but it is too small for more than five people to practice at a time. I keep his dream and, penny-by-penny, have been saving money and planning someday to fulfill my father's dream. And it did happen one day, thanks to one of my older students in the United States of America-Steve Hunting-that we were able to start to build a proper school. It was his donation and help to get us a loan that I was able to start to build our official school in Indonesia.

Ibu Mimi Suwanda

My mother Ibu Mimi Suwanda had to be a strong woman to keep our family together. Dealing with everyday life in Indonesia and taking care of 14 children is difficult. She comes from the village of Wrungkiara. Her father and many of her uncles were the freedom fighters against the colonization, before the Independence. She was of the Cimande family. (Fig. 4)

In some ways you might say that Cimande theory is as simple as hit and block, but it is a powerful art. The men and women of Cimande village hide the art of Cimande from the general public for reasons of not wanting anyone to know of their skill. Even if you were to ask them if they knew Pencak Silat, they would deny any knowledge of Cimande or Pencak Silat in general. Being humble is a big part of being in good standing with the community and it is important to be a respectful person in Pencak Silat, with no need or reason to prove what we know, because what we know is part of our daily life.

If you go to Cimande village, you won't find people looking and talking like they know how to fight, but rather like everyday people working together to survive and live an ordinary life. They are concerned with helping one another in the village and sharing their knowledge with their family and neighbors.

When we do become angry and lose control and seem to be going in the direction of braking the rules in our society, most Cimande people have the reminder in their hearts, through their training and initiation ceremony, not to go in the wrong direction. In fact, each Cimande practitioner goes through an important ceremony and follows 10 rules of Cimande, called the Talek and Kecer Mata. Cimande is the only style that has this particular ceremony and rules to follow in West Java. In respect of that tradition it is the responsibility of all Cimande practitioners to remember to follow and be guided by those rules. We believe if everybody in the Cimande family follows the Talek, they will not focus on or talk about somebody else and their problems, flaws, or mistakes or make any judgments against others and will thus be quiet busy improving and keeping themselves in the right direction.

Herlan Herlambang (Bambang) Suwanda

My brother, Bambang Suwanda continues to spread and keep the Mande Muda name alive in Indonesia by teaching publicly in Bandung. He also teaches in the junior and senior high schools as well as in the college of Pasundan in West Java. He practices different systems and forms from our parents and also from other teachers. Each of the individuals in our family has different material and techniques in Pencak Silat, but the characteristics of the movement and philosophy of the art are the same. I credit Bambang as being the one that has helped me to demonstrate and develop the material for the Jagabaya program. My brother Bambang is also very talented in Pencak Silat Mande Muda and is an excellent Pamonyet (monkey style) player. On Febuary 17, 1998 Bambang was recognized by IPSI Jawa Barat Ikatan Penck Silat Indonesia, West Java as an authentic expert instructor.(Fig. 5)

Rita and Ika Suwanda

My sisters, Rita and Ika Suwanda, have also continued to spread and keep alive the name of Mande Muda in Indonesia by teaching to the public in Bandung, in the school systems as well as in the College of Pasundan in West Java. (Fig. 6)

Rita is the third daughter of Pendekar Uyuh Suwanda, our father and Ibu Mimi Rukim Suwanda, our mother. Rita grew up in a family of martial artists, and virtually everyday saw our father train with our family members and close friends. Pendekar Uyuh would always kick Rita out from training because in those days only men were allowed to practice because of its hard training and explosive power. Rita would always like the challenges and also loved Pencak Silat. She would hide and learn the art by watching our father and by practicing the in secret. After some time, our father noticed that Rita was serous about training and finally allowed her and my other sisters to practice the secret art of Pencak Silat with him. Rita was also excellent in the Kembangan, Olahraga and Mande Muda systems. When Rita was 14 years old she began to compete in every competition sponsored by Ikatan Pencak Silat Seluruh Indonesia (IPSI). She became a champion in Kembangan and Olahraga. She then became active in the IPSI organization. After our father's death Rita taugh Pencak Silat Mande Muda in her own school and also developed the Pencak Silat Mande Muda program in Indonesia. Aside from learning Pencak Silat from our father and myself, Rita also studied with many other Pendekars in IPSI. Rita's husband, Dadang Gunawan, was also one of her teachers because he was one of our father's best students.

6

Shannon Suwanda

Shannon Suwanda is my loving wife who has made my life so complete and has helped me more than anyone to make my dream of spreading the art of Pencak Silat Mande Muda throughout the United States and Europe. She is an outstanding martial artist with outstanding talent. She is my driving force. She has been studying and has spent a great deal of time in Indonesia training,

studying, and spending time with my family learning the history and culture of our family system. She has been making so much progress in learning about the arts and the culture firsthand. Each person has to experience for him or herself the culture to understand anything about Pencak Silat from West Java. So many of my students have made the trip to Sunda, just like her, to learn and see what Penca is really about. I credit my wife Shannon to be my loving, straight and guiding light and because of our love we are able to plant the seed of Pencak Silat Mande Muda throughout the world and for many generations to come. (Fig. 7)

Guru Besar Pendekar Herman Suwanda

I was born on February 10, 1955 in Sumatra, Indonesia. However, I was born there only because at the time that was where my father was working. The rest of my family and I relocated to West Java shortly after my birth. I began my personal training in Pencak Silat under my father's direction in 1960. In 1965 I began to study with many other Pendekars from many different systems. Our goal was to train with as many Pendekars from as many different types of systems so as to learn as much as we could to preserve our cultural martial art. Many times the training was very physical and many times I wanted to quit, but my father would not let me. He told me that I must study the art, for it is my future. Our training methods were very hard and failing in training was failing in life. So with the encouragement from my father and mother I made the decision to keep going. My father sent me to many different Pendekars to learn, after which he would make me review the material with him everyday. After nearly 10 years of private training with my father and other Pendekars I began to teach in West Java. With a standard curriculum of Pencak Silat Mande Muda in which my father had developed, we decided that I must try to spread the art of Pencak Silat Mande Muda to America. So in 1980 I arrived in the United States and began teaching and producing instructors

Starting in a new land was very difficult. I could hardly speak English, and trying to communicate was difficult not only for me while teaching but also for my students while trying to understand me. But after many months of talking and communicating with my students I discovered that the training I was giving my

students was very hard and physically changeling for them. I quickly had to slow it down and teach myself what the Americans wanted to learn. I had so much to teach, but trying to teach an art that people are not familiar with and was too physically changeling, was also a learning experience for me. After time and help from some of my early students like Steve Hunting, Jim Wimmer, and Dan and Paula Inosanto, Later students like Paul Marrero and Tony Somera that would help me to construct a format and teaching style of my own that would prove to be beneficial to my new found home and students here in America. It was like the teacher becoming the student. Once I had developed my communications skills I was able to convey our family art of Mande Muda.

Many people trained with me only long enough to receive their certificates and I never saw them again for many reasons. The problem was that I don't know how much quality and personality of that person continues to fit in with the standards or responsibilities of my own judgments of what an instructor carrying this art should have. I just hope that they continue to spread the art as good people and of course I hope they still have good quality in the way they move and see things in Mande Muda. Many of these same people are still sponsoring my mission, because without these people I wouldn't be able to spread the arts, as I am responsible to do. I believe that in life people always need other people. And when it comes to martial arts, developing relationships and instilling respect is on the top of my list. Allow me to list how I see some of the issues that surround the discontinuing of training.

• Some instructors discontinue training because they feel they have learned enough from me.

- Some instructors discontinue because they have moved on to other states or countries and have a hard time continuing to progress in their learning without access to the material.
- Some instructors stop learning for whatever personal reasons that cause them to not want to have connection with Mande Muda anymore.
- Some instructors go away or discontinue, because I cut the connection stemming from my own judgment about what I think is important in an instructor of the art of Mande Muda.

Sometimes I have to say goodbye or tell them not to mention or use my name or Mande Muda for their own purpose. They forget that I'm also human,

and have feelings, and that I am an Indonesian man trying to survive in a foreign (Western) country. I need support and sponsoring (also, to know that they are doing the right things in the right ways as) in order to share the art with those who love Pencak Silat and want it to continue to grow.

My cultural background and differences also make it difficult to deal with those who are not knowledgeable of how to communicate their wishes or themselves to me. I have been learning the differences in culture and try my best to understand mannerisms, and in general the way people deal with one another within their own culture. Also, there are some things that should not have to be said; I guess you would call those unspoken boundaries, expectations, protocol, and respect for each other. Unfortunately, I found that I have had to outline these boundaries and expectations up front so that there are no misunderstandings later. Live and learn and learn to live.

I have to say that all those involved with Mande Muda, from the host who have sponsored seminars to instructors, both having strong connections to me as a person and to the art, those are the ones responsible for the continued growth of the art in their areas and countries. These are my right hand students, working hard doing their best to promote, expose, and share the art from the sake of the art, giving credit where credit is due. These are the people who are most responsible for helping Mande Muda remain strong outside of Indonesia. I offer my special thanks to all of the people whose support is very important and appreciated by me. Without them Mande Muda would not be growing the way it is today.

• The hosts of seminars.
• Instructors of Mande Muda, in particular the Jagabaya, Suwanda Academy affiliate instructors.
• Certified Instructors who have a current License.
• The people who participate in the seminars and who love Mande Muda
• The members of the Mande Muda Organization.

I just want to say thank you to all my students around the world who are helping me along with my family to protect the arts by continuing our traditional aspects of moral character and philosophy of Pencak Silat Mande Muda.

Chapter 11

Mande Muda Teachers and Association

Instructors Certificate

There is nothing wrong for you to learn Mande Muda from someone who has an Instructors Certificate. However, since they became certified, these instructors have been chosen by me in the past, but are not involved with the new organizational efforts or familiar with any of the new material in Mande Muda. As you know this art is growing so fast with the material and each year material can be so different from the pervious year and therefore not having that exposure or knowledge means that you cannot be well rounded in the art to attain the level of understanding I expect of an advanced instructor.

Licensed Instructor

I recommend that you learn from a licensed instructor. These are the instructors who continue to be active with me, learning the most recent material and following my directions and strongly sponsor my mission.

Jagabaya

The Jagabaya are the most current and up to date instructors of Mande Muda. That means that they are learning step-by-step with each level with a great deal of material that allows them the opportunity to develop themselves to the most advanced levels of the art. If you are looking for the highest-level instructor in Mande Muda to train with, you should seek out a Licensed Jagabaya Instructor.

Jagabaya is the first step in accomplishing the ultimate goal of Pendekar. First you must be selected to become a Jagabaya. To do this you must be interviewed and screened by Pendekar Herman Suwanda. If you are selected you will be trained in many different levels of Pencak Silat Mande Muda that are set by Pendekar Herman Suwanda. The training is intense and employs the elements of physical, mental, historical, cultural, and personal training with Pendekar Herman Suwanda. Learning about Pencak Silat requires a deeper understanding about the art and the true culture and history behind it. To do this you would need to go through the time consuming process of discipline and dedication to the art and in this way you will learn what Pencak Silat truly is. There are many elements required to learn during this program: Jurus, buah, kembangan, the understanding of rhythm, timing, moving in the right way, feeling in the movement and the positioning of the hand and feet.

Those elements are really important for the Pencak Silat that comes from West Java. We don't have a choice, because that is the way they do it in West Java and that is what we do in the United States. Jagabaya are special people, because the Jagabaya program is not for the public; the only people in this program are the people who have been selected in a tight and careful manner. Thanks to technology, I can be in many states at the same time. But the program has to go to the people who have been selected as instructors. I share with the Jagabaya the training that is normally secret and is supposed to be one-on-one training between the teacher and student. I am happy to see that the Jagabaya program is working and the Jagabaya is receiving the knowledge of the program. Because this program is not for everyone, the Jagabaya's are considered instructors under the Suwanda Academy. The headquarters of the Suwanda Academy is located in Cibodas, West Java, Indonesia. My focus is

specifically towards the academic and producing of good quality Pencak Silat instructors who can share the art with the people in Indoniesia, United States and Europe.

On February 6 and 7, 1999 the first ever Licensed Jagabaya Instructors Seminar and Conference was held and was hosted by Grand Master Leo M. Giron and Master Tony Somera at their Bahala Na Martial Art school in Stockton, California (Fig. 1). The following are the current and active Jagabaya Instructors that appeared in the 1999 Licensed Jagabaya yearbook.

    Dan Inosanto — Los Angeles, CA
    Paula Inosanto — Los Angeles, CA
    Fred Degerberg — Chicago, IL
    Shannon Suwanda — International
    Tony Somera — Stockton, CA
    Kathy Ohara — Hilo, HI
    Steve Robinson — Chicago, IL
    David Hatch — Detroit, MI
    Leroy Pasalo — Hilo, HI
    Jeff Brown — Dayton, OH
    Michael Hands — Long Island, NY
    Dennis Duria — Chicago, IL
    Arthur Chestand - Chicago, IL
    Chris Malgeri — Madison Heights, MI
    Bernard Chong — Honolulu, HI
    Bill Stutesman — Dallas, TX
    Lynda Hatch — Detroit, MI
    Ken "Doc" Dority — Dallas, TX
    Charles Chi — Lindenhurst, NY
    Dave Moore — Columbus, OH
    Rob Crown — San Francisco, CA
    Ginna Goodenow — Dallas, TX
    Charlie Fernandez — Arlington, TX
    David Goodenow — Dallas, TX
    Tom Doherty — Chicago, IL
    Craig Carpenter — Indianapolis, ID
    Phil Matedne — Stockton, CA
    Steve Braun — Baltimore, MD
    Leslie Buck — Austin, TX
    Tom Gallagher — Citrus Heights, CA
    Jose Connors — Dayton, OH
    Joel Clark — Los Angeles, CA

Leonard Trigg — Portland, OR
Keith Wetoskey — Waterloo, ID
Steve Tarani — Fountain Valley, CA
Wes Locke — Joplin MO
John L'Herault — Chicago, IL
Roy Hagan — St. Louis, MO
Paul Marrero — Scottsdale, AZ
Kelly Smith — Fort Worth, TX
Richard Hogg — Fort Worth, TX
Al Kelly — Brookville, ID

On February 6, 1999 during the first ever Jagabaya training camp was held in Stockton, California (Fig. 2). It was here that Pendekar Herman Suwanda announced that he was forming a new organization and naming it after his Pencak Silat training facility in Cibodas, West Java. In the past there has been many Mande Muda practitioners promoted to the rank of instructor. While these instructors were often capable martial artists, few had the understanding of the traditions and culture of Pencak Silat. It has been an ongoing goal for me to work toward and develop a program that would stress and highlight all the facets of Pencak Silat as taught in West Java. To separate and identify these new instructors from those who were certified in the past, I have created a series of titles starting with *"Jagabaya"* (*enter guard*) ranks and progressing to *"Punggawa,"* *"Satria"*(*warrior*), *"Pendedar Muda"*(*young clever minded person*) and finally *"Pendekar"*(*clever minded person*). I have stated: "Students that earn these titles are to be considered Instructors under the Suwanda Academy, located in Cibodas, West Java, Indonesia. Focus is specifically towards the academic development and production of good quality Pencak Silat Instructors who can share the art with the people in Indonesia, United States of America and Europe."

Assocation Building

It could be considered a life long dream for me to establish a group of associations to build the foundation of all practitioners of Pencak Silat. As Pecak

Silat continues to grow I feel it is necessary to build and establish a fellowship and partnership amongst a growing population of practitioners dedicated to promoting and propagating the same ideas that in many ways will connect us all with the same common goals.

Pencak Silat Mande Muda International Association Inc.

The Pencak Silat Mande Muda Assocation is the Suwand family martial art. Although created by Guru Besar Uyuh Suwanda in 1951, it has its roots in very ancient and traditional styles of Silat. Since 1980 Pendekar Herman Suwanda has been promoting this association to promote the Indonesian culture, including his teaching in martial art and historical education throughout world. After years of preparation and hard work, on January 29, 1998, The Pencak Silat Mande Muda International Association was officially filed and endorsed by the Secretary of State of the State of California in America. Pencak Silat Mande Muda International Association is governed by a set of by-laws that includes a board of directors.

This has been a dream for years to establish and organize this association in order for the association to grow throughout the world. I am so happy about making the association official and of course I had help dealing with all the obstacles of putting this association together. I have many people to thank, but the person that has helped me to make this dream come true is the one person that I care most about in my heart: Shannon (Vicente) Suwanda. Without her I would have had a very hard time in making this dream a reality. I would also like to acknowledge Steve Hunting, Tony Somera, and Barry Shreiar for their help and support with the final touches to make this dream come true.

This association includes memberships from all over the world. As a member you will be informed with a regular newsletter along with video training. The purpose of the newsletter and the video training is to allow you to follow what's going on with Pencak Silat Mande Muda, whether it deals with Mande Muda or Pencak Silat in Indonesia. But most importantly, the newsletter and videotapes give you the opportunity to learn more about the rich Indonesian culture. I am traveling so much, my body is always moving around, but I hope my Silat stays close to you even when I am not around. One of the unique elements of this association is that I would like input from you in regards to what you would like for me to write and for you to know in future newsletters. I will be glad if I can share what I know about Pencak Silat. The more information and knowledge you have about Indonesian culture, the more you will be able to understand Mande Muda and other styles of Pencak Silat. The hope for this newsletter is to educate and also to make it worth your time to join the Mande Muda membership. Let me plant this thought in you: Support one another and be happy.

The first Recorded Official Pencak Silat Mande Muda International Officers:

President – Herman Suwanda
Director – Shannon Vicente Suwanda
Vice President – Steve Hunting
Legal Advisor – Barry Shreiar
Board of Directors – Dan Inosanto, Tony Somera, Paul Marrero
Public Relations – Mike Young

The Official Logo of Pencak Silat Mande Muda International, Inc.

The Mande Muda logo has many symbolic meanings contained within it that represent the spirit of Mande Muda.

The Three Leaves Represent Options of Attack
1. Walk away from an attack
2. Talk your way out of an attack
3. Stand and defend yourself

The Cabang (Trisula) Represents Self-Defense

1. The white head represents using your head and thinking clearly, without clouded judgment.
2. The colors red and white are the national colors of the Indonesian flag.
3. The triangle represents your growth in Mande Muda starting at the bottom and evolving toward the top.

The Philosophy of the Logo

In the beginning you may start to learn Mande Muda for physical reasons. As you progress you grow and evolve on many levels. You become humble and know the harm you can cause if you were to fight.

You have grown to the point of becoming a better human being and do not want to cause harm to anyone. Many people fight because they question themselves and their art, but really no one needs to test either their ability or their art on another human being.

Pencak Silat Association of the United States of America PSA-USA Inc.

Because Pencak Silat competition is so popular in many areas of Southeast Asia, this association was created to promote and organize

Pencak Silat competition throughout America. Pencak Silat Association of the United States of America (PSA-USA) was established so that all groups and practitioners of all Pencak Silat can group together to form teams of competitors in order to compete on an international level to represent Pencak Silat in the United States (Fig. 5). For many years before the formation of PSA many of my students would travel to Indonesia to compete in international competition (Fig. 6). This is the major reason why PSA was formed. So that there could not be one group or one person that would be the head or majority rule of PSA-USA, this association is regulated by a set of by-laws that holds regular meetings and elects officers. With the help of Craig Carpenter, Paul Marrero, and Tony Somera the first draft of the PSA-USA by laws was formed on February 20, 1998. The first set of officers to represent Pencak Silat Association of the United States and America PSA-USA are as follows:

Indonesian Consultant – Eddie M. Nalapraya
Overseer of Organization in the US Herman Suwanda
President – Paul Marrero
1st Vice President – Steve Hunting
2nd Vice President – Tony Somera
Advisor – Dan Inosanto
Advisor – Paula Insoanto
Legal Advisor – Criag Carpenter
Consultant – Fred Degerberg
Consultant – Rick Tucci
International Competition Coordinators –
Mike Hand, Jeff Brown, Jim   Wimmer
Secretary – Shannon Vicente Suwanda
Treasurer – Kathy Ohara
Public Relations – Mike Young

Chapter 12

The Suwanda Academy

Padepokan Pencak Silat Suwanda Academy

Padepokan Pencak Silat Suwanda Academy sounds really good to me. Padepokan refers to a studio used for Silat training. This was my father's dream to have a padepokan for students in Indonesia to practice in and also for our students that come from outside Indonesia. If you go to Indonesia, especially to West Java, you won't see signs of Pencak Silat schools. I am sad that we don't have any studio or a place for our students to practice. For almost 18 years I have been carrying my father's dream and want to have a school in the mountains in Indonesia. In 1992 I bought some land but had many problems trying to raise the extra funds to build the padepokan, especially after taking care of my family and many other families in Indonesia. But after many sleepless nights, the dream of my father and I had finally been put on paper and I had the drawings of a Padepokan. (Fig. 2)

Finally, in June 1998 I went back to Indonesia and started to make the foundation build walls all from the piece of land that was my fathers dream It

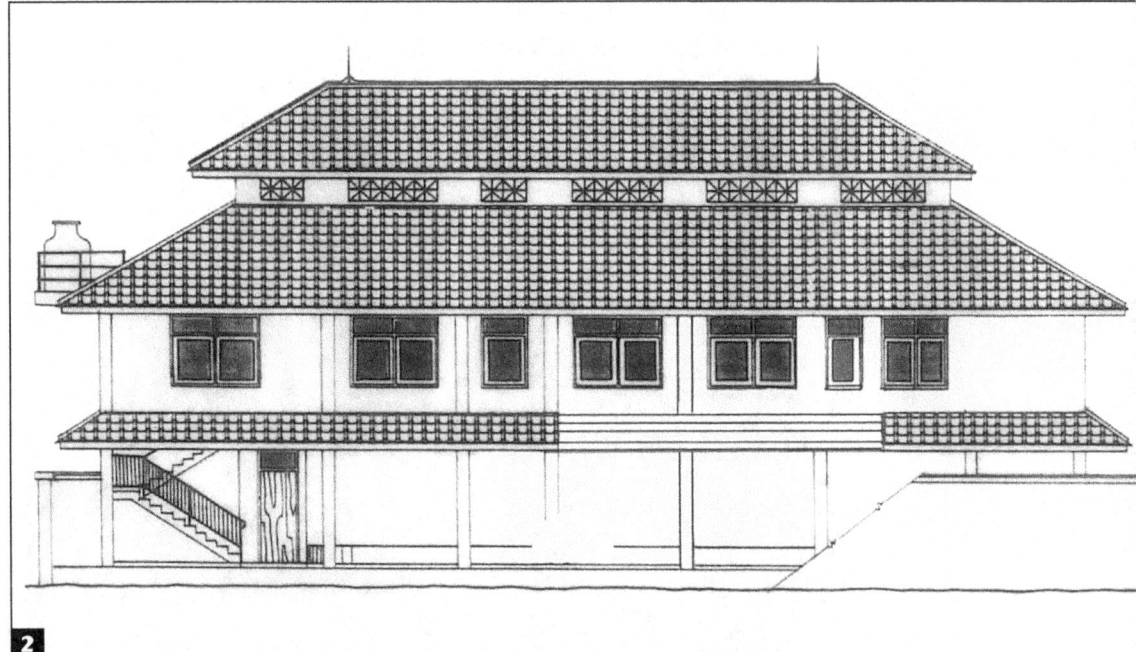

maybe just a wall and maybe I will be waiting for another 10 years to build the studio, but I don't care. This is a sweet dream with big planning for Pencak Silat. I will do to the best of my ability what I can do to complete my mission to make Silat grow in my own country and around the world. Like I have said in the past, most traditional schools teach in the living room, they never have more than two students because there is not enough room for more. If my planning goes through with God's will, I think this padepokan well be helpful for all Pencak Silat to have a studio to practice at and I will be more than happy to allow other schools use this beautiful padepokan. (Fig. 3).

The padepokan is about two hours from the city really in the village. Since it is in the mountains, the weather in the village where the padepokan is located is not as hot as the rest of Indonesia. The school is built on top of a mountain in Kampung Dago, Desa Suntenjaya, Lembang, West Java (Fig. 4).

This area is a beautiful agricultural area with mountains and a river running through the valley that the school overlooks. The air is so refreshing and cool- unlike Bandung, were there are many cars and extreme heat and humidity. Except for the animals that live around the school, it is fairly quiet with peaceful days and nights. It is the perfect environment for training and to get away from modern life and concentrate on learning. So it has perfect training conditions. I think my students who come from outside of Indonesia will enjoy the training area. It will be much larger and further into the mountains than the current training facilities. I hold camps in Indonesia twice a year during June and October (Fig. 5).

Outside of IPSI (Ikatan Pencak Silat Seluruh Indonesia) this is the first Padepokan Pencak Silat in West Java, or maybe even in Indonesia that is owned by an individual person or school. The academy is unique in that it has nine bedrooms, five bathrooms with warm water showers, and a large training area that can fit over 50 people training at one time (Fig. 6). The bottom floor is where all the training is done day or night. The second floor is for dining living quarters for those that come into Lembang, West Java to train (Fig. 7). This, in my opinion, is the most ideal place to train in West Java. My dream someday will be to make many people proud.

Building a huge place like this requires that so many ceremonies and cultural aspects be observed. Starting first with praying and preparing special food offering of yellow rice from almost

40 families in the village area and praying again in the middle of the land where the Padepokan would be in order to ask permission, as we are going to make noise, and to apologize to the ancestors for disturbing them during this process. Next we had to bury seven white chickens in the middle of the land were the Padepokan is being built in which we would do more praying.

The entire village comes and enjoys the food that is prepared for everyone. Everybody is happy to see the ceremony and eat. Of course, for us it is a lot of work trying to arrange all of these events, just to begin building the Pakepokan, but I respect the traditional ways and follow them.

One day I received a phone call from my mother. She said: "The employees are digging the ground deeper and deeper for the well, but no water is coming out." I replied, "That is strange, what should we do?" My mother already knew the answer for that and she said: "We need more ceremony, the ancestors are upset." I said, "Do whatever we have to do." And of course, that meant that she would oversee more praying, more offerings of respect, lots of cooking, and bringing more chickens. Believe it or not, the next day after the ceremony water came out from the well.

This is the way of life in Indonesia, connected to the earth and connected to our ancestors, looking to both of them to guide us. Everything has to be done the right way to make the project move smoothly and make the people living around it smile and happy.

The culture is so strong in Indonesia, for everything we do there is always something that needs a blessing and prayer (Fig. 8). This school is so much of a blessing, and I keep praying I can make the school successful so I can give back to my community and village the culture and to continue my mission of spreading the art and knowledge to the public all over the world. I consider every member and everyone who comes to a Mande Muda seminar, the ones supporting me through this project and with my dream.

I just would like to say "Thank you" to all of the Mande Muda instructors and members for supporting my efforts through seminar participation and continuing to learn Pencak Silat. I will do my best to share the arts and the culture of Indonesia. I hope that Pencak Silat will continue to spread and grow in a healthy way in the world. The Padepokan will be a useful place for Pencak Silat for many generations to come. Terima Kasih.

Suwanda Academy

We named the school the Suwanda Academy and believe it or not, my father's dream has materialized. This Academy is now the International center for Mande Muda training. Now we hold regular training and the Indonesian Mande Muda training camps there.

For two weeks at a time, day and night we are kicking, punching, choking, traveling, seeing performances, performing, meeting teachers, until everyone is exhausted and I have to say "enough for today." On the top of that, the student learn and see more culture and get to understand what I have been telling them about the hospitality of the Sunda people and the richness and beauty of the performing arts.

My goal is that all the participants that come to the Mande Muda Silat camp will understand more about Pencak Silat, culture, the beliefs behind it, and when they return to their homes they will understand more deeply about Mande Muda and Pencak Silat in general. So when someone tells them a story or information about Pencak Silat those people can use their own experience

to gauge the information by and if they know what they hear not to be true they can smile. They won't have to argue because they don't have to prove anything, they have been to that culture in Indonesia and have experienced it firsthand and understand it better and will know fact from fiction.

At the present time the Suwanda Academy is being used by the local schools that don't have enough space for all their students (Fig. 9), as well as by our instructors who are teaching their students and many children that we

have adopted. Basically, we have taken responsibility for twenty children, including educational needs from tuition, school clothing, to their transportation fees and more (Fig. 10). In return, the children have agreed to learn Pencak Silat and we hope that one day they will take responsibility in the school and teach others and help to run the school and continue spreading the art and preserving the traditional aspects that make it uniquely from our culture (Fig. 11).

The goal for this facility is to provide the place and means for sharing and spreading the arts and culture of the Sunda people. We hope for it to be there for many generations to come. We also lend the school to the local artist who teach and practice local music and performing arts, teaching and practicing Silat drums and instruments, and for all the Pendekars around West Java to gather and discuss Pencak Silat.

Talking all day and into the late evenings until they want to retire to one of the rooms where they can sleep and rest up for another day of continued deep discussions on important issues about Pencak Silat like the movements, terminology and more.

Whenever we are in Indonesia it is important that this type of activity takes place to ensure the continuance and growth of Pencak Silat, and we are happy that the Pendekars take advantage of this facility for this type of training.

Chapter 13

The 25 Styles of Mande Muda

The following are brief descriptions with illustrations of the primary characteristic of each of the 25 styles that make up Pendekar Herman Suwanda Pencak Silat Mande Muda system. Some of the styles presented are actual fighting methods; others are concepts or strategies to employ when engaged in an encounter.

Cimande

Cimande is a system of attacking the arms (figs. 1–6). Cimande is the name of a village, a river, and a style of Pencak Silat in West Java. Cimande has simple Jurus (forms) and Bua (applications). The Cimande style is found in

three different villages Cimande Tarik Kolot, Cimande Tengah, and Cimande Girang. Tanash Sareal is the area where Bah Kahir, the founder of the Cimande style, is buried. Cimande has the reputation throughout Indonesia for its skills in treating injuries to the bones. Masters use special oil called Balur (fig. 7) after training to heal injuries incurred to the bones of the forearms (fig. 8). Cimande is highly respected for both its bone healing and its Pencak Silat. There is a special ceremony called Kecer Mata, which is performed in the Cimande system to initiate members. The head of Cimande, Tarikkolot, prays during the ceremony as members are inducted (fig. 9). During this time the initiates drop water that has been blessed into their eyes (fig. 10). After this, the new members are given a Talek or set of laws to follow. This was and still is practiced, and is available only to those who are sponsored and vouch for by a person that has completed this ceremony.

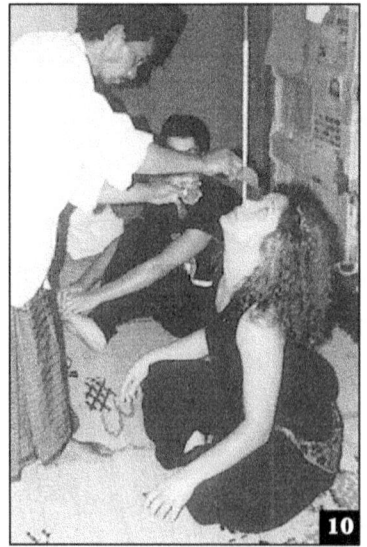

Cikalong

Cikalong is the name of a village and a style of Pencak Silat. Cikalong Pencak Silat practitioners move quickly and lightly, their methods are very effective in evading and taking down the enemy. This system is not related to any animal style and prefers attacking to the outside of an opponent's body. (Fig. 11–13)

Harimau

Harimau is a Sumatran ground fighting system. This system is based on te movements and tactics of the tiger. Harimau uses twisting leg grapples and lower body strikes to bring an opponent down so the Harimau fighter can finish him off. In this particular system of Harimau the hands are also used to help tie up the opponent while the legs are used to finish off the opponent or guard against more attackers. (Fig. 14–18)

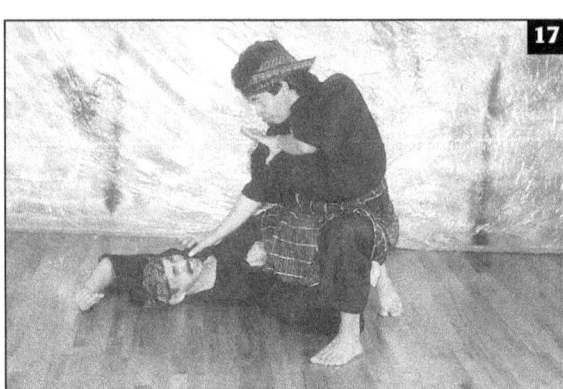
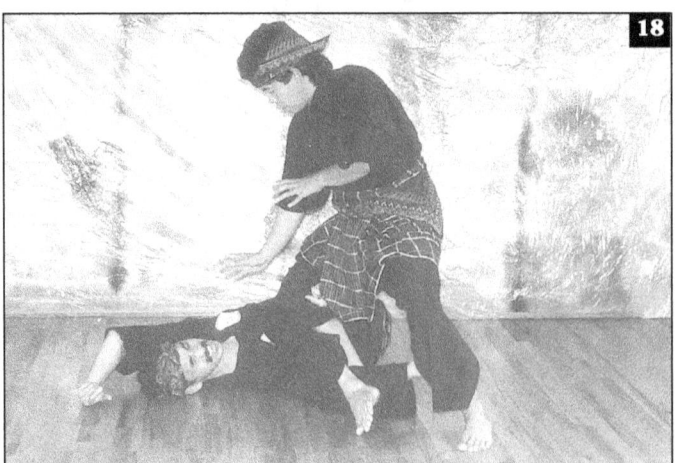

Syabhandar

Syabhandar teaches to attack an opponent from the centerline of his body. The style is named after the founder, Mama Syahbandar. Mama is originally from Sumatra but he traveled to West Java, studied Pencak Silat there, and then remained in West Java to teach. (Fig. 19–21)

Kari

Kari is a close-range locking style. This is another form of Tjikalong and is considered a "cheating" style. As the practitioner is attacked, he sticks his hands through the arms and passes the defense of the attacker, entangling him. Most of the techniques are used to seek instant lethality, concentrating on the throat, neck, and nose. (Fig. 22–24)

Madi

The Madi style is used to pull and jerk the opponent off balance so as to attack and utilize finishing strikes and locks to neutralize him. It is also a modern form of Tjikalong. It is characterized by quick footwork and tactics of jumping onto an opponent to bring him down to the ground. (Fig. 25–29)

Cipecut

Cipecut utilizes flexible weapons such as sarong and horsewhip. This style was developed from the Cikalong village, and incorporates many lethal whipping strikes to tie or lock the opponent's arms, legs, head, and neck that turn into choking maneuvers. Cipecut also uses loose clothing, towels, belts, waist cloths, men's ties, fanny packs, and of course the sarong. After the techniques are applied with the flexible weapon, the flexible weapon is used to hold your opponent at bay. (Fig. 30–33)

Timbangan

Timbangan means "scale" in Indonesian, but in Mande Muda terminology refers to the balance of the energy flow between practitioner and opponent. The Timbangan stylist prefers to redirect his opponent's energy thereby causing him to trip or fall to the ground. There is no contact in this system, thus making distance and timing crucial to the effectiveness of the art. To develop this timing the Timbangan stylist practices for hours on complex two-man drills to learn how to read and redirect his opponent's energy. When practitioners become comfortable with their technique, they engage in light sparring under the strict supervision of a Timbangan instructor. This is the energy flow between practitioner and opponent. (Fig. 34–36)

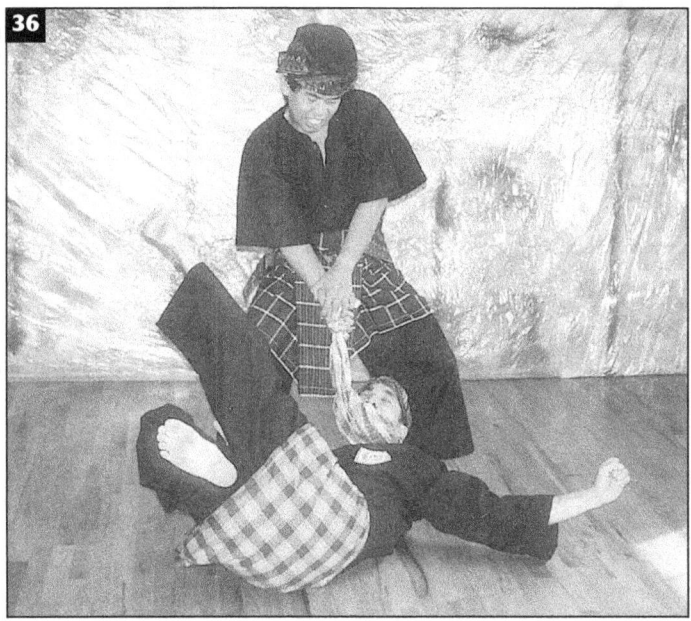

Nampon

Nampon are deep breathing exercises for straightening the body. This enables the practitioner to protect his body from receiving serious internal or external damage during combat. Mande Muda stylists also incorporate the Nampon style of Silat, wherein deep breathing exercises are coordinated with specific body movements to strengthen and invigorate specific sections of the practitioner's body. Training in this system will use specific hand motions that are coordinated with specific breathing patterns. Footwork is also added to the breathing patterns to make sure you can apply the breathing techniques in motion. Dynamic tension, along with relaxed body movement, is applied during the breathing exercises to strengthen specific muscles not normally exercised by conventional exercise methods. After three to six months of regular practice of Nampon, the body becomes strong enough to withstand a strong physical attack. (Fig. 37–42)

Sera

Sera is a hybrid system of Cikalong, Cimande, and Syahbandar. What makes the Sera style so effective is its precise use of exact angles to break down an opponent's attack. Even while attacking, a Sera player will try to attack at a specific angle to keep him out of harms way while at the same time putting the practitioner in an advantageous position to attack. (Fig. 43–48)

Rikesan

Rikesan is a style designed to directly utilize bone-breaking techniques. The word Rikesan means "breaking" in Indonesian, and incorporates techniques which live up to its name. The Rikesan player will wait for an attack, then apply a joint lock somewhere to the attacking limb, rendering the limb unfunctional. Not only will the Rikesan player attack the joints and bones of the opponent, he will also attack the sensitive nerve centers on the body to enhance the effectiveness of the technique. In addition, practitioners are taught what time of the day to strike and specific pressure points to further disable an attacker. (Fig. 49–51)

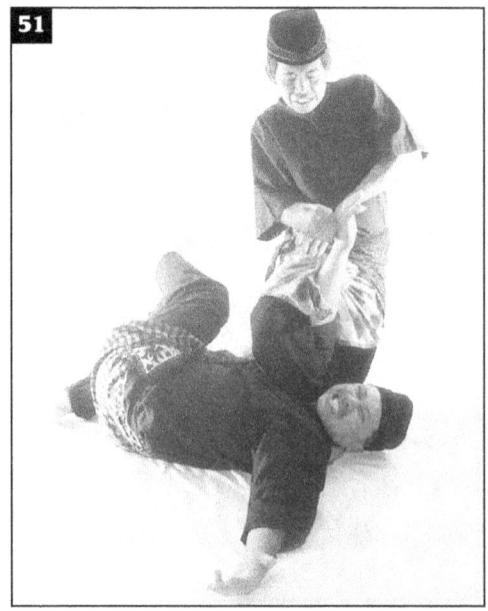

Tanjakan

Tanjakan means "hill" in Indonesian and is sometimes referred to as mountain Silat. The system was developed in the mountains, which caused the Tanjakan player to stay close to the ground because of maneuvering on uneven terrain. In the Tanjakan system, the player likes to grab an opponent, pull him off balance, and at the same time kick him. The Tanjakan player also likes to vary his stance from low to high. The constant change of height makes him a difficult target to hit. More importantly, utilizing the up and down motion of the body is used to gain momentum for a more effective strike. In Mande Mude language, Tanjakan means fighting close to the ground. (Fig. 52–56)

Ulin Naps

Ulin Naps can be best descried as breathing exercises used to control the player's emotions. In Mande Muda the player utilizes a series of breathing exercises to help the him control his emotions during an encounter or fight. Relaxation and breath control is the key to this system. The player is directed at first to control his breathing patterns while lying down, then from the sitting position, and finally standing upright. The breathing patterns are precise and systematic, designed to take the practitioner to a higher state of mind. When Ulin Naps is mastered, the player can control many of his involuntary bodily functions. (Fig. 57–60)

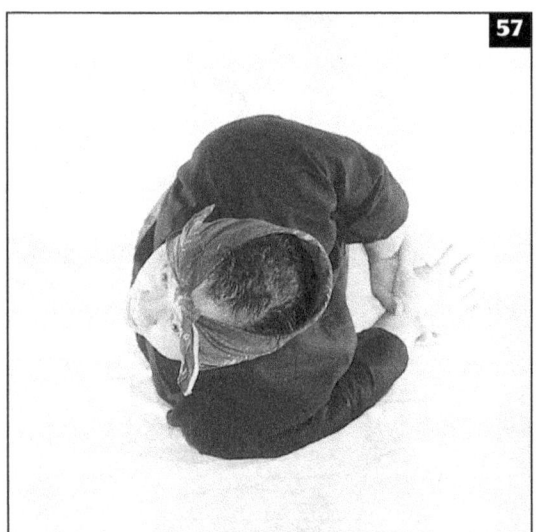
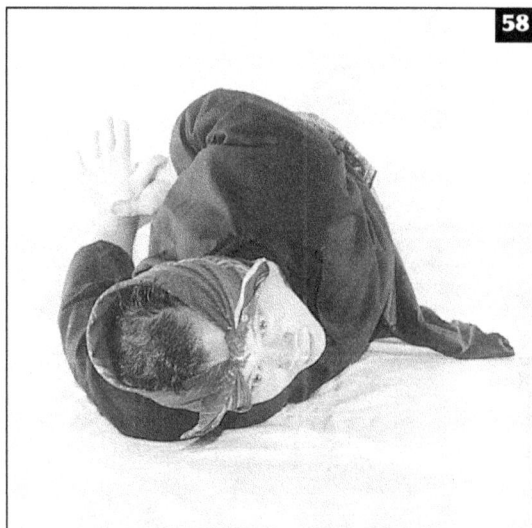

Ulin Baduy

Ulin Baduy is an extreme form of Silat, wherein the player goes directly at the opponent, straight to the point. The primary goal of this system is to take the opponent out as quickly as possible, footwork and specific angles of attack are secondary. Basic linear hand and foot techniques are taught in a direct and no nonsense manner, and are practiced in two-man sets called Buahs. The Buahs are very rough and physical and include hard contact training, especially in the shoulder area. The Ulin Baduy player primarily hunts for the opponent's throat, making it his primary target. (Fig. 61–64)

Galih Pakuan

Galih Pakuan is a weapons system that features 18 types of swords or golok-the favorite of Indonesian players. Golok is a long bladed, single edged knife with varying blade lengths a blade shapes. The average length of a golok is from 10 to 26 inches. The blade theory for combat in this system is taken from the Cikalong system, which emphasizes moving to the outside of an opponent to attack from a better angle. The principal high point of the system is when the practitioner can manipulate 18 different goloks at the same time while performing a pre-arranged set of movements. (Fig. 65–68)

Pamcan

Pamcan means "father tiger" fighting with the spirit of the tiger. The unusual element of pamacan silat is that unlike the tiger claw system of harimau, which teach the physical movements of the tiger and how they can be utilized for self-defense, Pamacan silat emphasizes the mental state of the tiger and using this state of mind to overcome an opponent. The player wants to literally embody the spirit of the tiger into his body and being. This is done through methodical process, with a qualified teacher guide, who guides the player through various mental states. The player puts himself into a trance like state and mentally becomes the tiger. (Fig. 78–81)

Pamonyet

Pamonyet means, "father monkey," and is the monkey fighting system based on the movements and mannerisms of the monkey. Fast, quick movements of the monkey are utilized along with fast punches, hooks, pinches, and ripping attacks. While hand techniques are primarily used in Pamonyet Silat, the legs are also developed to a high degree through the low squatting stance that practitioner moves into. Noise and distractions are used to disorientate the opponent, and these are done by screaming, slapping the body, or stomping the feet to temporarily divert your attention to quickly launch vicious attack. (Fig. 69–77)

The 25 Styles of Mande Muda

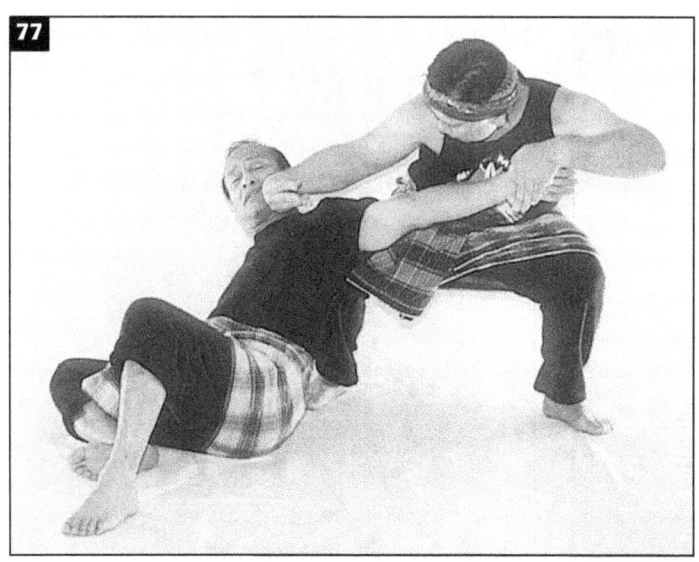

149

Syahbandar Baru

Syahbandar Baru is a new style from Sumatra based largely upon the snake, and emphasizes going to the opponent's inside centerline. It utilizes quick trapping and grabbing movements done with the whole arm, particularly with the elbows, and it is characterized by a wide, sliding stance. The player uses his entry from the outside and works his way into the centerline of his opponent. Some teachers from West Java taught this as the new style of Syahbandar. (Fig. 82–85)

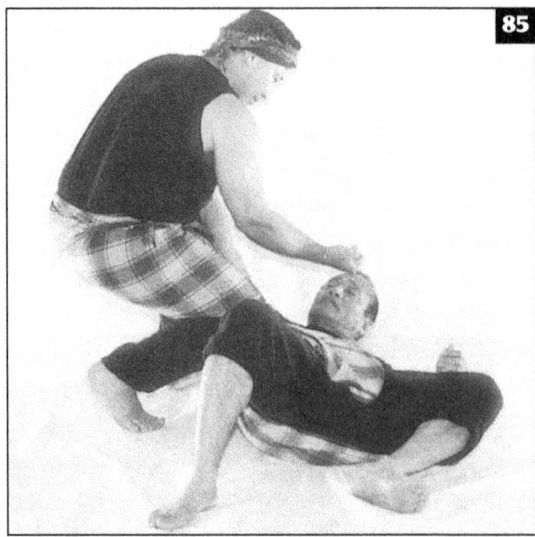

Cikalong Baru

Cikalong Baru is a new style of fighting to opponent's outside, the theory of which is to avoid or get away from the opponent's punches or kicks. A Cikalong practitioner will always try to move to the outside of an opponent, so that he doesn't have to worry about the opponent's other hand or foot attacking him. This style of Cikalong was taught as a new generation or highbred system. As the standard, Cikalong Baru is not related to any animal style. This Cikalong style is from new teachers or different teachers from the village of Cikalong. (Fig. 86–89)

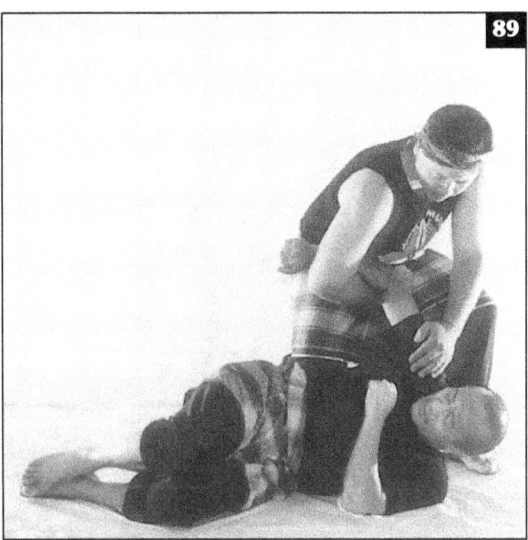

Harimau Baru

Harimau Baru is the new style of tiger or ground fighting. The reason why the name Baru (new) is used, is because it comes from different teachers. I learned this Harimau Baru many years after my father had taught me his system of Harimau from West Java. The two styles of Harimau are the complete opposites. In the new Harimau, the legs and feet are used to create the entry and locks. Practitioners use their legs and feet to take the opponent to the ground, following the entry you will use our legs and feet to lock your opponent. As with the old Harimau style, at this time you will determine whether to take this encounter to the next level or to terminate it. If you continue you will find that your hands and arms are free. This will allow you to counter your opponent or to engage the next oncoming attackers. (Fig. 90–92)

Sanalika

Sanalika is the wait and grab method, and is similar to Rikesan in that is a very defensive style that is unforgiving. It applies the use of grabbing, locking twisting, holds, and arm traps to disable and subdue an opponent. This style also teaches tolerance and how to control the emotions, similar to Ulin Naps. Once in the grasps of the player, the opponent will suffer extensive damage to their body if they attempt to escape. Once the Sanalika is applied, the locking will become the opponent's downfall and will result in the opponent's bones breaking. (Fig. 93–96)

Benjang

Benjang is the old style of Sudanese wrestling from the villages of West Java. During wedding ceremonies, as entertainment, the families would chose one member from each side of the family-one representing the bride and one representing the groom. The winner of the Benjang contest would be the sign of who would lead or be the head of the household. This entertainment was meant to be in fun, but in some cases the Begjang would prove to be a contest of family strength that sometimes would result in someone getting hurt. (Fig. 97–99)

Sampiyong

Sampiyong is the art of stick and shield fighting that incorporates a golok and a shield or a weapon to be used as a shield. In the Sampiyong style the defender prefers to stay to the outside away from the opponent's secondary weapon or the distance from where he can use his legs and feet. The Sampiyong player will use his shield to block or make his entry and follow up with a decisive blow to the opponent's weapon arm to disable the weapon hand. The defender will then follow up by striking to critical areas of the body and use his weapon to lock or control the opponent. (Fig. 100–103)

Sabetan

Sabetan is a style based on unexpected slicing actions. While this style is like Cimande, its striking angles are more to the side of the body and can be used with or without weapons. When only using your empty hands, the punching methods are very unorthodox, which makes Sabetan difficult to counter or defend against. When using a weapon (karamkirs) the method is also unorthodox, and also applied in a slicing manner. One of Sabetan's main characteristics is that, if you block with your left hand, you will also punch or cut with the left hand. Most people who have trained or watched practitioners in the art of Pencak Silat will think this is Cimande. Only the people that train in the art of Cimande or Sabetan will notice the differences between the two systems. (Fig. 104–107)

Ujungan

Ujungan is the art of single stick fighting, and incorporates the use and theory of the Syahbandar and Cikalong styles. This style is practice through a set of Buahs or forms. The two combatants practice by attacking one another in a control manner until each has mastered the style, at which time the combatants can engage in full contact counter for counter exchange. (Fig. 108–112)

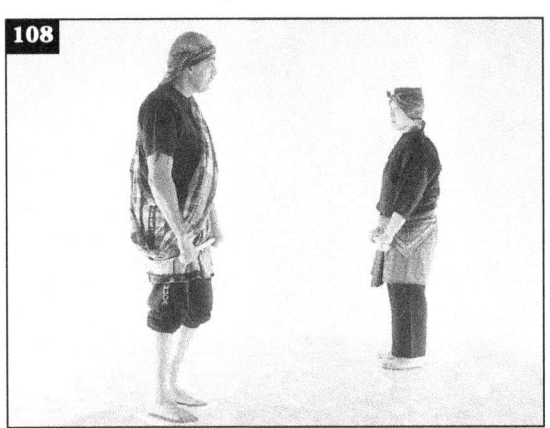

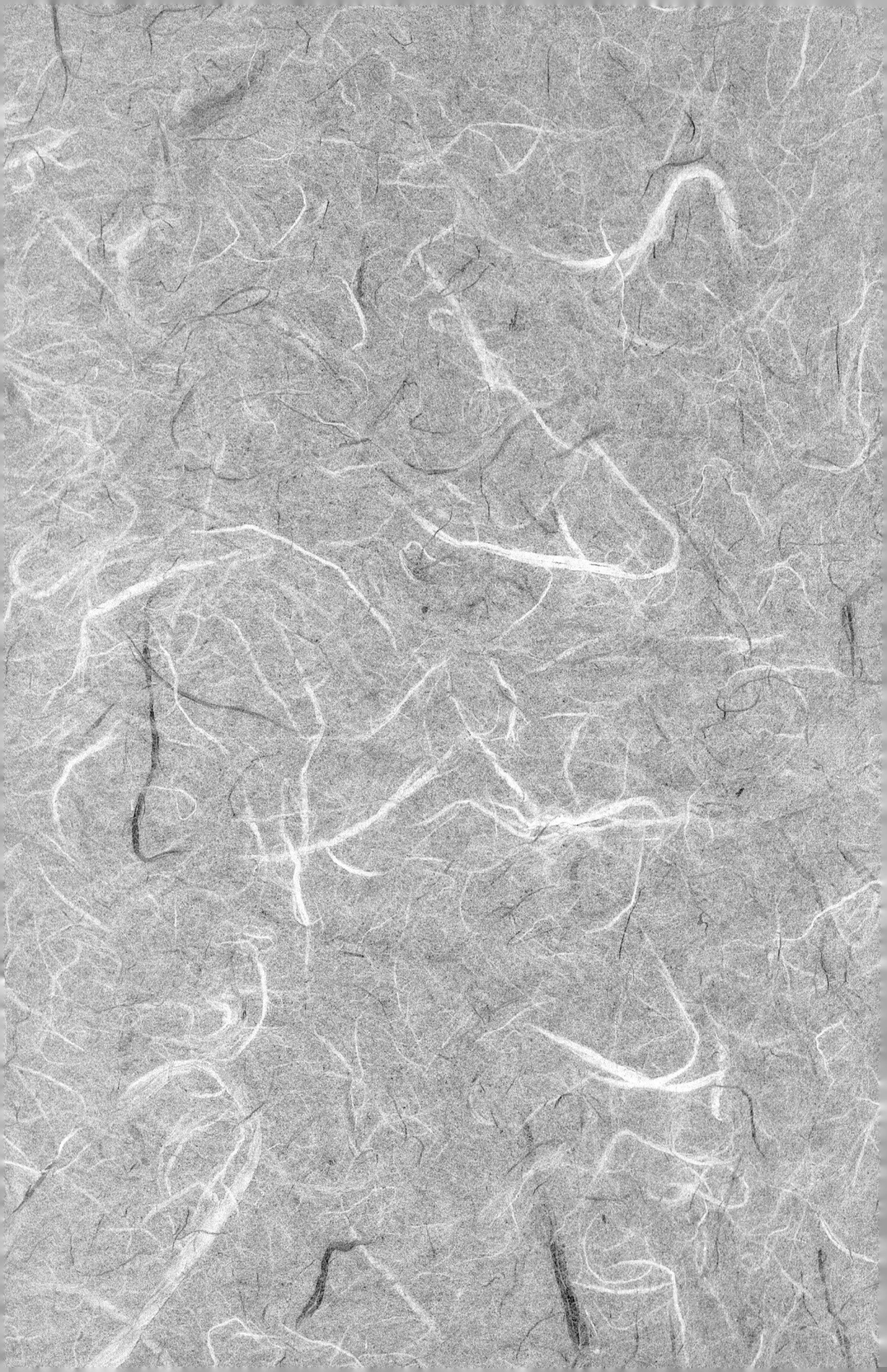

Part III

Foundations of the Art

Chapter 14

Official Uniform and Salutations

Uniform

Dress uniforms (fig. 1) are very important in Pencak Silat Mande Muda, as the uniform a practitioner wears identifies the art of Pencak Silat he practices. Depending on what style you play your uniform can be black shirt, black pants, and black peci (hat) (fig. 2). To play Mande Muda you would traditionally wear a black top and black pants (fig. 3) or a school tee-shirt and black pants, or black school sweat pants (fig. 4). A note to keep in mind as you prepare to get ready in your Pencak Silat Mande Muda dress, is to follow the instructions set forth in this section because the way you dress will determine everything about your Silat.

161

The Sarong

Sarongs come in many colors and patterns. Choose the one that you would like, there are not any particular colors or patterns that would normal offend anyone. The *Sarong is* worn in *Indonesia as normal casual wear* (fig. 5). You can wear it in your house (fig. 6) out in public, and even to church or formal occasions. And when you play Pencak Silat Mande Muda you are required to wear a Sarong, it serves many different purposes.

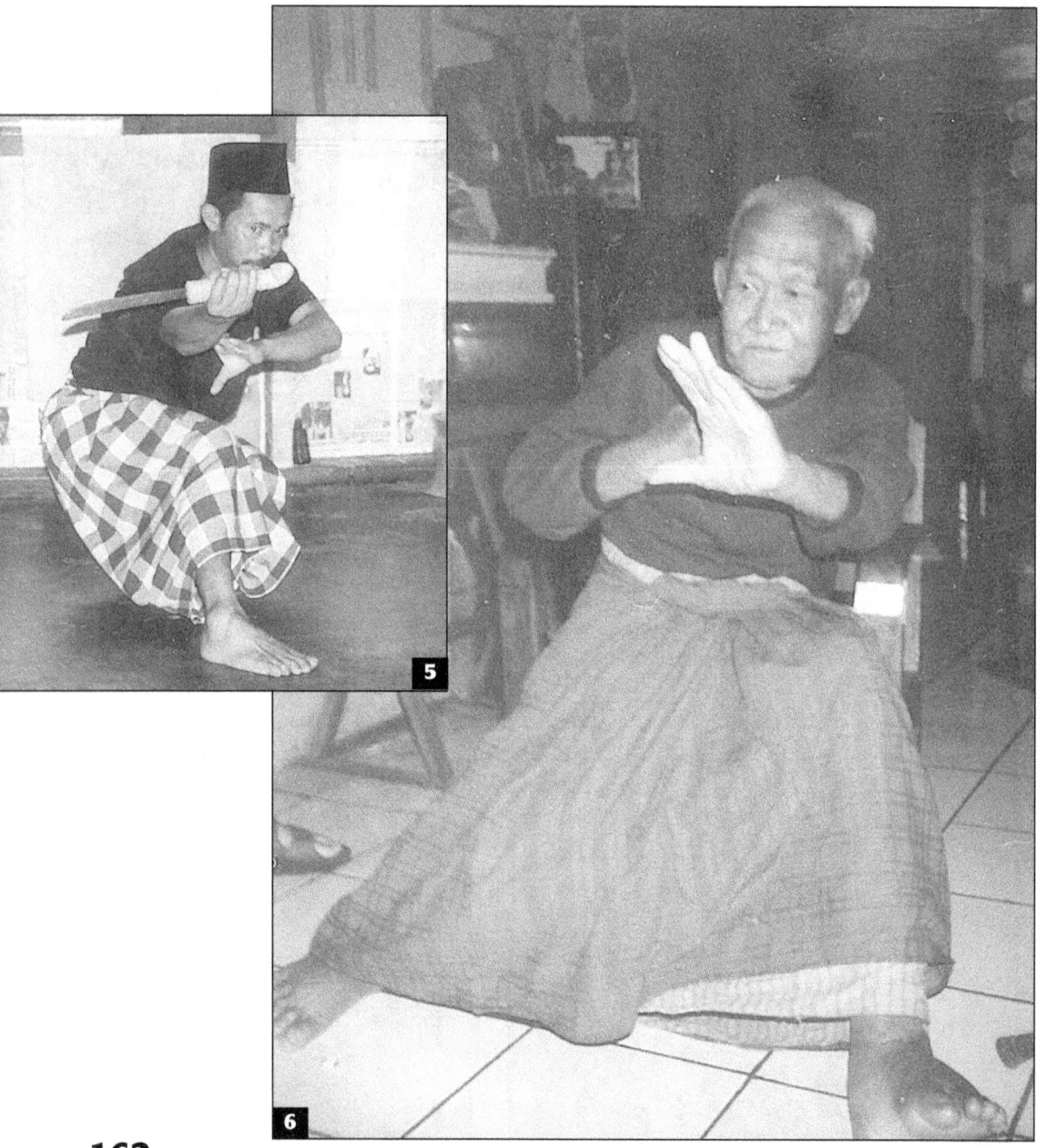

Wearing the Sarong

There are several ways to wear the sarong. The first application is causally wearing or carrying it. This can be accomplished by many ways, but in this illustration the Sarong is carried by hanging the Sarong over the left shoulder and under the right arm (fig. 7). This makes it very convenient to draw the sarong off of the body and apply the Cipecut style or whipping style of Mande Muda.

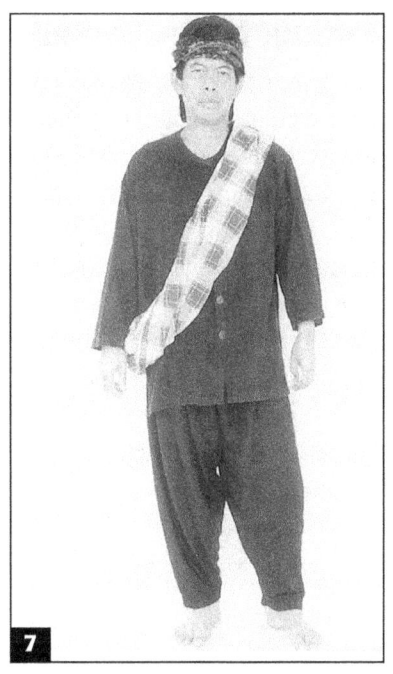

Cover Dress

This application of the Sarong can be used also in a causal dress by draping the Sarong over you body as to use it for cover, warmth, or just as a causal dress (fig. 8). This cover dress can also hide many different weapons very easily. Only be prepared to draw out or escape for this type of cover as it can also prove to be hazardous if you are unable to remove it fast enough to prepare for an encounter.

Putting on the Sarong

In most Pencak Silat schools in Indonesia, and especially as a Pencak Silat Munda Muda practitioner, you are required to wear the Sarong in the following way. First you must fold the Sarong in half or in a double lining, after which you step into the middle of the Sarong and pull it up to your waist. Pull the Sarong tightly and to your right side with your right hand (fig. 9). Next you must fold the Sarong back with your right hand to your left side, using your left hand to clamp it on your left side, your right hand fold back to the center of your body (fig. 10). Pull back from the left side of the Sarong and place the fold back to the centerline of your body and start to fold the Sarong under at your waist. Two folds should hold your Sarong in place (fig. 11). To finish off the dressing of the Sarong, ensure that the fold in the sarong is in the center of your body, this signifies the wearing of the sarong is from Central Java (fig. 12)

Official Uniform and Salutations

Formal Sarong Dress

The formal dress of the sarong is used for formal events and when attending prayers at the Mosque. The Sarong is worn in the same manner as in Mande Muda class, but it is hung in full length of the individual (fig. 13). To complete the formal dress the individual can wear a Peci or black hat (fig. 14)

165

Ikat Belt

A Mande Muda practitioner must wear an *Ikat belt*, which can serve three functions. One way is to hold and maintain your sarong in place and secured around your waist. Another is to use it as a weapon in the Cipecut style or whipping style in Mande Muda. The third way is to hold or hide weapons in the Ikat belt. The Ikat is in the shape of a triangle, but is identified with two ends and a point at the top of the triangle. Take the Ikat with your left and right hands at each end and wrap the ends to the right side of your hip. The top or point of the triangle should be placed on the side of your hip with the top pointing down to the side of your leg (fig. 15). With the ends in your hands tie it off on the right side of your hip. The tie should be in a slipknot for easy access to removal (fig 16).

Official Uniform and Salutations

Ikat Headdress

Ikat headdress is also very important. To wear your Ikat while training in Mande Muda, first start by folding over several times at each end of the tips with the tip of the triangle over your forehead (fig. 17) and wrapping the Ikat with the point up centered to the back of your head and grabbing the ends with your right and left hands (fig. 18). Wrap the two ends around the forehead (fig. 19). Continue to wrap around to the back and center of your head and complete the wrap by tying a double knot with the two ends (fig. 20). Lift and pull the front center point of the Ikat down to cover the two ends that were tied in a knot. Finish off the Ikat by dressing the rear point of the Ikat in a point (fig. 21).

Wearing your Ikat with the rear point pointing out will signify you as a warrior or fighter in Pencak Silat Mande Muda (fig. 22).

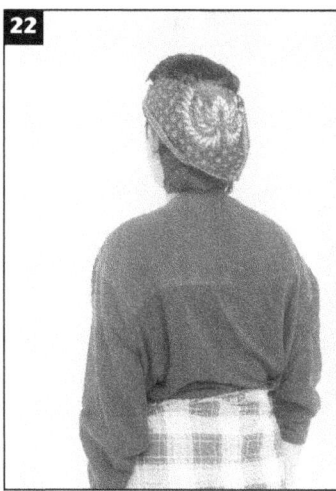

Ready to Train

After the Sarong, headdress, and Ikat belt are applied you are ready for training in Pencak Silat Mande Muda. Ensure that you follow the directions in wearing the correct uniform, as this will identify you as a Pencak Silat Mande Muda player.

Casual Position

In a casual position for taking instruction, or just standing for observation, you can stand with your feet a shoulder's with apart with your hands down at your sides (fig. 23) or with your right hand grabbing your left wrist directly in front of your body in a resting position (fig. 24). But, before training begins, it is always a nice jester to offer your teacher a cup of hot tea or coffee (fig. 25)

Challenging Position

Be careful when putting your hands on your hips (fig. 26) or crossing your arms (fig. 27), as these two positions invite a challenge. You will put yourself in a position of wanting to challenge the person or persons you are directing your body jester too.

26

27

Formal Greeting

The formal greeting (fig. 28) in a formal setting-weather it be in a class, visiting another school, social activity, or greeting a visitor at your home- begins by standing directly in front of the person you are greeting to show proper respects (fig. 29). Extend your right hand in friendship and grab the person's hand in a formal handshake, grab your right forearm with your left hand to show a non-aggressive action (fig. 30). Pull back with your right hand until your right fingers are in the middle of the persons palm, extend your left hand and place it on the outside of the person right hand (fig. 30). Bend at the knees and pull your hands back to the person's fingertips (fig. 31). Pull back your hands with the palms of your hands together and draw them back to your chest while slightly leaning your head forward (fig. 32).

Official Uniform and Salutations

Casual Greeting

The casual greeting is used as a normal greeting or when showing respect to a teacher, fellow student, or someone you meet in normal passing. This is done by placing your heals and your feet together. Bring your hands to the center of your chest and place your left and right palms together with your fingers pointing straight up. Slightly bend at your waist and lower your head (fig. 33). This causal greeting is the most preferred method while playing Pencak Silat Mande Muda. The salute is mutually returned.

Informal Casual Greeting (Single)

There is also an informal, casual greeting that is done by using a single hand motion. This is accomplished by standing in a causal position with your feet apart with the thumb of your right hand held next to your chest with fingers pointing in an upward motion. Your left hand hangs vertically down on your left side, in line with your left leg, palm facing against your left leg. To complete this informal casual greeting bow the head slightly forward and look at the person you are acknowledging (fig. 34). The greeting is mutually returned either by using the one hand or two hand method.

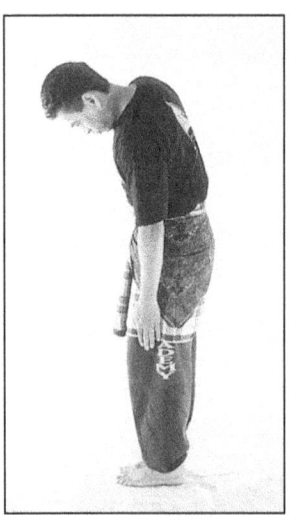

To Be Excused

There may be times were you would need to excuse yourself from the floor, leave the room, or even pass by your senior classmates or instructor. This is done from a standing position. When excusing yourself you must walk by the person you would like to be excused by. It is not necessary to walk up to or directly near this person; just walk from your current position and off the floor. Do this by placing your left arm down alone your left side, with your left palm against your left leg and bend your head. Do this only during the time you will pass your instructor (fig. 35). Your gesture will be noted and a hand movement or jester will be mutually returned.

Formal Salutation

Before any Juru, Kembanagan, or any formal presentation of Pencak Silat Mande Muda forms or dance you will be required to begin by performing a formal salutation. This is done by standing at attention with your feet together, you hands down by your sides, and your eyes focused straight ahead of you (fig. 36). Raise both arms to your side with palms facing up; your head is tilted back with your eyes looking directly up towards the heavens (fig. 37). Continue to raise your arms over your head and join your left and right palms together over your head (fig. 38). Retract your hands down to the center of your chest, keeping your left and right palms together with fingers pointing up and your head bent down with your eyes looking at your hands and offer respect (fig. 39).

Formal Salutation (continued)

Next separate first your palms by lifting apart starting from your small finger until your palms facing down (fig. 40). Rotate your hands by keeping the back of your hands together and continue making the circle with your hands fingers pointing down (fig. 41). Continue the circle with the fingers of your left and right hands pointing toward your chest (fig. 42). To complete the formal salutation draw both hands back to your sides, palms facing up just above your hips (fig. 43). You are now ready to begin your formal performance.

Official Uniform and Salutations

Ready Position

The ready position is assumed at the beginning of any movement of Jurus (forms) or application of Kambangan (dance), known as Buah, or any movement that will engage the training between two or more students. The ready position is a non-aggressive posture. The position is more of a formal or ready stance prior to the beginning of any martial movement. The ready position is assumed by standing in an upright position, heels and feet together with both hands at the side of your body, palms facing up (fig. 44). The ready position can also be performed with the hand closed and in a fist.

Chapter 15

Warm-up Exercises

Prior to the start of training in Pencak Silat Mande Muda you should first consult your physician. These warm-up exercises can be very strenuous to any student, whether beginner, intermediate, or advanced. Before the start of each training session the student of Pencak Silat Mande Muda will be required to run through a few basic warm-up drills and exercises to loosen and stretch the muscles and body. By taking the initial time to warm-up and do these exercise using proper techniques as described in the following pages, you will decrease the chance of injury as a result of pulled muscles and damage that may occur during your training time. While doing these warm-up exercises for the first time, please use caution and do not try to apply the stretching of the muscles at 100% of the illustrations-start at 50% or less. Listen to your body and how it tells you that the pain is to much and you will need to back down to a lesser application of these warm-up exercise. As you continue to exercise you can increase your warm-up stretching until you reach 100%.

Satu

In a ready position (fig. 1) step with your left foot to 9 o'clock, your hands are in a ready position. Lean forward and kneel down with your right knee on the ground (fig. 2).

177

Lean your body to the left and lay flat on the ground with both feet and legs on the ground (fig. 3). From the laying flat position roll your hips to the right and lift yourself up slightly with your left shin and right knee (fig. 4). Retract down to the right and stretch your pelvis by rotating your hips to the right and left (fig. 5). With your left hand grab your right foot by reaching back to your left side, stretching the right leg and lean forward (fig. 6).

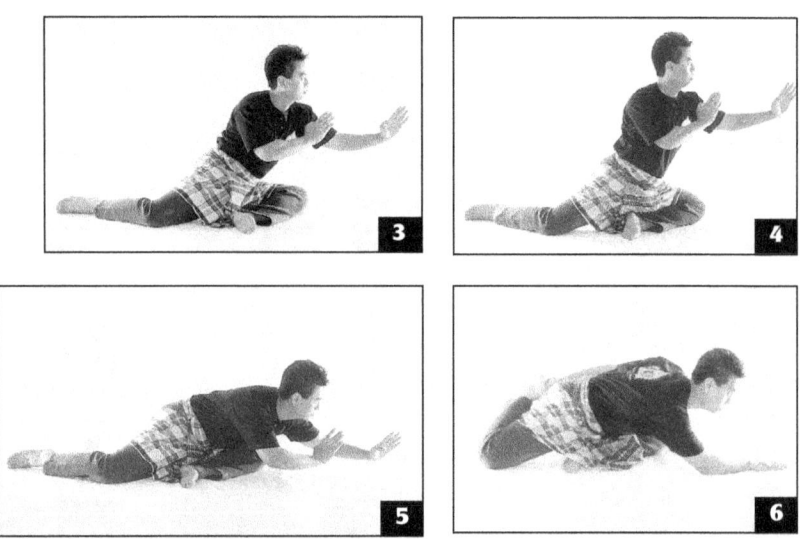

Repeat this exercise on the other side by changing body positions. (fig 7–12

Dua

From a sitting position where you left leg is straight, pull your right foot and place it on your left thigh (fig. 13). Rotate the right ankle both forward and backward. With your right foot on your left thigh, reach forward and grab your left ankle (fig. 14). Grab your left ankle and stretch forward (fig. 15). Repeat this process on the other side by switching your right leg forward and pulling your left foot and placing it on your right thigh (fig. 16). Rotate the left ankle both forward and backward. With your left foot on your right thigh, reach forward and grab your right ankle (fig. 17) and stretch forward (fig. 18).

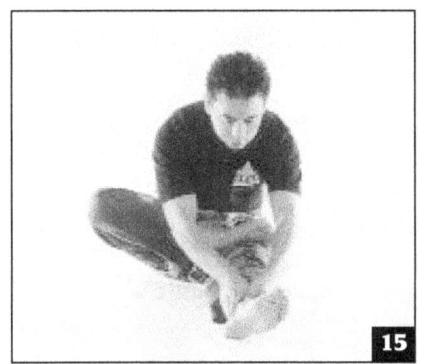

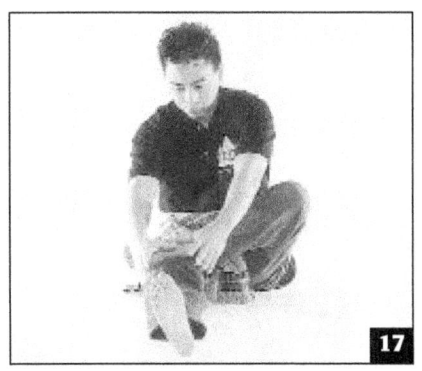

Tiga

In a sitting position, and from your Dua exercise, position right leg forward and left ankle on your right thigh (fig. 19). Position both hands flat, directly behind you and lift up with your right leg and lean forward with your body (fig. 20). By stretching your back and legs turn your body to your right side and place your left foot flat on the ground (fig. 21). Rotate by pivoting on your right knee and turning your body to the right (fig. 22). Rotate 360 degrees around to your right side and with your right foot forward, left leg to the side (fig. 23).

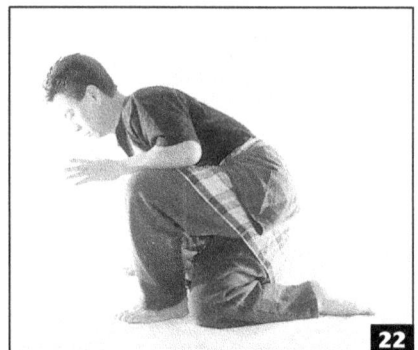

Sit directly down in a Depok position with right leg over left thigh and hands in a ready position (fig. 24). To return back to your original position, push up with your right leg and left knee and lean forward into a ready position (fig. 25). Start to rotate your body 360 degrees to your left side and pivot on your left foot and right knee (fig. 26). Sit directly down into a depok position, left leg over right thigh, hands in a ready position (fig. 27). To compete this side, maintain your leg position and turn your body to your right side and stretch down and back (fig. 28).

Empat

From a sitting position, place your left leg forward and your right ankle on your left thigh (fig. 29). Position both hands flat directly behind you and lift up with your left leg and lean your body forward (fig. 30). Stretch your back and legs by turning your body to your left side and placing your right foot flat on the ground (fig. 31). Rotate by pivoting on your left knee and turning your body to the left (fig. 32). Rotate 360 degrees to your left with your left foot forward and your right leg to the side (fig. 33).

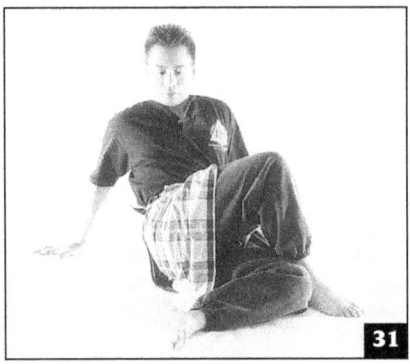

Slide directly down in a depok position, left leg over right thigh and hands in a ready position (fig. 34). To return back to your original position, push up with your left leg and right knee and lean forward into a ready position (fig. 35). Start to rotate your body 360 degrees to your right side and pivot on your right foot and left knee (fig. 36). Sit directly down into a depok position with right leg over left thigh with your hands in a ready position (fig. 37). To complete this position, maintain your leg position and turn your body to you're left side and stretch down and back (fig. 38).

Lima

Begin this stretching exercise from a standing position (fig. 39). Standing on your right leg lift your left leg, grab your left ankle, and position your left ankle over your right thigh (fig. 40). Lean forward and bend your right knee (fig. 41). Balance your weight on your right foot and bend on your right knee, both hands on the ground (fig. 42). Lift up with your right leg and push up with both of your hands (fig. 43). Standing on your right leg grab your left ankle and pull stretching the left leg (fig. 44). Repeat.

Enam

Begin this stretching exercise from a standing position (fig. 45). Lift up your right leg, grab your right ankle, and position your right ankle over your left thigh (fig. 46). Lean forward and bend your right knee (fig. 47). Balance your weight on your left foot and bend on your left knee, both hands on the ground (fig. 48). Lift up with your left leg and push up with both of your hands (fig. 49). Stand on your left leg and grab your right ankle and pull the stretch the right leg (fig. 50). Repeat.

Tujuh

In a sitting position, keep your left and right feet together and your left and right hands together (fig. 51). Lean your body forward by pushing with both feet and thrusting your body (fig. 52). Roll completely forward with both left and right knees and forearms on the ground (fig. 53). Stretch forward with both left and right forearms and spread your left and right knees out as wide as possible while keeping your back straight (fig. 54).

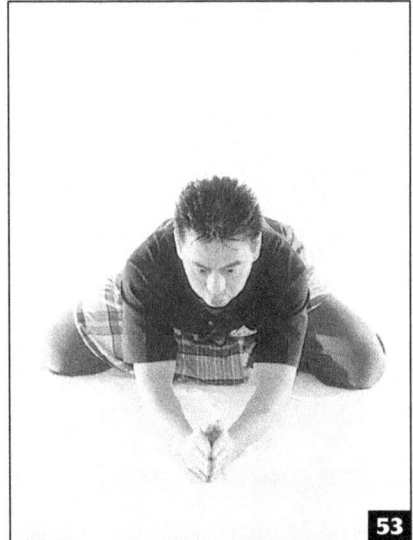

Warm up Exercises

To return to the original position, start to pull back with your body (fig. 55). Lift your forearms off the ground and pull back with your body until you are on your shins (fig. 56). Pull yourself back by using your body motion and pulling back with your legs (fig. 57). Returning to your original position (fig. 58).

Delapan

In a sitting position, keep your left and right feet together and hold your feet with your hands (fig. 59). Position your left hand flat behind your left calf and with your right hand flat behind your right calf (fig. 60) Push up with both left and right hands and lean forward using your feet for leverage (fig. 61) Return down to your original position (fig. 62) Repeat this exercise (fig. 63).

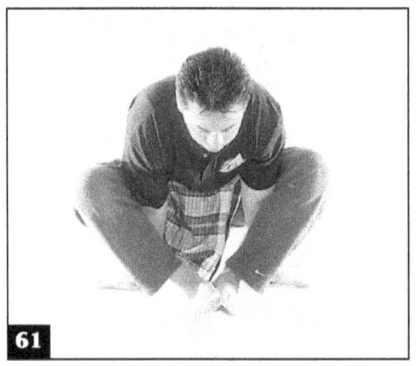

Sembilan

In a sitting position, keep your left and right feet together and hold your feet with your hands (fig. 64). With your left hand, reach under your left calf and pull on your left foot and with your right hand, reach under your right calf and pull on your right foot. The body is kept in a compressed position (fig. 65) Lift the body and pull on both right and left feet, lifting your back in a straight position (fig. 66). Return down to your original position (fig. 67). Repeat this exercise (fig. 68).

Sepuluh

Stand in a ready kuda kuda (horse stance) position with your left and right palms together (fig. 69). With pressure, point both hands forward (fig. 70). Rotate both left and right hands and point in a downward position applying pressure (fig. 71). Bend forward at the waist while maintaining pressure with both hands (fig. 72). Reach with both hands forward, including stretching the back forward (fig. 73). Arch the back upwards and turn both hands in an upward position (fig. 74). Lift your back straight up with both hands still applying pressure while pointing to the heavens (fig. 75). Repeat this exercise.

Warm up Exercises

Sembelas

Stand in a ready kuda kuda (horse stance) position with your left and right palms together, fingers pointing up (fig. 76). Reach down to the left, putting your left arm underneath your left leg, your left hand flat next to the outside of your left foot, and your right hand directly flat and down shoulder with apart from your left hand (fig. 77). Lean forward and press down toward the ground with your chest as if you were doing a pushup (fig. 78). Return to the upper position by pushing up to lock out at the arms (Fig. 79). With your right hand, reach for your left hand and grab your left ankle (Fig. 80). Grab the left ankle while both left and right hands pull forward (fig. 81). Lean to the left until you become flat on the ground with the legs and pulling forward (fig. 82). Release the tension and repeat this exercise (fig. 83).

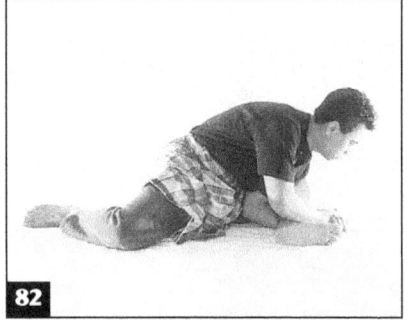
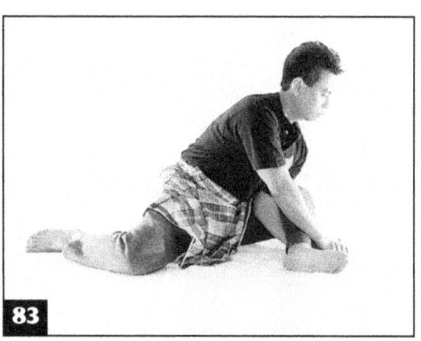

Dualeblas

Stand in a ready kuda kuda (horse stance) position with your left and right palms together, fingers pointing up (fig. 84). Reach down to the right, putting your right arm underneath your right leg, your right hand flat next to the outside of your right foot, your left hand directly flat and down shoulder with apart from your right hand (fig. 85). Lean forward and press down to the ground with your chest, much like doing a push up (fig. 86). Return to the upper position by pushing up to lock out at the arms (fig. 87). With your left hand, reach from your right hand and grab your right ankle (fig. 88). Grab the right ankle with both right and left hands pulling forward (fig. 89). Lean to the right until you are flat on the ground with the legs and pull forward (fig. 90). Release the tension and repeat this exercise (fig. 91).

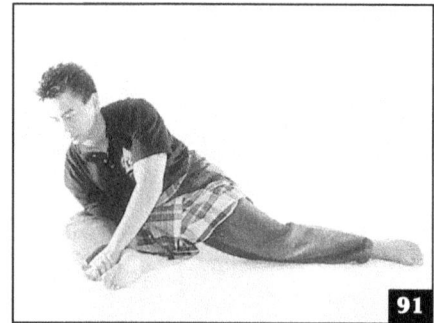

Tigabelas

Begin in a ready position with legs apart in a kuda kuda (horse stance) with your left hand in front of the right hand (fig. 92). Turn to your right side, your chin over your knee, your knee over your toes (fig. 93). Reach with your right hand underneath your right leg (fig. 94). With your left hand over the top of your back, reach with your right hand backwards to grab your left hand (fig. 95). Lock your left and right hands together and pull or compress your body (fig. 96).

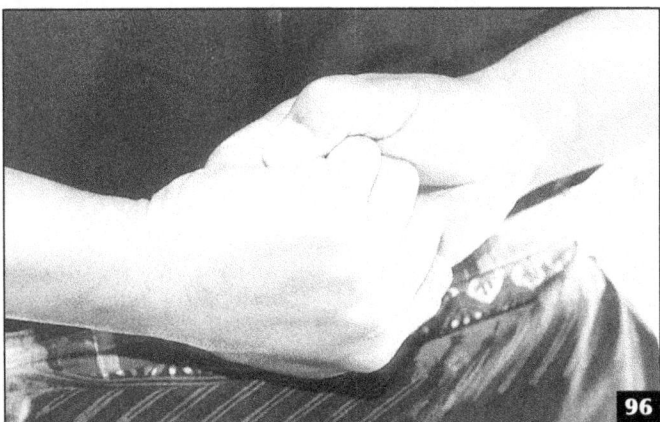

(continued)

Tigabelas (continued)

Release and return to the starting kuda kuda position, this time with your right hand in front of the left hand (fig. 97). Turn to your left side, your chin over your knee, your knee over your toes (fig. 98). Reach with your left hand underneath your left leg (fig. 99). With your left hand under the left leg and right hand over the top of your back, reach with your left hand backwards to grab your right hand (fig. 100). Lock your right and left hands together and pull or compress your body (fig. 101). Repeat this exercise.

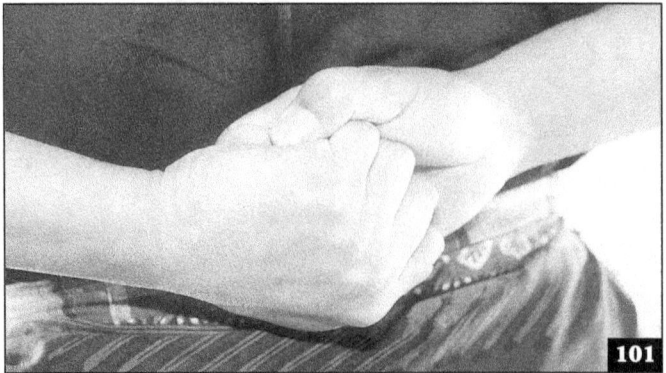

Empatbelas

From a squatting position feet flat on the ground, bend at the knees, hands flat on the ground (fig. 102). Jump with your right leg straight out to your right side, your left leg is bent and tucked under your body, your hands flat on the ground (fig. 103). To return, jump back to your original starting position (fig. 104). Jump with your right leg straight back, positioning your right leg directly behind you, your left leg is bent and tucked under your body, your hands flat on the ground (fig. 105). To return, jump back to your original starting position (fig. 106). Jump with your left leg straight out to your left side, your right leg is bent and tucked under your body your hands flat on the ground (fig. 107). To return, jump back to your original starting position.(fig 106) Repeat this exercise.

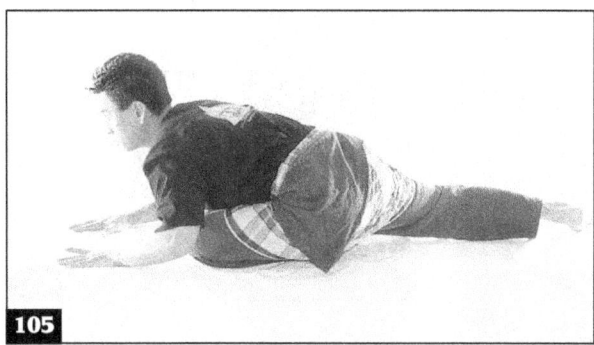

Limabelas

From a squatting position with feet flat on the ground, bend at the knees with hands flat on the ground (fig. 109). Position your left leg through the center of your two arms and your right leg directly behind your body with both legs flat on the ground (fig. 110). Return back to your original starting position by lifting your lower body with your arms (fig. 111). Position your right leg through the center of your two arms and your left leg directly behind your body, both legs are flat on the ground (fig. 112). Return back to your original starting position by lifting your lower body with your arms (fig. 113). Repeat this exercise.

Enambelas

From a squatting position, feet flat on the ground, bend at the knees, keeping hands flat on the ground and fingers pointing directly in front of your body (fig. 114). Relocate your hands to the side of your feet with your elbow pushing back on the inside of your knees (fig. 115). Lean as far as you can to your left, trying to touch the ground with your left knee (fig. 116). Return back to your original starting position (fig. 117). Lean as far as you can to your right, trying to touch the ground with your right knee (fig. 118). Repeat this exercise.

Tujuhbelas

Begin in a sitting position with your left and right feet together and your left and right hands together pointing directly in from of you (fig. 119). Position your arms directly in front of you, hanging over your shins, keeping your body and back in a relax position (fig. 120). Lift your body straight and flex your back, grabbing at the same time your left and right ankles (fig. 121). Repeat your position with your arms directly in front of you hanging over your shins and your body and back in a relax position (fig. 122). Repeat this exercise.

Delapanbelas

From a kuda kuda ready position, start with your right hand out in front of your left hand, which is placed next to your chest (fig. 123). Lift your right leg up until your right foot is elevated next to your left knee (fig. 124). Step down with your right foot to your right side in a deep kuda kuda position (fig. 125). Lift your left leg up until your left foot is elevated next to your right knee (fig. 126). Step down with your left foot to your left side in a deep kuda kuda position (fig.127). Repeat this exercise.

Sembilanbelas

Begin this exercise by repeating the delapanbelas exercise. In a kuda kuda ready position start with your right hand out in front of your left hand, which is placed next to your chest (fig. 128). Lift your right leg up until your right foot is elevated next to your left knee (fig. 129). Step down with your right foot to your right side in a deep kuda kuda position (fig. 130). Lift your left leg up until your left foot is elevated next to your right knee (fig. 131).

Warm up Exercises

Step down with your left foot to your left side in a deep kuda kuda position (fig.132). Keeping your left knee bent, lift your right leg up until your right foot is over your left knee, insert your right hand under your right foot and pull up with your right hand to stretch your right leg (fig. 133). Holding on to your right foot, slowy step down with your right foot to your right side, keeping the tension on your right shoulder and right leg (fig. 134).

Resume your kuda kuda with your right hand out in front of your left hand, which is placed next to your chest (fig, 135).

(continued)

Sembilanbelas (continued)

Keeping your right knee bent, lift your left leg up until your left foot is over your right knee, insert your left hand under your left foot and pull up with your left hand to strech your left leg (fig,. 136). Holding on to your left foot, slowly step down with your left foot to your left side, keeping the tension on your left shoulder and left leg (fig. 137). Resume your kuda kuda with your right hand out in front of your left hand, which is placed next to your chest (fig. 138). Repeat this exercise.

Duapuluh

Begin in a deep kuda kuda stance with your right hand out in front of your left hand, which is placed next to your chest (fig. 139). Lean your body to the right side keeping your right foot flat on the ground and keeping your body weight over your right leg, while maintaining your right hand in front of your body (fig. 140). Next, lean your body to your left side without raising the level of your head, keeping your left foot flat on the ground. Keeping your body weight over your left leg, switch to your left hand out in front of your right hand, which is placed next to your chest (fig. 141). Repeat this exercise, maintaining your level of your head.

Chapter 16

Hand Movements and Strikes

Sered

Sered (fig. 1) is *a circular strike that generates from the centerline of your body.* The rotation of the strike is vertical and comes from under the opposite hand. This type of strike is used for close quarter encounters and is incorporated with the Syabandar style of Mande Muda. The Sered strike is most effective while in side kuda kuda (horse stance) position.

Begin the sered movement in a ready position (fig. 2). Step out with your left foot into a kuda kuda stance, placing your left hand is in an open palm position and next to your chest, and your right hand is in an open palm position directly in front of your chest and level with your shoulders (fig. 3). To perform the sered strike, draw your right hand back to your chest (fig. 4), and in a circular motion rotate the right hand in a vertical motion, striking from under your left hand (fig. 5). Repeat this motion on both sides using the left and right hands.

Sered (continued)

The buah (technique) application will start with an opponent striking with his right hand (fig. 6). As your opponent strikes, evade by stepping out to the side with your left foot, while your left hand does an outside parry the opponent's fist and your right hand begins the sered strike from under the opponent's strike (fig. 7). To complete the strike, generate power by hitting the opponent's chest with an open palm strike (fig. 8). This strike is also preformed with the left hand and stepping out to your right side.

Hand Movements and Strikes

Suliwa

Suliwa (fig. 9) *refers to a circular motion*. This motion begins by pulling from a horizontal circular motion. The motion is pulling from the top and also can be used parrying from the top. The idea is to pull or parry with the lead hand in a circular motion, grabbing or parrying the opponent's arm and locking it close to your body, while the opposite hand breaks or blocks the opponent. This suliwa motion is best used to the outside of the body, much like the Cikalong style, but can also be done from the inside like Syabhandar style. The suliwa hand movement is most effective while in a front kuda kuda stance.

Begin the suliwa movement in a ready position (fig. 10). Start by stepping forward with your right foot to 1 o'clock, your right hand is over your left hand (fig. 11). Your left hand will make one complete circle, your right hand will retract to your right side next to your right shoulder, palm facing forward. At the completion of your left hand rotation, your left hand extends shoulder high with palm up (fig. 12). Repeat this motion on both sides using the left and right hands.

Suliwa (continued)

The buah application will start with an opponent striking with his right hand. As your opponent attacks you step with your right foot to 1 o'clock, your right hand outside parries the opponent's strike (fig. 13). Grab the opponent's right wrist with your right hand and strike with your left open hand to the opponent's right elbow, your left palm is facing up (fig. 14). Repeat this movement on both sides, using both the left and right side of the hand.

Besot

Besot (fig. 15) *is similar and the motions are the same as suliwa*, except that the circular motion is a shorter version that the full circular motion as in the suliwa application. This movement is used to grab or parry and also for breaking or blocking the opponent's arm or hand. This besot motion is a short and to the point application, and is preferred to be used on the inside of the opponent's body. While similar to the centerline attack of the Syabhandar style, the besot application can also be used on the outside of the body, much like the Ciklong style.

Begin the besot movement in a ready position (fig. 15). Start by stepping forward with your right foot to 1 o'clock, your left hand extended palm up, your right hand is between your chest and left arm (fig. 17). Your right hand will retract in a pulling motion to your right side, your left hand will extend to the front with an open palm (fig. 18). Repeat this motion on both sides using the left and right hands.

15

16

17

18

Besot (continued)

The buah application will start in a ready position facing your opponent (fig. 19). As your opponent attacks you with his right hand, step with your right foot to 1 o'clock, extend your left hand with palm up to block the inside of the opponent's right arm. Your right hand will go between your extend left arm and chest in a counter clockwise motion and will retract in a pulling motion to your right side. You are now ready to counter or strike your opponent (fig. 20). Repeat this movement on both sides using the left and right side of the hand.

Kobok

Kobok (fig. 21) is *a frontal circular motion that is used for blocking kicks or inserting into the legs or arms, and is used as a lever to throw your opponent off balance or to tie up his arms*. This type of hand and arm motion is also used for striking, and uses the forearms to push your opponent off balance. Many times the shoulder is incorporated with the motion to take down the opponent and finish him off using Harimau techniques.

Begin the kobok movement in a ready position (fig. 22). Immediately step with your left foot to 9 o'clock in a kuda kuda stance. At the same time lift your right arm and circle it in a clockwise motion, your left arm remains next to your waist (fig. 23). Continue the clockwise motion with your right arm until in comes in line with your left knee. Meet your left hand and right forearm at knee level and lean forward (fig. 24).

Kobok (continued)

To repeat this motion on the opposite side, rotate on the ball of your feet and turn your body in the direction of your right leg. Reposition your right arm over your right leg and your left arm so it is in line with your left leg (fig. 25). In a counter clockwise motion with your left arm, strike to your right side until in comes in line with your left knee. Meet your right hand and left forearm knee level and lean forward (fig. 26). Repeat this motion on both sides using the left and right hands.

The buah application will start with an opponent striking with his right hand. Evade and step directly to 11 o'clock with your left foot, outside parry the opponent's strike with your left hand, and start the clockwise rotation of your right arm (fig. 27). Lean forward and continue with the left arm strike to the opponent's groin area (fig. 28). Continue to lean forward, dropping your right knee to the ground and strike the opponent's right thigh with your right shoulder. Your arm is to be inserted between the opponent's left and right leg, after which you turn your right arm so your right hand will hit the back of the opponent's left knee and push forward (fig. 29). Repeat this movement on both sides using the left and right side of the hand.

Pukul Satu

The pukul satu is *a single strike that is from the Cimande system*. This strike is used in an aggressive posture to help train with a partner. One person will need to assume the part of an aggressor so the two can exchange their techniques.

The strike starts from a ready position with both hands positioned above your waist with palms up, fist closed, and feet together (fig. 30). This strike is also executed with footwork. Step forward with your right foot to 1 o'clock, bend slightly with the right knee and punch straight ahead with your right hand held chest high (fig. 31). After punching with the right hand draw it back to its original position next to your right hip (fig.32). Next, step forward with your left foot to 11 o'clock, bend your left knee slightly and punch straight ahead with the left hand held chest high (fig. 33). Draw the left hand back to its original position next to your left hip and step back with your left foot so you will be in the original starting position (fig.34). Repeat this movement on both sides using the left and right side of the hand.

Pukul Dua

The pukul dua is a double strike from the Cimande system. As in the satu pukul, one person will serve as an aggressor so as the two can exchange their techniques.

The double strike starts from a ready position with both hands positioned above the waist, palms up and feet together (fig. 35). The double strike is also executed with footwork. Step forward with your right foot to 1 o'clock, bend the right knee slightly and punch straight ahead with both fists chest high (fig. 36). Draw the punch back to its original position next to their respective hips (fig. 37). Step forward with your left foot to 11 o'clock, bend your left knee slightly and punch with both fists chest high (fig. 38). Draw the punch back to its original position next to your left and right waistline (fig. 39). Repeat this movement on both sides using the left and right side of the hand.

Pukul Back Fist

The back fist pukul (strike) (fig. 40) is one of the fastest and most powerful closed fist strikes in Pencak Silat Munda Muda. And like the majority of strikes, this particular strike comes from the Cimande system. The target is usually to the face of the opponent, but is also used to target vital areas of the body.

The strike starts from a ready position with both hands positioned above your waist, palms up fist closed and feet together (fig.41). Step forward with your right foot to 1 o'clock, raise your right arm until it is in a horizontal position at shoulder level, your left hand is in an open position directly in front of your mid section and ready to catch the strike (fig. 42). As you strike with the right hand, drop your weight into the center line of your stance, striking your left hand with the back first pukul (fig. 43). To repeat this strike reposition yourself to the ready position (fig. 44).

40

41

42

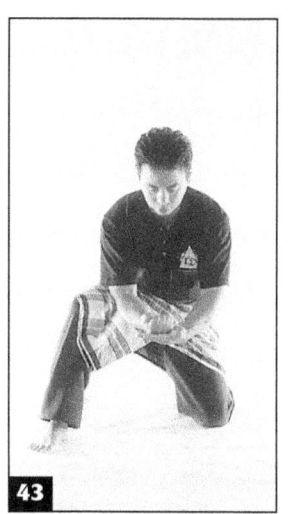

43

44

Pukul Back Fist (continued)

Step forward with your left foot to 11 o'clock, raise your left arm until it is in a horizontal position at shoulder level. Your right hand is in an open position directly in front of your mid section and ready to catch the strike (fig. 45). As you strike with the left hand, drop your weight into the centerline of your stance, striking your left hand with the back first pukul (strike) (fig. 46). Repeat this strike on both sides using the left and right backhand pukul (strike).

The buah application will start in a ready position facing your opponent (fig. 47). As your opponent strikes with his left hand, step with your right foot to 1 o'clock, downward check with your right hand and grab your opponent's left wrist (fig. 48). With your right had strike quickly to the bridge of the opponent's nose (fig. 49). Repeat this movement on both sides using the left and right side of the hand.

Hand Movements and Strikes

Pukul Kanan/Kiri

Pukul Kanan (fig. 50) is *striking from the right-handed side*, and Pukul Kiri is *striking from the left-handed side*. This type of strike is also from the Cimande system. The target is usually to the side of the head but is also used to hit vital areas of the body.

The strike starts from a ready position with both hands positioned above your waist, palms up fist closed and feet together (fig.51). Step forward with your right foot to 1 o'clock. Strike with the right hand using the side of the fist. The left hand moves in a counter clockwise position chest high (fig. 52). To repeat this on the opposite side, reposition yourself to the ready position (fig. 53). Step forward with the left foot to 11 o'clock, and strike with the left hand using the side of the fist. The right hand moves in a clockwise position chest high (fig. 54). Repeat this strike on the left and right side of the fist striking with the side of the fist.

50

51

52

53

54

Kobok (continued)

The buah application will start in a ready position facing your opponent (fig. 55). As your opponent strikes with his left hand, step to 1 o'clock with your right foot and downward check his left forearm. Grab the opponent's wrist and chamber your right arm on your right side ready to strike (fig. 56). Strike with your right hand using the side of the fist to the left side of the opponent's face. Maintain the grip on the opponent's left wrist with your left hand (fig. 57). Repeat this movement on both sides using the left and right side of the hand.

Sikut Vertical Elbow Strike

The sikut *vertical elbow strike* (fig. 58) is executed with both left and right elbow using alternating footwork.

Begin in a ready position with both hands positioned above the waist and to your sides, feet together (fig. 59). Step with your right foot to 1 o'clock, bend the right knee slightly while at the same time lifting your right elbow horizontally in line with your right shoulder. Your left hand in a forward position palm up ready to intercept the vertical elbow (fig.60). Lean forward by bending your left knee and place the majority of your body weight in your centerline. Strike down with your right elbow, placing your left hand to the inside of your right knee to catch the elbow strike that will target this area (fig. 61). Draw your body and your hands back to their original position (fig. 62).

58

59

60

61

62

Sikut Vertical Elbow Strike (continued)

Step with your left foot to 11 o'clock, bend the left knee slightly while at the same time lifting your left elbow horizontally in line with your left shoulder, your right hand in forward position palm up ready to intercept the vertical elbow (fig. 63). Lean forward bending your right knee and place the majority of your body weight in your centerline. Strike down with your left elbow, placing your right hand to the inside of your left knee to catch the elbow strike that will target this area (fig. 64). Draw your body and your hands back to its original position next to your waistline (fig. 65). Repeat this movement on both the left and right elbow.

Hand Movements and Strikes

The buah application will start in a ready position facing your opponent (fig. 66). As your opponent strikes at you with his right hand, apply an inside forearm block with your left forearm (much like the besot hand movement), and step forward with your right foot to 1 o'clock (fig. 67). Slide your left hand to your opponent's right wrist, your thumb pointing upward. Place your hand on the back on the opponent's neck and push his head and his right arm in a clockwise motion (fig. 68). To finish with a vertical elbow strike, step back with your right leg so your right knee is on the ground. Place your left hand under the opponent's neck and finish him off by striking down on his face with a vertical elbow strike (fig. 69)

The Horizontal Elbow Strike

The horizontal elbow strike (fig. 70) is executed with both left and right elbow using alternating footwork.

Begin in a ready position with both hands positioned above the waist and to your sides, feet together (fig. 71). Turn your body to the right and step with your right foot to 3 o'clock and execute a left horizontal elbow strike at your right open hand (fig. 72). To repeat these movements on the opposite side, start to turn the body to the left and pivot on the balls of your feet. Your left hand should be open and going in a counter clockwise motion elevated to your head. Your right arm should be horizontal to your midsection and ready to pivot on the balls of your feet, turning your body to your left side (fig. 73). Lean to your left side and strike with your right forearm to your open left hand (fig. 74). Repeat this movement on both your right and left side pivoting on the balls of your feet.

Hand Movements and Strikes

The buah application will start in a ready position facing your opponent (fig. 75). As your opponent strikes at you with his right hand, apply an inside forearm block with your left forearm (much like the besot hand movement) and step forward with your right foot to 1 o'clock (fig. 76). With your right hand catch the opponent's head with your open right palm and, in a clockwise motion, turn the opponent's head to your right side (fig. 77). To finish the horizontal elbow strike, place your right open hand over the left side of the opponent's head or forehead. Strike with your left forearm with a horizontal strike to the back of the opponent's head (fig. 78).

Gunting Strike (continued)

Gunting (fig. 79) is executed by crossing your two forearms, much like a scissors movement. The application of gunting can be performed by striking with the lead fist to a vital area of the body or by grabbing or parrying with either hand to vital areas of the body. Gunting works very well with any footwork, but is most effective using the betrik (back leg striking) footwork.

Begin in a ready position with both hands positioned above the waist and to your sides, feet together (fig. 80). Step forward with your right foot to 1 o'clock. Strike with the side of your fist to the centerline of your body at shoulder level using your right hand. Your left hand is open and covering the centerline of your body (fig. 81). Return to the ready position with both hands positioned above the waist and to your sides, feet together (fig. 82). Step forward with your left foot to 11 o'clock. Strike with the side of your fist to the centerline of your body at shouldr level using your left hand. Your right hand is open and covering the centerline of your body (fig. 83). Return to the ready position with both hands positioned above the waist and to your sides, feet together (fig. 84). Repeat this movement using the left and right lead hands.

79

80

81

82

83

84

Hand Movements and Strikes

The buah application will start in a ready position facing your opponent (fig. 85). As your opponent strikes at you with his right hand, step to 1 o'clock with your right foot. Use your left hand to outside parry the opponent's right hand. Prepare your right hand to strike the inside of the opponent's triceps (fig. 86). Finish this technique by striking the opponent's right inside triceps. Your left hand should stay on his right hand to ensure your safety (fig. 87).

Chapter 17

Foot and Leg Movements and Strikes

Sapu (fig. 1) means broom or to sweep. In Pencak Silat Mande Muda terminology, sapu comes from the meaning of kaki or leg. The sapu movement is part of the Cikalong, Syahbandar, and Harimau styles. There is a system of jurus (forms) that need to be mastered before moving beyond the sapu movements in order to integrate the sapu movements with other styles of Pencak Silat Mande Muda.

Sapu Dalam

Sapu dalam is *to sweep to the inside*. Using the inside or bottom of your foot, execute a circular sweeping motion to the inside of the opponent's foot before it hits the ground. The target is the lowest part of the foot.

Begin in a ready position with both hands positioned above the waist and to your sides, feet together in a stationary position (fig. 2). Place your left hand forward palm up and your right hand chambered next to your right shoulder much like the suliwa hand position. Raise your right heel off the ground (fig. 3). Pick your right leg so that your right knee is horizontal with your right leg (fig. 4). Start a counter clockwise motion with your right leg (fig. 5).

Sapu Dalam (continued)

To complete the sapu dalma on the right side continue with the counter clockwise motion with your right leg until your right foot crosses the centerline of your body. Your right foot should be as close to the ground as possible with your right foot in a vertical position. Bend your left knee slightly in order to help you maintain balance (fig. 6).

To repeat the sapu dalma on the left side place your right foot on the ground. Place your right hand forward with palm up and your left hand chambered next to your left shoulder. Raise your left heel off the ground (fig. 7). Pick up your left leg so that your left knee is horizontal with your left leg (fig. 8). Start a clockwise motion with your left leg (fig. 9).

To complete the sapu dalma on the left side continue with the clockwise motion with your left leg until your left foot crosses the centerline of your body. Your left foot should be as close to the ground as possible with your left foot in a vertical position. Bend slightly with your right knee in order to help you maintain balance (fig. 10). Repeat this movement several times on both the left and right side.

Foot and Leg Movements and Strikes

The buah (technique) application will begin with your opponent directly in front of you (fig. 11). As your opponent attacks you with a right punch, counter his punch with a suliwa hand movement. At the same time as your opponent steps forward with his right foot, immediately engage the bottom or inside of your right foot to an inside sapu dalam on your opponent's foot, while the opponent's foot is still off the ground (fig. 12). Before your opponent's foot touches the ground, sapu dalam his foot quickly with the bottom or inside of your right foot to the your left side, throwing your opponent off balance (fig. 13). Repeat this sapu dalam movement several times on both the left and right side.

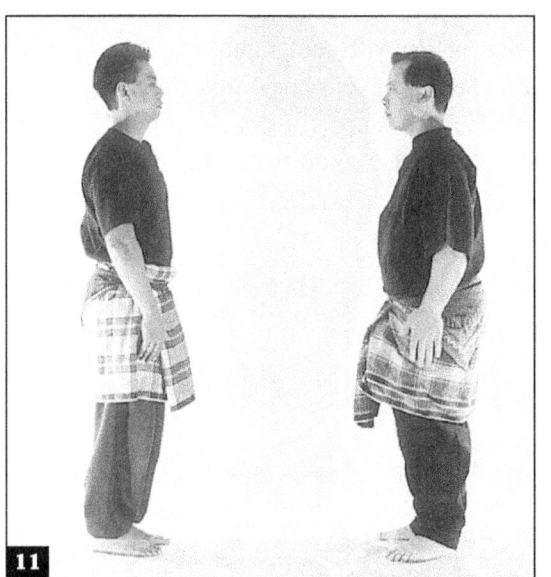

Sapu Luar

Sapu luar means to *sweep to the outside*, wherein you apply a circular sweeping motion to the outside of the opponent's foot. With this motion you are to use the outside of your foot and target the outside and lowest part of the opponent's foot.

Begin in a ready position with both hands positioned above the waist and to your sides, feet together (fig. 14). Place your left hand forward with palm up and your right hand chambered next to your right shoulder. Raise your right heel off the ground (fig. 15). Pick your right leg up so that your right knee is horizontal with your right leg (fig. 16). Cross your right foot in a clockwise motion over to your left side (fig. 17). To complete the sapu luar on the right side continue with the clockwise motion with your right leg until your right foot crosses back through the centerline of your body. Your right foot should be as close to the ground as possible with your right foot in a vertical position. Bend your left knee slightly in order to help you maintain balance (fig. 18).

Foot and Leg Movements and Strikes

To perform the sapu luar on the left side, place your right foot on the ground. Place your right hand forward with palm up and your left hand chambered next to your left shoulder. Raise your left heel off the ground (fig. 19). Pick your left leg so that your left knee is horizontal with your left leg (fig. 20). Cross your left foot in a counter clockwise motion over to your left side (fig. 21). To complete the sapu luar on the left side, continue with the counter clockwise motion with your left leg until your left foot crosses back through the centerline of your body. Your left foot should be as close to the ground as possible, with your left foot in a vertical position. Bend slightly with your right knee in order to help maintain your balance (fig. 22). Repeat this sapu luar movement several times on both the left and right side.

Sapu Luar (continued)

The buah application begins with your opponent directly in front of you (fig. 23). As your opponent attacks you with a right punch, counter his punch with a suliwa hand movement. At the same time as your opponent steps forward with his right foot, immediately engage the outside of your right foot with an outside sapu luar on your opponent's foot while it is still off the ground (fig. 24). Before your opponent's foot touches the ground, sapu luar his foot quickly with the outside of your right foot to the your right side, throwing your opponent off balance (fig. 25). Repeat this sapu luar movement several times on both the left and right side.

Ledot Leg Movement

This leg movement (fig. 26) is similar principal to the kobok hand movement. After using a pacok or front kick, you insert your leg between the opponent's legs and turn your leg and body to push your opponent off balance or to the ground. Ledot is used also as an entree to Harimau.

Begin in a ready position with both hands positioned above the waist and to your sides, feet together (fig. 27). Place your left hand forward with palm up and your right hand chambered next to your right shoulder. Pick your right leg up so that your right knee is horizontal with your right leg. Extend your right foot forward much like a front kick (pacok) (fig. 28). To complete the ledot on the right side, continue pivoting on your left foot to 9 o'clock and rotate your hips and right leg counter clockwise (fig. 29).

To execute the ledot movements on the left side, place your right foot on the ground. Place your right hand forward with palm up and your left hand chambered next to your left shoulder. Pick your left leg up so that your left knee is horizontal with your left leg. Extend your left foot forward like a front kick (pacok) (fig. 30). To complete the ledot on the left side, continue to pivot on your right foot to 3 o'clock and rotate your hips and left leg clockwise (fig. 31). Repeat this ledot movement several times on both the left and right side.

Ledot Leg Movement (continued)

The buah (technique) application will begin with your opponent striking at you with his right hand. Perform a left handed lead suliwa hand movement to the opponent's striking arm (fig. 32). Insert your right leg between the opponent's legs, striking your opponent's groin area while maintaining the suliwa arm lock on your opponent (fig. 33). Rotate your right leg and hips to the left, your left foot to an open position, and push down with your right leg on the inside of the opponent's right thigh, and your right foot pushing down on the opponents back knee (fig. 34). Repeat this ledot movement several times on both the left and right side.

Foot and Leg Movements and Strikes

Kuda Kuda Horse Stance Position

Kuda Kuda (fig. 35) can be translated to horse stance and or the action of walking. Kuda Kuda is a key element of the Sayahbandar style of Pencak Silat Mande Muda. Spread your legs apart as to put your left knee over your left toe and your right knee over your right toe. Sit or drop your centerline into a squatting position. In a normal Sayahbandar movement, the feet will do all the work to advance you forward while maintaining your kuda kuda stance. This kind of stance, along with advancing footworks, is very deceiving and very fast.

Begin in a ready position with both hands positioned above the waist and to your sides, feet together (fig. 36). Step out wide with your right foot to 3 o'clock. In order to execute a good kuda kuda stance, endeavor to position both left and right knees over your left and right toes. Place your left hand forward with palm up and your right hand chambered next to your right shoulder (fig. 37). Hold this position for several seconds. Return to a ready position by retracting your right foot to your left foot with both hands positioned above the waist and to your sides, feet together (fig. 38).

235

Kuda Kuda Horse Stance Position
(continued)

To perform this kuda kuda stance on your left side, step out wide with your left foot to 9 o'clock, and endeavor to position both left and right knees over your left and right toes. Place your right hand forward with palm up and your left hand chambered next to your left shoulder (fig. 39). Hold this position for several seconds. To return to the ready position, retract your left foot to your right foot with both hands positioned above the waist and to your sides, feet together (fig. 40). Repeat this kuda kuda movement several times on both the left and right side.

The buah (technique) application will begin with your opponent facing you in a ready position (fig. 41). The opponent will step forward with his left foot and strike with his left hand. As your opponent strikes at you, step out deep with your right foot to 9 o'clock and check with your left hand to the opponent's left forearm (fig. 42). Continue with your suliwa hand movement and strike with your right hand to your opponent's left elbow and slide your left hand down to grab your opponent's left wrist. Lower your body and squat down to get into your kuda kuda stance (fig. 43). Repeat this kuda kuda movement several times on both the left and right side.

Teteg Foot Striking

Teteg (fig. 44) means to compress or compression. The teteg theory is based on the heel of the foot first and rolls into the toe, in other words heel roll to toe. The teteg movement is part of the Cikalong, Syahbandar, and Harimau styles in Pencak Silat Mande Muda. There is a system of jurus (forms) that need to be mastered before moving beyond the teteg movements in order to integrate them with other styles of Pencak Silat Mande Muda.

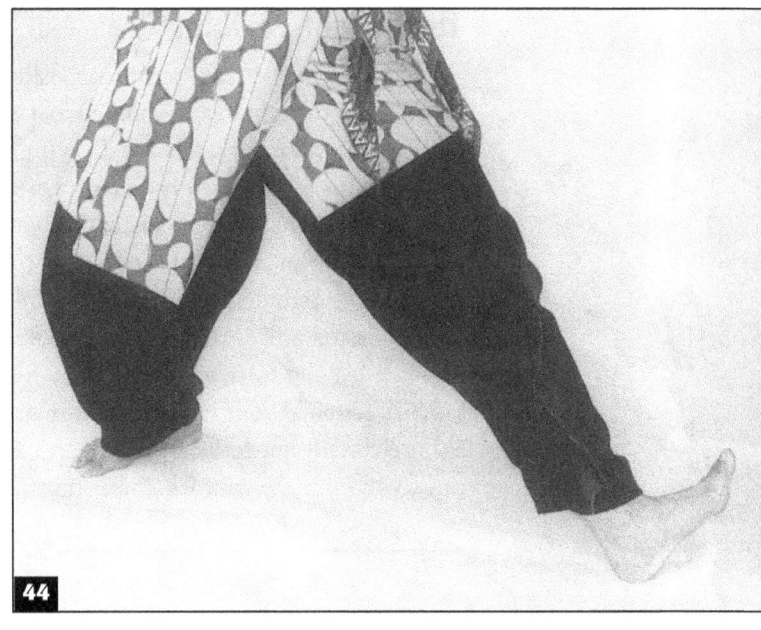

Begin in a ready position with both hands positioned above the waist and to your sides, feet together (fig. 45). Place your left hand forward with palm up and your right hand chambered next to your right shoulder. Position your right leg so that your right knee is diagonal with your right leg. Extend your right foot forward and point your right heel to the ground with your right toes pointing up (fig. 46). Your right leg should be straight and your heel will impact the ground first at a 1 o'clock and is ready to pivot to your right (fig. 47). Bend your right leg and turn your right foot to the right and lean your right knee in the same direction as your right toe is pointing, this is the teteg foot movement (fig. 48). Be careful not to bend too far or lean in the wrong direction. This may cause injury to your leg, knee, and ankle.

Teteg Foot Striking (continued)

To perform the teteg on the opposite side, return to a ready position by retracting your right foot to your left foot with both hands positioned above the waist and to your sides, feet together (fig. 49). Place your right hand forward with palm up and your left hand chambered next to your left shoulder. Position your left leg so that your left knee is diagonal with your left leg. Extend forward your right foot and point your right heel to the ground your right toes pointing up (fig. 50). Your left leg should be straight and your heel will impact the ground first at an 11 o'clock and is ready to pivot to your right (fig. 51). Bend your left leg and turn your left foot to the left and lean your left knee in the same direction as your left toe is pointing, this is the teteg foot movement (fig. 52). Be careful not to bend too far or lean in the wrong direction. This may cause you injury to your leg, knee and ankle.

Foot and Leg Movements and Strikes

The buah (technique) application will begin with your opponent facing you in a ready position (fig. 53). The opponent will step forward with his right foot and strike with his left hand. As your opponent strikes at you, step with your left foot behind his right foot, placing the top of your right foot just above his right heel and check with your left hand to the opponent's left forearm (fig. 54). Continue with your suliwa hand movement and strike with your right hand to your opponent's left elbow and slide your left hand down to grab your opponent's left wrist. Pivot your left heel and foot around your opponent's right foot. Lean your left knee toward your left toe. This will create the compression lock on your opponent's right foot, knee, and leg (fig. 55). Repeat this teteg foot movement several times on both the left and right sides.

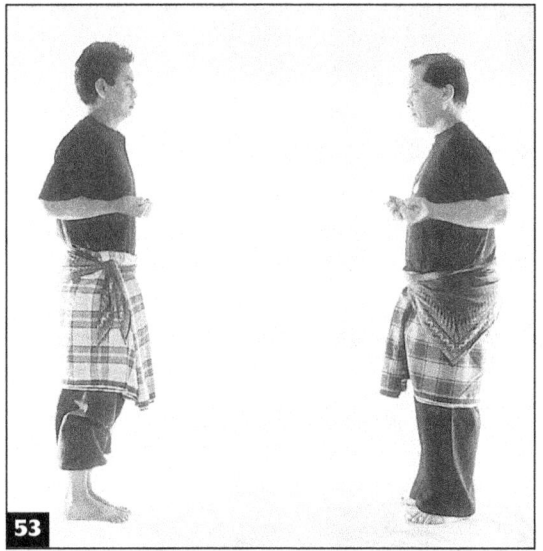

Bentrik Back Leg Striking

Bentrik (fig. 60) is to *strike and retract*, and its theory is based on *the back whip, weather with the leg or arm*. The bentrik movement is part of the Cikalong, Syahbandar, and Harimau styles in Pencak Silat Mande Muda. There is a system of jurus (forms) that need to be mastered in order to integrate the bentrik movements with other styles of Pencak Silat Mande Muda.

Begin in a ready position with both hands positioned above the waist and to your sides, feet together (fig. 61). Cross your right forearm over your left forearm at chest level with both palms facing toward your face. Elevate your right heel off the ground while bending your right knee and keeping your toes on the ground (fig. 62). Step forward with your right toes to 12 o'clock. Your back foot is pointing at 9 o'clock and your right foot is also pointing at 9 o'clock. Your right arm extends forward with an open palm, your left arm is chambered back to your left shoulder with an open palm. Both arms are in a horizontal position (fig. 63). At the same time, strike the ground with your right heel, your right foot should be pointing at 9 o'clock, your right leg is straight, close your left and right hands into a fist signifying grabbing (fig. 64).

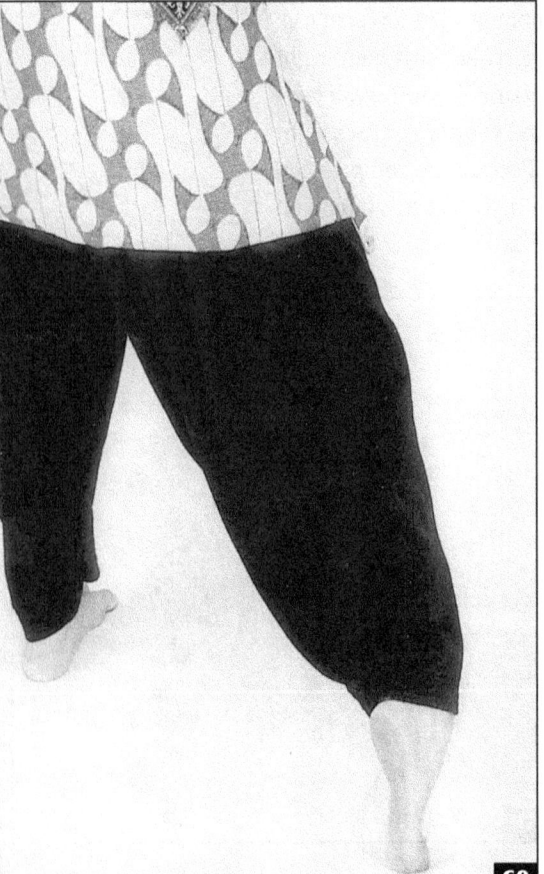

Foot and Leg Movements and Strikes

To perform this bentrik movement on the opposite side, reposition your right foot forward to 12 o'clock. Cross your right forearm over your left forearm chest level with both palms facing towards your face (fig. 65). Step through with your left foot to 12 o'clock, toes pointing at 3 o'clock, left heel off the ground. Your left arm extends forward with an open palm, your left arm is chambered back to your right shoulder with an open palm. Both left and right arm are in a horizontal position (fig. 66). At the same time, strike the ground with your left heel, your left foot should be pointing at 3 o'clock, your left leg is straight, close your right and left hand into a fist signifying grabbing (fig. 67). Repeat this bentrik movement several times on both the left and right side.

Bentrik Back Leg Striking (continued)

The buah (technique) application begins with your opponent facing you in a ready position (fig. 68). The opponent will step forward with his right foot and strike with his right hand. As your opponent strikes, grab the opponent's throat with your right hand and outside parry his punch with your left hand. Step with your foot behind the opponent's right leg, placing the back of your leg too the back of the opponent's leg, your right heel is elevated, and both your left and right foot are pointing to 9 o'clock (fig. 69). At the same time, heel strike the ground and strike the back of the opponent's leg with the back of your leg. Grab the opponent's throat with your right and pull. With your left hand grab the opponent's right wrist (fig. 70). Repeat this bentrik leg movement several times on both the left and right side.

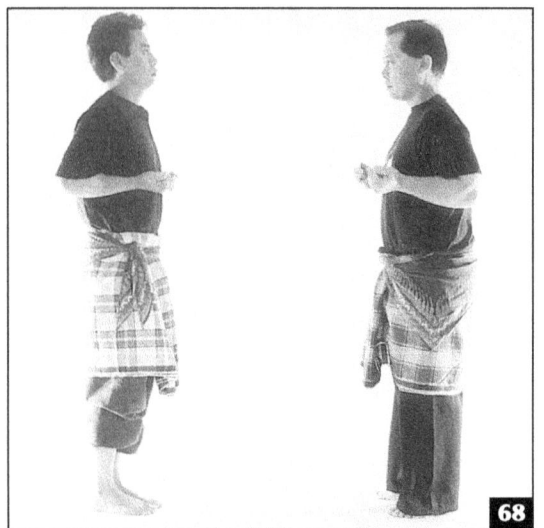

Pacok Kick to the Shin

Pacok (fig. 71) simply means *front kick to the shin*. The pacok theory is based on the front kick to a low vital area of the opponent's body or limbs. The pacok movement is a part of the Cikalong, Syahbandar, and Harimau styles of Pencak Silat Mande Muda. In this particular kick, your front foot you will lift and kick forward while pulling back your toes. The kick should be with the ball of your foot, your back leg is slightly bent, and the kick is to be not higher than a person's knee. There is a system of jurus (forms) that need to be mastered in order to integrate the pacok movement with other styles of Pencak Silat Mande Muda.

Begin in a ready position with both hands positioned above the waist and to your sides, feet together (fig. 72). Place your left hand forward with palm up and your right hand chambered next to your right shoulder. Pick your right leg up in preparation of a low front kick (fig. 73). Snap your right foot forward and kick low, no higher than your knee. Retract your kick quickly (fig. 74).

Bentrik Back Leg Striking (continued)

To repeat the pecok on the opposite side return to a ready position begin by retracting your right foot to your left foot with both hands positioned above the waist and to your sides, feet together (fig. 75). Place your right hand forward with palm up and your left hand chambered next to your left shoulder. Pick your left leg up in preparation of a low front kick (fig. 76). Snap forward your left foot and kick low, no higher than your knee. Retract your kick quickly (fig. 77). Repeat this pecok movement several times on both the left and right side.

The buah (technique) application will begin with your opponent facing you in a ready position (fig. 78). The opponent will step forward with his right foot and strike with his right hand. As your opponent strikes, counter with a suliwa hand movement. Your right hand grabbing the opponent's right wrist and your left hand striking to the opponent's right elbow. Kick to the opponent's shin or knee with your right foot, pulling your toes back and kicking with the ball of your foot (fig. 79). Repeat this pecok leg movement several times on both the left and right side.

Dengkul Strike with the Knee

Dengkul (fig. 80) is to *strike with the knee*. The dengkul theory is based on the front knee strike to a vital area of the opponent's body or limbs. In most cases the dengkul will be directed to the head. The dengkul movement is a part of the Cikalong, Syahbandar, and Harimau styles of Pencak Silat Mande Muda. There is a system of jurus (forms) need to be mastered in order to integrated the dengkul movements with other styles of Pencak Silat Mande Muda.

Begin in a ready position with both hands positioned above the waist and to your sides, feet together (fig. 81). Extend your left arm forward with palm up at shoulder height. Strike up vertically with your right knee horizontal to your thigh and knee. Slap your right knee with your right hand to signify the knee strike (fig. 82).

To repeat this movement on the opposite side, extend your right arm forward palm up and shoulder height. Strike up vertically with your left knee horizontal to your thigh and knee. Slap your left knee with your left hand to signify the knee strike (fig. 83). Repeat this dengkul movement several times on both the left and right side.

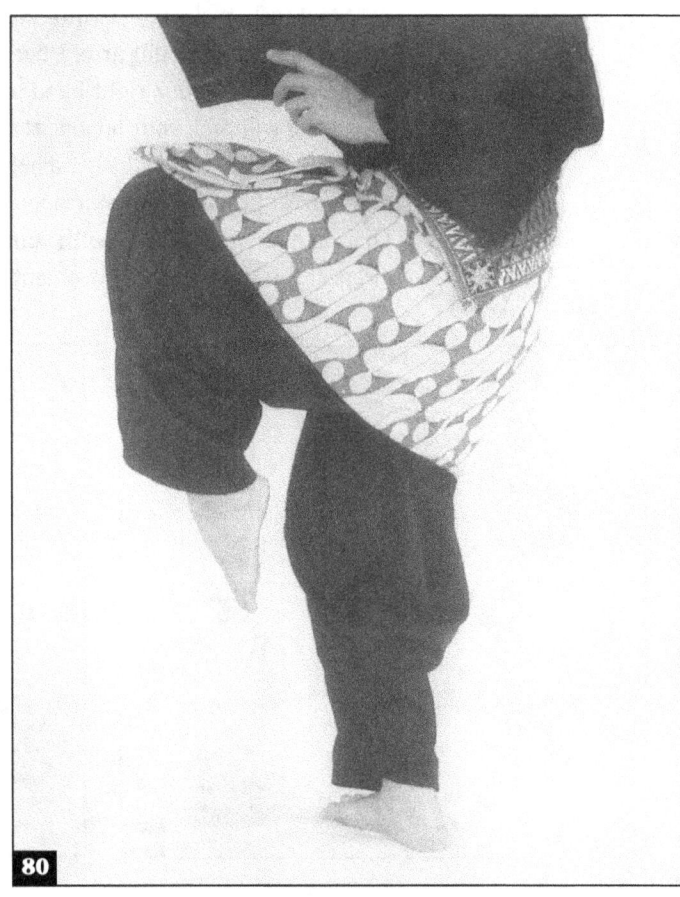

Dengkul Strike with the Knee (continued)

The buah (technique) application will begin with your opponent facing you in a ready position (fig. 84). The opponent will step forward with his right foot and strike with his right hand. As your opponent strikes, step with your left foot to 12 o'clock. Use your left hand to do a besot inside block to the inside of the opponent's right arm. Chamber your right hand across your chest (fig. 85). Strike with your right hand to the right side of the opponent's face. Your left hand will grab your opponent's right forearm and right knee start to lift up (fig. 86). Place your right hand behind your opponent's head and pull his head to your right knee. Lift your opponent's right arm with your left hand to lock his right shoulder. Strike with your right knee to the opponent's head (fig. 87). Repeat this dengkul leg movement several times on both the left and right side.

Pring Compression Movement

In Pencak Silat Mande Muda terminology pring is a counter movement that is cause by the opponents hooking or grabbing the leg (fig. 88). The pring theory is based on a counter movement that will compress or push the opponent down to the ground and is used in conjunction with hand movements. The hand movements can encompass blocking, grabbing, punching, or the use of the kobok movement. This pring movement can do major damage to the opponent's foot, ankle, knee, and hip. The pring movement is a part of the Cikalong, Syahbandar, Harimau styles and is also a trademark of Kembangan of Pencak Silat Mande Muda. There is a system of jurus (forms) that need to be mastered in order to integrate the pring movement with other styles of Pencak Silat Mande Muda.

Begin in a ready position with both hands positioned above the waist and to your sides, feet together (fig. 89). Extend your left arm forward with palm open, your right hand should be next to the right side of your forehead with palm open. Strike with your right leg using a pecok front kick (fig. 90). Lean forward and drop down on your right foot to the ground. The instep of your foot should point to your right. Be careful not to bend too far or lean in the wrong direction, as this may cause injury to your leg, knee, and ankle (fig. 91).

88

89

90

91

Pring Compression Movement (continued)

To repeat the pring on the opposite side, return to a ready position begin by retracting your right foot to your left foot with both hands positioned above the waist and to your sides, feet together (fig. 92). Extend your right arm forward with palm open. Your left hand should be next to the left side of your forehead with palm open. Strike with your left leg using a pecok front kick (fig. 93). Lean forward and drop down on your left foot to the ground, the instep of your foot should point to your left. Be careful not to bend too far or lean in the wrong direction, as this may cause you injury to your leg, knee, and ankle (fig. 94). Repeat this pring movement several times on both the left and right side.

Foot and Leg Movements and Strikes

The buah (technique) application will begin by you doing a pecok or front kick to your opponent. Your opponent will evade and hook his left arm under your right left (fig. 95). To counter the opponent's hook on your right leg, reposition your right foot to the outside of the opponent's left knee (fig. 96). Begin to complete the pring movement by pushing down with your right leg to the side of the opponent's knee. Be careful not to push too hard it may cause damage to your opponent's knee. Use your right hand to pull back on the opponent's forehead (fig. 97). Repeat the pring counter movement several times on both the left and right side.

Depok

Depok has both a side sitting position (fig. 98) and a frontal sitting position (fig. 99). In Pencak Silat Mande Muda terminology, depok means *sitting and preparation position both for rest and aggressive counter attacks*. The depok movement is that of a defensive movement, but can easily change into an aggressive offensive movement that is quick and deceiving. It can be used

as a lure to attract or attack an opponent that will ultimately end in the style of Harimau. The depok theory is based on a counter movement induced by an opponent. But the counter movement can also be used as a way to enter into Harimau. This depok movement can do major damage to the opponent's foot, ankle, knee, and hip. The depok movement is a part of the Cikalong and Syahbandar styles but is also a contributing movement in the Harimau style. There is a system of jurus (forms) that need to be mastered in order to integrate the depok movement with other styles of Pencak Silat Mande Muda.

Begin in a ready position with both hands positioned above the waist and to your sides, feet together (fig. 100). Start with your right arm in front of your chest and left arm to your left side, and begin a clockwise motion with both left and right arms. Step directly back with your right foot to 6 o'clock (fig. 101). Continue with the clockwise arm and hand motions until your left hand is in front of your forehead and your right arm across your midsection. Sit down into the position with your left leg in a vertical position over your right leg, which is flat on the ground (fig. 102).

Depok (continued)

To perform the depok on the opposite side, start by standing up (fig. 103). In an upright body position pivot on your feet and turn your body in a clockwise motion. Start to turn your arms and hands in a counter clockwise motion (fig. 104). Continue with your clockwise body motion and start to make your decent to the ground. Your arms and hands will continue with the counter clockwise motion (fig. 105). Sit down with your left arm in front of your chest and right arm across your midsection. Your right leg is in a vertical position over your left leg, which is flat on the ground (fig. 106). Repeat this movement several times on both the left and right side.

Foot and Leg Movements and Strikes

The buah (technique) application will begin with your opponent facing you in a ready position (fig. 107). The opponent will step forward with his right foot and strike with his right hand. As your opponent strikes, step with your left foot to 11 o'clock, evading the strike. Use your left hand to do left hand outside parry to the outside of the opponent's right wrist (fig. 108). Step with your right leg past the outside of your opponent's right leg. Your left knee is on the ground and your left shin is over the opponent's right foot (fig. 109). Retract and push with your right thigh to the opponent's right outside left using your body weight to force the opponent to the ground. Your left shin will be resting on the opponent's right leg and your right thigh is resting on the opponen's right knee. Use the right hand to strike or grab the opponent's arm or body (fig. 110). Be careful as this depok movement can cause injury to the opponent's ankle, knee, hip, and leg. Repeat this depok counter movement several times on both the left and right side.

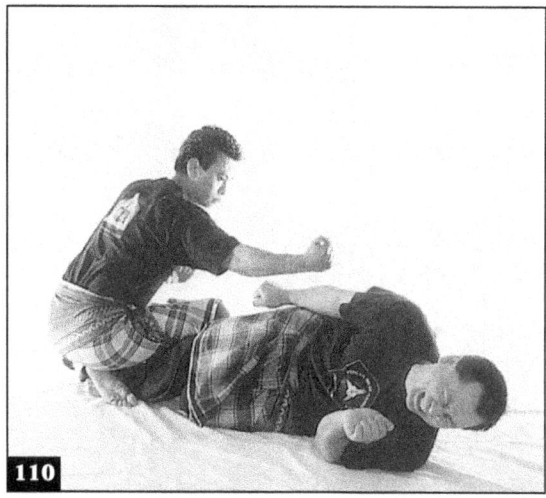

Chapter 18

Body Positions

The following section presents one body position from each of the 25 styles of Pencak Silat Mande Muda. These body positions may be the position that the practitioner would take at the beginning of a conflict or during its action. These body positions are not necessarily the body positions that the practitioner will display or use during a conflict, but will identify the types of styles in which the practitioner may choose to use during the conflict. The body position reflects the type of posture that is taken during any given moment of the individual style and could be used as a point of reference in any of the 25 styles of Pencak Silat Mande Muda.

Cimande

Cikalong

Harmau

Sera

Syahbandar

Kari

Madi

Cipecut

Timbangen

Body Positions

Nampon

Rikesan

Ulin Napas

Tanjakan

Indonesian Martial Arts: Pencak Silat

Pamonyet

Pamacan

Ulin Baduy

Syahbandar Baru

Galih Pakuan

Indonesian Martial Arts: Pencak Silat

Benjang

Harimau Baru

Sampiyoung

Cikalong Baru

Body Positions

Sabetan

Sanalika

Ujungan

Chapter 19

Forms and Training

Jurus

The term juru (fig. 1) come from the *Bahasa Indonesia language*, and refers to *form* or *motion*. Jurus consist of a series of martial movements that are practiced alone (solo). Their use is to practice the contest of engagement, but the application is hidden in the form. The Mande Muda practitioner will progress through several elements of hand, foot, and body movements to incorporate the different basic hand, foot, and leg strikes along with hand, foot, and leg attacks. Body positions will also be included and will use the various body positions to execute the correct hand and leg movements to work together in a counter and aggressive movement.

The jurus of Mande Muda begin with empty hands. After many hours of training under strict supervision, the practitioner in the intermediate and advanced stages of jurus can include the use of weapons, including bladed weapons. The juru is very important to learn first because it teaches you the basic motions or movements through training in the basic fundamentals of Mande Muda. Jurus offer training in repetition, and this helps in the development of both the body (muscle) and the mind (neuro memory) of the practitioner. The juru is a set execution of movements. As the practitioner masters the jurus the next level of training with the juru is call buah. The jurus can be found in all of the 25 styles of mande muda. The following juru is in movement succession (fig. 2-6).

Buah

The term buah (fig. 7) comes from Bahasa Indonesia and *refers the fruit of the flower*. In terms of Silat, this refers to the *application or technique of a movement pattern (juru)*. Buah or Buahana is the Sudanese terminology for application of Penca and is the same movement or technique that is used in the Jurus, but now it is done with a partner. After the jurus are practiced with skill and agility the practitioner will now incorporate what he has learned in the juru with a training partner to help practice the techniques of the juru. This type of training will help in the development of real life and simulated combat activity. The practitioner will learn what it is like to have an opponent strike, kick, block, and counter his techniques. The buah is performed first with caution and care of each practitioner. As each of the players gets better in executing the movements of the buah the speed will increase. Care is taken during each buah because as the speed increases, so does the intensity of the buah. The Munde Muda practitioner uses the buah to mentally seek out new and other opportunities of countering his opponent, and this is called pechahan. The following is the buah from the jurus in the reverse juru section (Fig. 8–11)

Pechahan

Pechahan means *to create from one*. In other words, you can take one technique and create an unlimited number of counter techniques or permutations of each of the counter techniques. In order to prepare for the pechahan you must first know the original or root techniques of any particular Juru and also its buah as a guide. Pechahan can be the finishing or continual movements of any one technique. You will use the elements of take downs, breaking bones, kicking, punching, locking, parrying, and evading using your own creativity. In a real fight you cannot plan on what to do, you need to create, but you must create from the root techniques. Pechadan is a method of training that is base on learning the root movement. The best way to describe pechahan is by first holding a glass of water. The glass represents a technique. Now drop the water glass on the floor. It now shatters into a thousand pieces. If you do a technique and as a result see another way of doing it, you just created a permutation and another way of doing a counter technique. The mental images you get from doing a technique are endless. This is the essence of pechahan.

Kembangan

Kembangan (fig. 12) is derived from the *Bahasa Indonesia word "kembang,"* meaning flower and to bloom. Kembangan is to dance, and the dance originated as a means of relating tales of victory from the battlefield and came to be set to music as part of the celebratory mood. The move of dance or "kembangan" clearly indicates to other silat practitioners that the style is from West Java (fig. 13).

Kembangan (continued)

The dance also serves as a library of movements and combative techniques for the Pencak Silat Mande Muda practitioners.

In Pencak Silat Mande Muda the dance is one of the most important foundations of training available in the art (fig. 14). The kembangan is a part of the school curriculum in West Java (fig. 15). The students learn kembangan only for the physical activity and most of them will only do this because the school requires it. In most cases this is as far as the student will take the art. Only a small percentage of students will continue to learn more about he kembangan by seeking it out a martial art teacher. Every movement in the kembangan contains a self-defense technique. The kembangan dance is used for training in much the same way as many other martial arts form training. One major difference that separates Pencak Silat Mande Muda kembangan from other martial art dances is the special music that is played along with it, that teaches the practitioner the timing and power (fig. 16).

Forms and Training

Many different instruments that include drums of different shapes produce music for the kembangan. There are six kettledrums called a kendang (fig. 17), a gong (fig. 18) and a reed instrument called a terompet (fig. 19). The Pencak Silat Mande Muda student learns how to apply power from the rhythm and tempo of his or her kembangan music. When the student's moment of power or impact comes in a technique, the music tempo will increase and so will the intensity of the student's kembangan (fig. 20). As the music rhythms increase, this will play to the student's kembangan in a way to give the student power and the student will sometime dance in a trances like state of mind (fig. 21). Many times the student will take on the traits of an animal much like a tiger. As the music continues to play the student will become more relaxed and grain confidence and focus on the power. The elements or methods of striking, blocking, counter blocking, kicking, evading, parrying, footwork all comes from the power of the music in the kembangan (fig. 22).

Kembangan (continued)

Mande Muda students practice the kembangan until they feels that they are one in the same and are happy with the kembangan. Next the student will go through a ceremony that is designed to "marry" the student to the kembangan. The student and the music will become one. This means that the student believes that the kembangan and its techniques will be unbeatable in combat. At this point the student knows that his kembangan can rely on the techniques inspired by the kembangan to save the student from any situation that will confront the student. During the night of the "marriage of the kembangan" the student must repeat the kembangan many times (fig. 23). The number of times depends on which day of the week the student was born. Each time the kembangan is done the student of the kembangan must set a small stone down in front of his teacher. The student is not allowed to talk until the ceremony is over. He is able to eat and drink but nothing must leave his body. After the kembangan is completed the teacher will take the student to a river and dunks his head seven times, as each day of the week is an individual day of power (fig. 24).

Pencak Silat without Kembangan is not "Penca" that comes from Sunda (West Java). Kembanagn is really important for Penca from Sunda and many people say the root of their Penca comes from Sunda, but at the same time they don't know what Penca realy is. You have to learn Kembangan to understand what Penca is. Penca without kembangan is just like a country without its flag. Remember, kembangan is not as easy as the buah to learn. Let me instill this thought in your mind: it is really easy to learn how to kill people, but the hard part is to learn how not to be killed.

To do kembangan is nice and feels good because you move with the music, like you do with rock n' roll. Every muscle is an electrical impulse in the body that moves so fast and makes breathing become very difficult and quick. On top of that there are many people watching your every movement, and this for sure will make you feel like you need to go to the bathroom because you are so nervous.

Rules of Kembangan

There are terms and rules of kembangan first of all you should know the kembangan is made up as different parts. Again, here we are speaking about the type of kembangan from West Java, Sunda. I will present the terms as they are usually presented in the traditional Sunda Ibing or Kembangan. Although, sometimes just one section of the ibing or kembangan is performed, this will depend on the performer.(Fig. 25)

Paleredan

The first section that is usually performed in kembangan is called paleredan (fig. 26). The term refers to the music in which the movements are performed. The paleredan movements are really gentle but aggressive and at the same time the movements are done to the seven-count rhythm ending with the gong. The gong is your clue to stop and begin another section of movements.

Tepak Tilu

The second section is called tepak tilu (fig. 27). This set of movements will immediately follow the paleredan movements, and are performed much faster with quick and aggressive actions. The movements in the tepak tilu are done to a three-count rhythm and will also end a gong.

Padundung

Padundung is *the third and final section of the ibing or kembangan* (fig. 28). It is also the fastest section and is the climax of the ibing or kembangan. Your clue is every other beat of the gong. In this section you normally use weapons, and is where the fighting would normally start. Traditionally, the music would start to announce to the opponent it was time to enter the fighting arena. During the padundung section, practitioners would fight so seriously during the ibing or kembangan that one might die.

Hence, the meaning of Maenpo, which means "forget to play." The word penca refers to training in the jurus and ibing or kembangan and the word Maenpo refers to the application. People who come from this area also know the word Maenpo Silat can

be found in Sumatra, Malaysia, and the Philippines. The influence is now a common term that is used "Pencak Silat" and is used in Indonesia.

Another rule in performing the ibing or kembangan is that normally you would go to the performing area and tell the drummer what type of rhythm he should play for you, or you can give him hand signs. Using two fingers indicates you would like to perform the tepak dua. Showing three fingers indicates you would like to perform the tepak tilu. Or you can just tell the drummer what rhythm you would like.

In any case, you will need to remember that the Penca was often performed for ceremonies and rituals in the villages and would last all night long, commonly starting at seven P.M. and lasting until five the next morning.

Ibing

Ibing (fig. 29) *is also a Sunda term we use in West Java to refer to the kembangan.* In order to truly know Penca from West Java a person must learn to feel the rhythm and motion in and of the form first hand with the live musicians. (Fig 30). There is not a sequence of set movements, but rather there are many rules to follow and you don't have a choice if you are performing Pencak Silat from West Java. If you don't follow the rule you will lose, as it would be like doing the Salsa dance with Jazz music. If the Pencak Silat comes from Sunda (West Java), one must know these words:

Peleredan-
Tepak Dua-
Tepak tilu-
Bombang-
Padundung-
Golempang-
Tepak hiji-

These words are classical of the Ibing (Kembangan) and relate to the

specific parts of the form alone. Also included and just derived are New Jurus and New Ibing (Kembangan) born from a belief of uniting the art. No more individual characteristics from particular areas, as was once readily apparent.

Ibing and Kembangan Training

When you go to train in Penca, the first thing the instructor is going to teach you is kembangan. During each class session you will first learn the "one gong" application to kembangan. One gong refers to seven movements, done over and over again until you have preformed them all correctly. This can go on for several days, weeks, or months. After the instructor feels that you have mastered the first set of movements your next step will be to learn the second section or the tepak tilu. Once again, this section will be done until you have preformed it correctly, or until the instructor feels you have mastered it. After the first two sections of the kembangan training is complete you will learn the last phase known is padundung. The same training will be in effect as the first two sections. The instructor will train you until he feels that you have mastered the final section.

After you have learned all sections of the kembangan you are ready to do your own ceremony. This is why it can take between one to two years just to complete one system or style. In some cases it can take even longer, and this depends on the student and instructor. Some schools teach the ibing or

kembangan without teaching the applications of the movements. Unfortunately, many students are not taught the applications of the movements, just the traditional ibing or kembangan.

I can remember back in the 1960s when my parents sent me to one school to learn Cikalong in the village of Situsaeur, Situgunting, Bandung, West Java (Fig. 31). I had to walk three hours from my house carrying a bag of rice, cigarettes, and some money just to pay for my training! When I got to my teacher's house, someone was already there practicing, so I had to wait until that person was done until I could start my lesson. This was after three months of just sitting at my teacher's house before he would even accept me as his student. Normally, we would learn in the living room of our teacher's, one student at a time. And of course we had to move all the furniture our to the house so we would not damage any of it. The atmosphere was relaxing and you could take a break if you wanted to or the teacher would just decide to tell you to "stop, enough for now."

Today, most traditional Pencak Silat schools are still like this. You almost can not find a studio or even a sign that there is a school teaching the traditional Indonesian martial arts of Pencak Silat. The most beautiful and modern Pedepokan studio is located in Jakarta belonging to IPSI (Ikatan Pencak Silat Seluruh Indonesia). They are trying to rebuild the reputation of Pencak Silat in a better image. This is to lessen the embarrassment that some of the young people feel when they are learning Penca, as they have come to associate the art with village life. Also because the art was used in many wars and had become known with an association of killing and creating criminals during wartime.

In general today there are still some very traditional Pencak Silat schools in the way they teach and promote their system. If you go to the Cimande village or any village and you want to see Pencak Silat, it may not be an easy thing to do. Many of the schools that teach Pencak Silat are taught in the homes of the teachers. Closed to anyone that tries to watch or tries to see what Pencak Silat is all about.

So, in general, kembangan or what some people call ibing, cannot be taken away from the Penca that comes from West Java. I would like all of my students and everyone that is training in the Mande Muda system to know at least one kembangan or ibing. This will mean to me that my students are deeply motivated and dedicated to learn more about my Indonesian culture and arts.

I will always teach the deep traditions in Mande Muda. I will continue spreading the art in that way to the world so the traditional Pencak Silat will remain from many generations to come and will live forever in those that play Mande Muda. My hopes are that within the next generations to come of Indonesians, they will also keep the tradition of our blood and our family as

Sunda people. Without our trademark of characteristics in Pencak Silat, we will have lost our identity. I am so happy that many Westerners are learning the traditional art and not just wanting to learn to break necks or try to nail each other with words and actions but rather, learning on a deeper level. By learning Ibing (Kembangan) the culture will not disappear.

The Way I See It

In general the kembangan or ibing is not an easy thing to do because first you have to remember the movement and then you have to step in the correct rhythm. But if you go through with this type of training this will mean that you are learning what Pencak Silat is, not just how to perform techniques. Techniques are easy to learn, but you need to learn about our culture, our history, and our way of life. This is why I have brought Mande Muda to the world so you will know what I feel is the most important training and to make sure that you have good information about Pencak Silat. The culture and values behind Mande Muda encourage having good relations with other human beings. It seems that the more you learn about Pencak Silat the less you would want to hurt someone. We learn Pencak Silat so we will not need to use it. So, the way I see it, to know Herman Suwanda is to know Pencak Silat Mande Muda. And when you have mastered this you will ultimately learned the correct meaning of Pencak. (fig. 32)

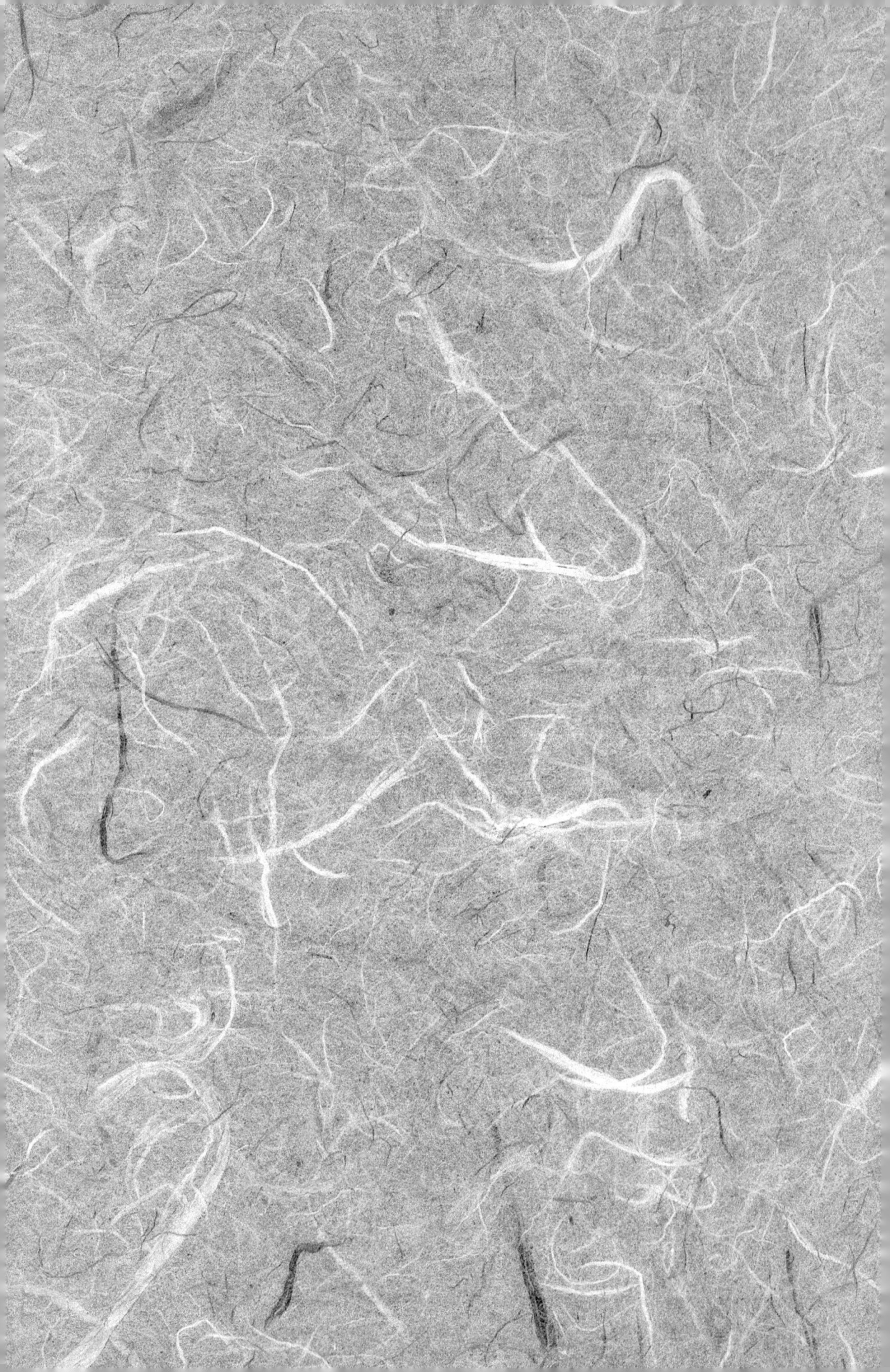

Part IV

Interviews with Herman Suwanda

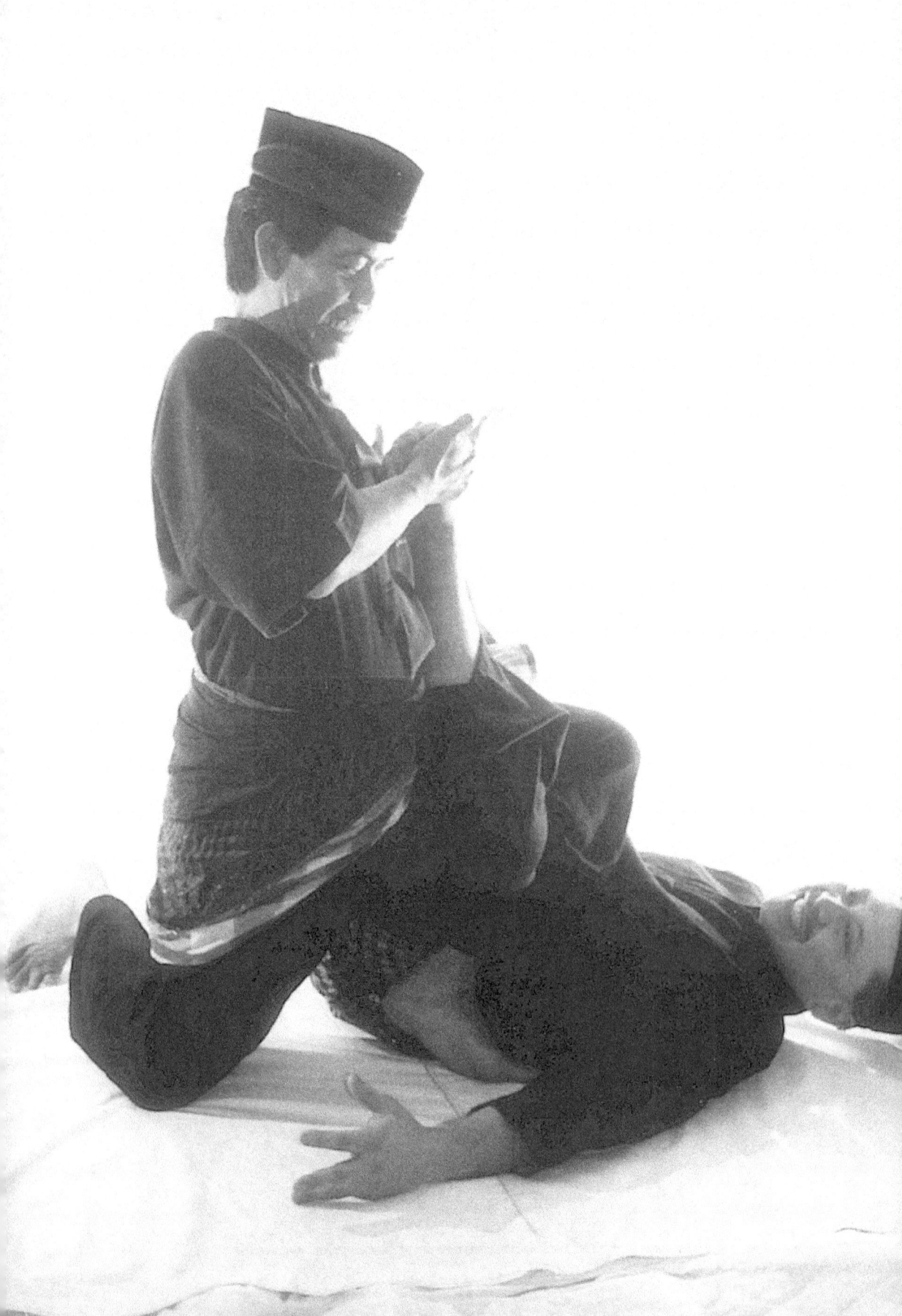

Chapter 20

Harimau Old and New

By Antonio Somera

Silat is a way of life for those people that live and work in the small towns and remote villages of Indonesia. But for Pendekar Herman Suwanda it is a way of life that has carried him from the lush jungles of West Java to the concrete jungles of America. His teaching in Mande Muda Pencak Silat include 25 styles that he now teaches to the public.

In this interview, we will cast light and remain focused on two similar styles in particular from the Mande Muda system: Harimau (tiger techniques that are low to the ground) and Harimau Baru (new style of tiger or fighting that is low to the ground).

There have been many different interpretations of Harimau. But for those of you that would like to take a walk in the jungles of Indonesia with me, listen to the sounds of the jungle, maybe you will be able to hear the roar of a tiger or even more frightening the feeling of being hunted by this inquiring spirit. The following is the last interview I conducted with Herman Suwanda.

Somera: Why do you teach Harimau and Harimau Baru?

Suwanda: I teach Harimau because this is the Harimau system from my father and our family Ancestry. The Harimau from my father is what I consider the old Harimau and I teach old Harimau to preserve our family's culture, history and ancestry. The reason why I teach the Harimau Baru is because I had learned this style of Harimau from many other teachers and this new system of Harimau is different then the old Harimau system. With the two systems of Harimau it will complete or add to making any practitioner of Silat aware of the capabilities that they possess. The other factors are that I find that these two styles of Harimau are very effective. I also enjoy learning and sharing new types of styles to the general public that has it's proven effectiveness.

Somera: Where does your Old Harimau come from?

Suwanda: The old Harimau comes from my father and our ethnic group. The only reason why I call it old Harimau is because I learned it back in the 1960s, in which this was the first Harimau I was exposed too. I was born in Sumatra, however, I was born there only because at the time this is where my father was working. The rest of my family and I relocated to West Java shortly after my birth. So my family is from West Java and the Harimau that my father taught me hails from West Java. The original Harimau system that my father taught me from West Java is called Macan or Pa Macan. But, if you go deeper into the jungle or into the remote villages they call it Maung which means Tiger.

Somera: Where does your Harimau Baru come from?

Suwanda: My Harimau Baru comes from many different teachers. The reason why I call it Baru is because I had learned this Harimau many years after my father had taught me his system of Harimau from West Java.

Somera: How can you describe in general the difference between the old and new Harimau?

Suwanda: Many of the old and new Harimau traits can be related to the type of training that is done. Much of the training is done with physical preparation. This physical training is done to get your body into the physical shape in order to properly demonstrate the correct Harimau movements. Many of the techniques are that of the tiger, crawling, locking, jumping, scratching and just as importantly hunting or stocking their pray. The main differences of the old and new Harimau is the principles of how these two styles will begin there entrees, how they will apply there locks or controlling the opponents body and how they will finish there techniques.

The old style uses the hands for the entry and locks, but is not necessarily based only on the use of the hands, the legs also play a very important part of locking the opponent and to determine if the encounter should be taken to the next level. However, it uses the hands more than the new style of Harimau. The new style of Harimau will hold with the hands but lock with the legs. The new style can use the hands for locking but much less than the older style of Harimau. In both styles the hands will force you to the ground and the hands will lock the opponent until at which time you would determined whether to take the encounter to the next level or to terminate the contest. This will also free your legs and feet to help in the controlling of your opponent. Using this type of strategy will free either your hand or legs and feet for the next on-coming attacker or attackers.

The new style of Harimau is the total opposite. In the new Harimau the legs and feet are used to create the entry and locks. You may use your legs and feet to take your opponent to the ground, following this entry you will use your legs and feet to lock your opponent. As in the old Harimau at this time you will you will determine whether to take this encounter to the next level or to terminate. If you continue you will find that your hands and arms are free. This will allow you to counter your opponent or to engage the next on-coming attackers.

The theory is that anything the hands can do so will the feet. The principals are the same but the application of control is determined by the application of attack. If you did not know of the two you can watch the old and new Harimau and not know the difference. To the general public it would look the same. Knowing both styles will only make your Harimau complete.

Somera: What would you like for the general public to know about old and new Harimau?

Suwanda: The old Harimau and the Harimau Baru will mean that the training will be very painful. But when you train and it hurts you will appreciate the finished techniques of Harimau. Just like going to college, you study trying to learn the subject. But after you graduate from college, you will feel good knowing that you have studied hard and accomplish your goals and have mastered your subjects. Same with Harimau, your body will be sore and hurt from the training because you and your body are not prepared for the tremendous conditioning and training application of Harimau. The reason for this is that you're true concept of Harimau may be different. In Mande Muda old Harimau and Harimau Baru, it is very hard physically. The training is on the ground. Stepping, crawling, different angles and using the legs and lower portion of you body. This exercise will improve your ability to move on the ground, up and down as well as to lock or to control your opponent. This type of training may be very hard and painful. The Harimau training is hard and most people here in America are surprised that the training or preparation is do difficult. After you condition your legs and body to this type of training, the Harimau techniques will be accommodating to your body. You will have accomplished what many have not.

Somera: What does Harimau mean?

Suwanda: The word Harimau means "tiger." But, Harimau to the Indonesian people can mean many different things. Harimau can mean any style of Indonesian Marital Arts. It can mean a family's type of training; it can mean a family's way of life. Depending on the location, the peoples beliefs and respect for their culture will determine there own means and interpretations by world of "Harimau."

Somera: Do all Indonesian people train in Harimau or some type of martial art?

Suwanda: Most families will have some type of Harimau or martial art training. The reason because so many families will train in Harimau or martial arts is very simple, for protection of their families. Many of the families will try to hide or train in secret. This is because most of the training is done in there own homes or in different areas in the jungle. This is also why the Harimau is done in a very close manner. The house is small and the areas of training constrict the movement. This means that when Harimau is played the

Harimau is done very close. Also the Indonesian people believe that any fight will end up on the ground. And the more you fight on the ground the more powerful you will become. This is why I continue to go back to Indonesia and train. I want to give back to my people there art of Harimau and martial arts.

Somera: Do you think that the American people can train in Harimau?

Suwanda: Yes, it will be hard at first but after they continue to train it will become a little easier as time goes on. But, they will need to continue and not stop or it will be like starting all over again. This is why I teach Harimau techniques first. The American people like to learn the techniques first then they like to learn how to condition themselves. However, like all Silat, Harimau is not for everybody. The American people seem to enjoy locking each other up on the ground. I do not always start with the conditioning as it sometimes scares some people away before they have had a chance to play with the techniques. Or to experience the finish product.

Somera: Is there a system of Harimau Hands?

Suwanda: Yes, Harimau hands are used on the more aggressive aspect of attacking. The Harimau hands are used to tie-up your opponent's hands, arms and upper body. This can be used either standing up or on the ground. You can apply your Harimau hands also to the feet of the opponent. The theory can be used with the legs and feet as well as I have mentioned earlier, what can be done with the hands should also be possible with the legs or feet.

Somera: How does other Harimau systems compare to your Harimau?

Suwanda: All Harimau systems are different. You can go to any village and train in Harimau and it would be different wherever you go. This is why our Indonesian Harimau is so rich. Not all Harimau is the same, so it is very hard to compare.

Chapter 21

Sabetan: The Unexpected Slice

By Antonio Somera

To open a martial art magazine today and not have something in it about Pencak Silat is very rare. This is due in great part to once was the hottest practitioner of Pencak Silat around. "I am doing this to set the record straight", explains Herman Suwanda,

It all began in 1980 when Herman Suwanda came over from Indonesia and landed in San Francisco California. His mission nearly 20 years ago was to spread his family's art of Mande Muda, which means "new Cimande" (Cimande is a name of a village and martial art style in Indonesia). His introduction to American customs played a tremendous role in developing his own way of teaching his family art. He would first travel into many different Martial Art studios to demonstrate the unique style of Mande Muda. Also trying from time to time to pick up a demonstration during other cultural events and festivals. "It was very hard back then no one knew me or of my style of Silat," said Pendekar Suwanda. Pendekar means wise man. During this early time Pendekar Suwanda would teach more of the traditional method of Pencak Silat. Using traditional forms, dance and drills. To his surprise the American public did not want this type of Silat. The American public wanted more of the warrior style of Silat. They wanted to learn more of submission locks holds and breaks. In order for Pendekar Suwanda to survive he had to find his way through the concert jungle of America. He would need to find his formula to be successful or his ultimate fear of returning to his country empty would be a reality. As fate would have it, Pendekar Suwanda would find his way and be the leading authority in American and throughout the world of Pencak Silat Mande Muda.

Pendekar Suwanda's family art of Mande Muda stands virtually alone in Indonesia style of Pencak Silat. His teachings would include stops from Hilo Hawaii to Long Island, New York and back to California were his only stops will be at the World acclaimed Inosanto Academy in Los Angles and his final stop in Stockton, California. Pendekar also has been spreading his art in Canada, which will also be a stop. Pendekar's newest challenges to spread his family art is his travels to Berlin, Germany and to the World's International Workshop

Festival to be held this year in England and finishing up in Dusseldorf, Germany.

Yes, Pendekar Suwanda has come a long way from his village in Bandung, West Java, Indonesia to being one of the most leading authorities in the Americas. To date Pendekar Suwanda teaches 25 different systems in his family art of Mande Muda.

1. Cimande–attack 80% to the arms
2. Cikalong–attack to the outside of the opponents body
3. Harimau–fighting like a tiger style from Sumatra
4. Syahbandar–attack an opponent from the center of his body
5. Kari–close-in locking and fighting
6. Madi–pull and jerk the opponent off balance
7. Cipecut–flexible weapon i.e., sarong or whip
8. Timbangan–energy flow between practitioner and opponent, a spiritual aspect
9. Nampon–deep breathing exercises for strengthening the body
10. Sera–hybrid system of Cikalong, Cimande and Syahbandar
11. Rikesan–bone breaking
12. Tanjakan–fighting close to the ground
13. Ulin napas–breathing exercise that controlling emotions
14. Ulin Baduy–straight to the point of combat
15. Galih Pakuan–weaponry fighting system, 18 golok
16. Pamonyet–monkey fighting system
17. Pamacan–fighting with the spirit of the tiger from West Java
18. Syahbandar Baru–new style of fighting to the center
19. Cikalong Baru–new style of fighting to the outside
20. Harimau Baru–new styles of tiger or ground fighting
21. Sanalika–wait and grab style
22. Benjang–sundanese wrestling
23. Sampiyong–stick and shield
24. Sabetan–unexpected slicing
25. Ujungan–single stick fighting

The hottest style to be released to the American public is called Sabetan. This style is one of the most fascinating systems of hand movements I have every seen. The flow is very fast and unexpected. I can see why the American public is following Pendekar Suwanda so as to try and catch the essence and elements of Sabetan. The following is a brief interview that will focus on the Sabetan system.

Somera: Pak Herman, how would you best describe Sabetan?

Suwanda: Sabetan means slice, this style is like Cimande. Sabetan's striking angles are more to the side of the body and can be used with or without weapons. When only using your empty hands the punching is used in a very unorthodox method. Which makes Sabetan very hard to counter or defend. It can be refereed to as the unexpected punch. When using a weapon or karamkirs (weapon used for Sabetan) the method is also unorthodox, but used in a slicing manner. This can also be refereed to the unexpected cut or slice. One of Sabetan's main characteristic is that, if you block with your left hand you will punch or cut with the left hand. And the angle of attack will be unexpected energy. Most people that have trained or watched practitioners in the art of Pencak Silat will think it is Cimande. Only the people that train in the art of Cimande will notice the difference between Cimande and Sabetan. This is a relatively new system in the 24 styles and systems that encompass Mande Muda.

Somera: Where did Sabetan originate?

Suwanda: From my Father Uyuh Suwanda he develops it from the style of Cimande during the early 1970s in Indonesia. My father was the founder of Sabetan number one to number eight. But he and I always wanted more. So, I followed my father's wishes and continued to finish his work. From the 1970s to 1980s I finished my father's dream by completing numbers nine to number 30.

Somera: How many Sabetan techniques are there?

Suwanda: There are a total of 30 Sabetan techniques that are used as the foundation. But, off of those 30, there are 10 different counter techniques. And I also emphasize the use of the left and right hand, giving the total of 600 Sabetan techniques that I teach. Which only uses the upper body.

Somera: Is Sabetan a hard or soft style?

Suwanda: Sabetan is a soft style, just the opposite of Cimande, which is a very hard style. Sabetan encompasses the elements of, striking, deflection, parrying, evasion and blocking. It also adds the use of correct and incorrect timing.

Somera: What does Sabetan add to your system?

Suwanda: Timing. As a beginner in Sabetan your hand speed will be slow. But as you work and practice your hand speed will increase. You will notice that your timing will be very sharp. Your hand speed and timing will develop, your speed will increase and to add to all of this, the elements of Sabetan will improve your energy of marital arts.

Somera: Why was Sabetan created?

Suwanda: My father and I wanted a more advance system of hand and knife application. Meaning, using more of the soft and creative points of attack or hunting which means targeting an area.

Somera: How often should you practice Sabetan?

Suwanda: If you can, everyday. You can practice it with or with out a partner. Practicing with your partner is called Sabetan Bua which means engaging with another person and without a partner is called Sabetans Juru that means root of the motion.

Somera: What is the concept of Sabetan?

Suwanda: The unexpected slice that will block and punch with the same hand. Having an unexpected punch without obstructions and without any sudden jolts or breaks in the flow of the techniques. The words I would use best to describe Sabetan are harmonious, tranquil and mild.

Somera: Is there any footwork used in Sabetan?

Suwanda: Yes, our footwork in Sabetan consists of moving left to right and right to left. We use angles of positioning mean 45, 90, 180 and 360 degrees, and also degrees of zig zagging. In general the footwork would be like street fighting. This would mean whatever feels most comfortable during the time of application. But, for now I only teach the upper body movements to the general public they will need to know this first and then I will soon be teaching Sabetan footwork.

Somera: How do you think the students of Sabetan feel about it?

Suwanda: Some students like and some don't. The reason why some students don't like it is because it is hard to learn and somewhat confusing. The techniques are against everything you have be taught. It's the opposite of any western theory of fighting systems. But on the other hand, most of my students really like Sabetan. The reason for this is that, it will increase you hands speed. Elevate you awareness, sharpen you skills and like I have stated it is very unexpected. Sabetan is new and exciting. And for this the students getting excited about learning more about the advance techniques of Sabetan or Manda Muda creates interest that they all enjoy.

Somera: Is Sabetan a style of fighting?

Suwanda: No, it's a drill. For a new student Sabetan it is good to learn because it teaches you how to punch. For a advance student it a style to add to your personal self defense system of action. It's not learning how to fight. It's learning how to react.

Somera: What do you consider to the requirements of Sabetan?

Suwanda: You would need to practice continually. Without practice you would lose your focus. It's like riding a bicycle, if you don't practice all the time you will fall down. You just can't pick Sabetan in just one day or one month. You need to make a commitment to train in Sabetan. Because it's not for everyone. But the finish product within you will shine.

Somera: Why should I practice Sabetan?

Suwanda: Knowing Sabetan will enhance all the many other styles in Mande Muda and not only Mande Muda, other style of Martial Arts.

Somera: What are the principals of Sabetan?

Suwanda: Don't punch in the normal way. If you punch in the normal way it is not Sabetan. This is the key to Sabetan.

Somera: How would you practice Sabetan?

Suwanda: It's better to start with empty hands. But after you get very good I would suggest in some cases to practice with Sabetan training knives. The Sabetan training knife will teach you the respect of the Karamkris. It will also give you a unique understanding of your hand speed.

Somera: Is there a weakness to Sabetan?

Suwanda: Yes, for right now because I have only recently release this to the general public. Most of the Sabetan partictioniers only know the hand and upper body movements. It will be in the best interest of anyone who will practice Sabetan to also learn Sabetan footwork.

Sabetan is one of 25 systems of Guru Besar Pendekar Herman Suwanda's family style of Pencak Silat Mande Mude. Guru Besar Pendekar Herman Suwanda is the head instructor of Mande Muda. He began his personal study of Pencak Silat under his father in 1960. In 1965 he began to study under other pendekars and continues his studies even to this day. He began teaching in 1974 in Indonesia and has traveled to the United States to teach in 1980. He has taugh seminars throughout the world and would hold training camps in Indonesia and the United States.

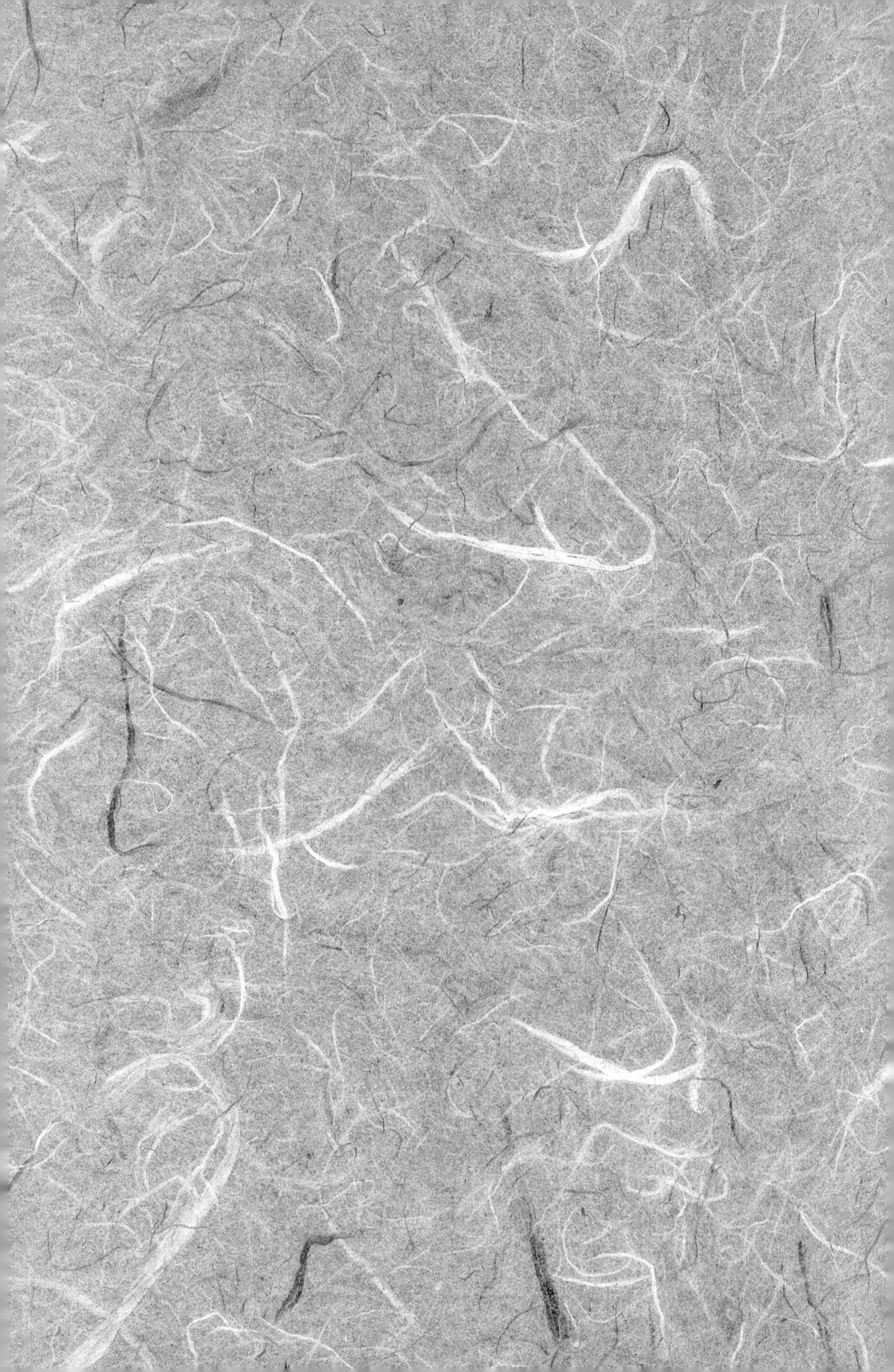

Part V
Reflections of a Pendekar

Chapter 22

My Teacher and Friend

In July of 1981 I had just returned to the USA from two months in Malaysia where I had gone in search of silat. To my disappointment, I found that those of non-Muslim faith were not allowed to practice or even see silat. On my very first day back, while on a walk down Telegraph Ave, I spotted a handbill posted on a telephone pole-"Learn Indonesian Pencak Silat." That led me to a local dance studio where I found Herman Suwanda teaching rudimentary dance moves to a small group once a week. Being impatient, I inquired about private lessons and his wife, Suzanne, informed me that a private lesson cost the same as a class lesson. I never went back to class again.

From then on, we met two or three times a week at their one bedroom apartment in Oakland. The heat was on full blast in the middle of summer, and the windows were closed and fully steamed up from a huge pot of chicken or some other meal boiling away on the stove. Herman feared the cold more than the complaints of the property manager. This was my first introduction to training pencak silat in the tropics!

Herman spoke about five words of English, and I had perhaps five words of Malay, but we got along just fine, and the one hour lesson would routinely become three. Occasionally, Suzanne would be home from work and she provided very helpful translations and cultural insight. One evening, they put on a tape of *kendang pencak* music and danced the long *paleredan* for me in the living room. I was astonished how the two of them could move so closely and with such complexity in such small quarters. Being a musician, I was hooked.

For the most part, our time was spent learning the 10 *jurus kaki* (foot moves) and 20 *jurus tangan* (hand moves), the normal beginners program from Herman's father, Pak Uyuh. Herman also began teaching me paleredan, the slow "mystical" dance. Mid-way through practice, we would take a break for tea, and Herman would tell many tales of his home and his family and of learning silat from many different teachers. Our mood was always jocular. At the time, neither of us had a job, so we would often while away the afternoon this way, sometimes running late enough that Suzanne would get home from work in time to give me a translation and wrap up of the mysterious events of my day with Herman (fig. 1).

Then one day he sat me down on the floor, became quite serious, and said, "OK Jim, this *cimande*." Of course, I had no idea what he meant, but I soon found out that I had reached the point where silat departed from the other martial arts I had studied. Several of the exercises were designed to toughen and condition the forearms by means of practicing forceful bone blocks. After the first practice session, I was quite shocked to see that my forearms had swollen to grotesque dimensions. The pain was intense and the situation seemed so surreal. Convinced that the damage was sufficient, he produced a bottle of special healing oil, *balur cimande*, and then proceeded to apply an excruciating massage which compressed the swelling back into the arm. I left practice that day seriously shaken, only to discover that this *cimande* was to become a consistent part of every practice, a seemingly unending trance state of pain that went on until Herman decided to quit. It took about three to four weeks of this kind of training with him before my arms stopped swelling and I no longer required that dreaded massage. Only many months later did Suzanne explain to me that it is actually the right of the student to say "enough," and the teacher will finally quit pounding on you. At least until the next lesson...

In all the years I knew Herman, he only gave me a test once. After six months of practicing like this, I went to Germany for professional reasons for several years. Herman decided I needed a test before going, so we went in my backyard, where he blindfolded me. For a half hour or so, he silently circled around me, all the while suddenly calling out the number of one of the *jurus* and simultaneously throwing the appropriately matched attacks at me. I had virtually no time to respond, and it was quite difficult to keep track of

Herman's whereabouts while blindfolded, so I got tagged a few times. Herman seemed satisfied, and said my name would be registered in the book in the main school in Bandung, West Java. He then presented me with a small Mande Muda patch and a cassette of the *kendang* music for my dance, both of which I treasure to this day. He also directed me to get involved with any martial art while in Germany, since I certainly wouldn't find any silat there. Throughout our entire friendship, Herman always encouraged me to check out all martial arts for their beauty and diversity. After my return from Germany, this would lead to many adventures.

After finishing in Germany, my wife and I took a prolonged trip through the Indian Subcontinent and Southeast Asia before our return to the US. On the last leg of our journey we traveled to Java so I could satisfy my curiosity about the origins of the silat I had learned from Herman. I had kept the Mande Muda school address in Bandung, and the fellow at tourist information was mightily amused that I wanted to go there instead of to the usual tourist shows. "Don't get beat up," he advised with a laugh, "let me know if you get lost."

We were heartily welcomed at Mande Muda by Pak Uyuh Suwanda, who treated us like old friends when I said I had trained with Herman. Herman had told me many tales of his father; how he had been a pirate in Sumatra, whose job it was to sneak on board merchant vessels and put out the lights before his comrades also boarded (fig. 2). Also, how it was more important to him that young Herman learn silat than attend school I heard about the severe penalties for not practicing. Now, sitting in the office with him, he still looked very much the part. The room was lined with photos and trophies and a couple of guys were sitting at a table poking at a cricket fight in a goldfish bowl. A conspicuous open window over the river provided a handy wastebasket for everything. Pak Uyuh used to threaten to throw little Herman out this window when he was bad, and Herman would in turn confiscate his sister's lipstick and cosmetics and toss them through it into the river. It made for a very interesting window into the culture for us, as well!

Next door, we were introduced to Kang Aming, master carver of the *wayang golek*, the ornate wooden puppets (fig. 3). He and Herman learned this craft as apprentices together, and many years later, Herman still devoted a great deal of time to this art in America, cutting incredible detail into the wood with a single knife, delicately painting life into their features with bright colors, and tailoring beautiful little traditional costumes. Like Kang Aming and his father, Pak Uyuh, he could also make them dance and come to life with silat moves.

During our week in Bandung, I came every day and learned jurus in the back room of the house, most of which I forgot because I only saw them once, and besides, I was worried about banging myself up on the bare concrete floor. I also remember it being difficult to see, since my glasses were constantly steamed up in the tropical heat and so much sweat ran into my eyes.

In the evenings, we were treated to silat performances, *jaipongan* dancing, and demonstrations of *ilmu dalam*, or inner knowledge, including *potong besi*, the breaking of a cast iron pump handle with the practitioner's forearm. I flinched, remembering the many sessions of painful *cimande* practice with Herman. During Independence Day celebrations, they executed skillful *demonstrasi*, choreographed combat in which the women beat the daylights out of all the men. The crowd loved it.

After Java, our journey was over and we returned directly to the USA. We were given some things to take to Herman, who in the meantime had moved to Capp Street in San Francisco. We left Indonesia feeling we had made a strong connection to "mysterious" Asia, filled with colorful memories from this strange and beautiful place.

During our search for a place to live we lingered for some time in the San Francisco area-long enough for me to learn more of the dance and a double *golok* (a long, machete-type field knife) dance from Herman. At the time, in late 1985, he was working in a tire shop and we would joke about his get-up in greasy overalls (fig. 4). Herman was always Herman, though, and he was regularly awarded employee of the month and took great pride in this accomplishment. In the meantime, his English had gotten very good, though still full of the Indonesian mannerisms and humor that ultimately became a trademark of his teaching style. He was excited that we had visited his home and told many stories of his youth in Bandung. It became clear that Herman was so much more than a martial artist-he was a healer, a musician, an artist, and cross-cultural!

He had an arrangement with a gym around the corner from the apartment so we could practice in the evenings when nobody was around. Our very first meeting there, Herman told me to put on a body protector since we would warm up with some sparring. It was new for me to spar with Herman, but I had mixed it up pretty successfully in a very competitive martial arts club in Germany and felt pretty tough. I certainly didn't feel that a body protector was necessary. Herman insisted, and to this day I'm glad he did. Right off the bat, he nailed me with a peculiar sidekick, which folded me in half and sent me straight to the floor, stunned. I came to know this kick very well, but never figured out how to defend against it. I'm certain to this day that the kick was one of the true mysteries of Asia. Herman had an uncanny ability to predict where you were going, to manipulate that moment so that you moved to his advantage. You always got a funny psychological moment and knew too late that you were had. You could see that kick coming, yet were helpless to defend. It always got you in the floating rib, always felt like being kicked by a horse, and it never, ever missed. Herman liked to say he had a patent on it. Over the years I saw that kick many times, and a parade of challengers who hit the ground hard, just as I did.

We ended up settling in Southern California, and I was afraid my silat education was terminated since the journey to San Francisco for lessons was too great. However not long afterwards, Herman and his wife separated and he moved to Los Angeles. So every Sunday, I made a habit of getting up at 6 a.m. and driving 1 1/2 hours to his studio apartment just off Lincoln Blvd in Mar Vista. We would have tea and I'd help him figure out how to pay the bills and deal with other problems of everyday life. He already had a couple of students in L.A., and we just met in a nearby park, rain or shine, hot or cold.

Soon afterward, he moved to a cottage behind a house in Venezia Way, and we traded the lawn of the park for the unforgiving concrete of his driveway. Herman had a very strong drive to teach the silat of his family tradition but he enjoyed adapting everything to the West. So, for instance, he would have us sit in the car and learn self-defense moves while behind the wheel. Herman was never happy unless you learned the applications so well that you caused him pain. If you were trying some chokehold on him and he said "I'm still talkin,'" it was a sure sign you didn't get it yet. With his newly acquired English, he loved to pepper the practice sessions with phrases from the latest movies, like "You're history, dude," or "Hasta la vista, baby." We had so much fun hitting the concrete that the neighbor lady would look over the fence to see what all the laughter was about.

At some point a few of us got the bright idea to pool our resources and get Herman a video camera for Christmas (fig. 5). He immediately began filming the practice sessions and we each got a copy. Herman realized the importance of such a device and dreamed of a project where he would document the many styles of silat on video for future generations. He felt strongly that the standardization of the art for sporting purposes would ultimately lead to the loss of many styles.

In about May 1987, I showed up at Herman's place for practice, and he waved a letter at me saying "Come on, Jim, let's go to the silat world championships in Malaysia. First time ever for an American team-you can try out your silat!" If there's anything that ever made Herman angry, it was a lily-livered chicken student, so in spite of an apparent lack of fellow team-mates, I said I'd be happy to go. Regaling me with stories of broken bones and ambulance rides for the less skilled participants, he obviously thought it would do me a world of good to get out there and duke it out with some invulnerable tiger fresh from the Sumatra jungles. This despite the fact that I was already too old for the one (!) age group for sparring. "Just lie about your age, Jim" was his unrelenting answer to my protests. I could already feel the noose tighten around my neck...

I began a six-month preparation for this event by practicing in the noonday sun through the summer and got a tough sparring partner from the local full contact scary karate school. He was very pleasant and we regularly beat each other bloody in the back yard. It didn't seem to matter compared to the certain hospital sojourn awaiting me in Malaysia. On Sundays, meanwhile, Herman fine-tuned my dance moves and taught me all the dirty moves I would need to disable the competition without the judges seeing. He also found four other students who didn't seem to mind facing the unknown, so we had an impressive American team of five, the smallest out of the 22 countries represented (fig. 6).

The Indonesian government subsidized our flights to Kuala Lumpur and put us up in the Merlin Hotel, a fancy high-rise in the center of town. The event itself was held in the national stadium and was free and open to the public, so there was always a huge crowd. Ever true to my teacher, I lied about my age and had already made it through weigh in and a medical inspection when the military police checked the date of birth in my passport and disqualified me for sparring competition. Feigning my disappointment to Herman, I still qualified for seni, the forms and dances competition.

This was more than a martial arts tournament. It was a true conference of diverse cultures, a cornucopia of silat styles on display. The Merlin was full of silat teams, and the foyers in front of the elevator doors provided excellent carpeted practice space for competitors. At every floor, the doors would open to a different scene–the beaming victor fighting off three attackers, breathtaking dances, sword duels with sparking blades, sparring practice, and the like.

The rules had been changed without our knowledge, so we all had to drop what we had prepared at home and rework our entire program within 24 hours. The situation was quite tense. For the competition, Herman made sure we had plenty of *oleh oleh*, gifts of t-shirts and American cigarettes for the *kendang* musicians to encourage them to play nicely for us. Sure enough, the performance went off well and we secured a good place in the standings (fig. 7). The next team didn't have any gifts and they looked bad because the band stopped playing a few bars into their performance. It pays to have a coach who's in the know.

After the tournament was over, we all hopped over to Bandung for a visit to the home school. As usual, Herman was anxious for us to practice in a "real" setting, so he arranged a meeting with a gentleman from the village of Cimande. Even though my forearms were reasonably conditioned by then, practicing with this man made my bones feel like they were flexing to the point of breaking. The pain was tremendous and the sweat was blinding me in the tropical heat, but by some miracle I made it through the session of arm cimande without passing out. When he indicated that he'd like to see if my leg stances were good, I thought he wanted to check out my form. Next thing I knew, he landed a terrific blow with his shin directly to my shin. My leg shot up to shoulder height from the force of his kick and I crashed against the wall before crumpling in a heap on the floor. I excused myself as gracefully as possible under the circumstances and escaped with a large contusion. We witnessed a student crying from the pain of this practice, but certainly no one thought of him as a sissy. When I asked Herman why we didn't practice this way at home, he replied that he had always hated it. "Too ugly. Too much pain, Jim." But he did enjoy watching us give it a go.

That same day, still limping on that devastated leg, I encountered Herman and Pak Uyuh in the office. Herman informed me that my kicks were too weak, and to remedy this, he and Pak Uyuh had decided that it would be best for me to spend a week fasting and meditating. I panicked, knowing that this meant spending the rest of my hard-earned vacation locked in a dark room, taking nothing for nourishment except hot water and fresh hot chili peppers. I begged and I pleaded, saying I would die if I didn't get a little vacation at the beach. To my great relief, they decided to let me do the *kawin ibing* instead–the marriage to the dance.

After our all too brief vacation, two of us returned to Bandung. According to our day of birth, we each had to do our long dance a pre-ordained number of times. I was lucky–I only had to make it through 33 repetitions, but my friend was stuck with 99! All between midnight and the morning call to prayer at the mosque, around 5 a.m. We arranged for a huge feast, each purchased an expensive Havana cigar, and we met at the home of Dadang Gunawan and Herman's sister, Rita Suwanda, who would become the future *guru besar*. We enjoyed a festive evening together with many silat friends. Just before midnight, we were jokingly advised to go to the restroom a lot and drink as much as possible, for after midnight, nothing was to leave the body except the out-breath and sweat. And nothing could be taken in except in-breath and boiling hot water from a ready thermos. A large piece of *keminyan* was burned, a peculiar smelling incense meant to attract the spirits, but which also smoked with an acrid intensity that burned the eyes and caused a sharp cough at the slightest inhalation. Our friends all went to bed in adjacent rooms, where they could hear our efforts from their places of rest. Pak Uyuh placed himself on a stool directly in the doorway to the next room. Herman had always assured me that this was a place of strong spirits, that to sleep in the doorway with your head in one room and your feet in the other would give you powerful dreams. At the stroke of midnight, when the rooms were dense with keminyan smoke, Pak Uyuh lit one of the Havanas and began chanting. At the end of each dance, I took one of 33 stones and placed it at Pak Uyuh's feet, who gave a blessing to continue. I could hear my poor friend in the next room, racing to get through his 99 stones, so I tried to at least make my dance powerful and particularly focussed. After 15 stones, I only wanted to make it through. At prayer call, when I crouched for Pak Uyuh to pour several buckets of fragrant flowers and water over me, I felt deeply grateful to still be able to walk. My fellow student and I then took 33 and 99 one thousand rupee coins and were instructed to go downtown and dispense them to beggars, one at a time. This took up a good deal of the morning and we were looking forward to getting back to the feast, from which the spirits only ever took a nibble, leaving the rest to us. We arrived to find that Herman and Pak Uyuh and the whole gang had consumed the whole thing! Not only that, they proceeded to rib us about how feeble we looked, doing the dance on chicken legs and cutting a ridiculous figure. Expecting to be honored for passing the test, we were laughed out of the house. And now we were married to the dance.

It is said that marrying the dance gives *pamur*, the sheen of the Damascus blade, to your dance forever more, and that audiences will always perceive your performance as beautiful, even if you stumble and fall on your nose. Later that same day, we had the opportunity to practice our moves with a live *kendang* band. After just finishing a night of 33 times through my *kembangan*, no more than three steps into it with the live band and I totally forgot what I was doing. I waved my arms helplessly and somehow feebly faked it through to some sort of miserable conclusion. To my great surprise, many of the onlookers congratulated me on my performance, remarking that they could "see" that I had a great teacher. I guess marrying the dance paid off after all, and I didn't have to spend the remainder of my vacation in Java shut away in a dark room, fasting and drinking boiling water.

There was only one detail remaining before returning to the USA-packing up a large bag of "toys" for the silat group back home. The list was considerable: 7 or 8 keris, a dozen *golok* knives, various spearheads, truncheons, hooks, daggers, and other such items. Herman told me not to worry, that Pak Uyuh would write me a letter allowing me to carry it all onto the airliner. I couldn't hide my disbelief, but was astonished to discover that, upon presentation of this letter, my wife and I were ushered right through security and into the plane. Only then did the stewardess relieve me of my bag of knives and stashed them in the pilot's cabin!

Back home, practice went on as usual in the driveway. Somewhere along the line, someone acquired some mats, so the falls became more comfortable. Herman often seemed annoyed about the misinformation he perceived was being spread in the USA about silat, so he began branching out and teaching seminars and doing performances whenever possible. When Dan Inosanto invited him to teach regular classes at the academy in L.A., Herman was excited about the possibility, but nervous about the exposure to so many new people. The day we made our first appearance there, I picked up Herman as usual. He was quite jumpy about going, so on our way out the door I gave him an encouraging pat on the back, only to discover that he had concealed a *kujang* (the hook dagger, national symbol of Sunda) under his shirt in the small of his back. "Never trust your students, Jim," was his usual comment. Secrets of the masters revealed!

Sure enough, the new students looked really tough, but Herman quickly adapted to such groups. However he resented the rumors that his group was only a dance class, not necessarily for the serious martial artist. He felt strongly that the influence of Bruce Lee had contributed to an overwhelming interest in technique application in the United States, leaving dances and the culturally artistic side of martial arts neglected. He decided that unpacking his own well-guarded techniques was the only way to any degree of commercial success, so unpack he did–with a vengeance. It was as if he transformed into a different teacher altogether, teaching so many exotic techniques with such mind-boggling speed that the student usually remembered only one or two of them.

For years, I enjoyed the dubious honor of being his demonstration partner, which often meant screaming in agony for the education and amusement of my fellow students. Herman had always taught us to look for the "key" to the technique, to always use my brain to extricate myself from a "problem." Now, if I had even the inkling of a key while we were demonstrating to a group, he would demonstratively whisper "Don't think, Jim!" into my face, and I knew that to wiggle meant certain intense pain. Herman would never allow an escape in front of an audience. The only time anybody else got to be the dummy for the duration of class was when a student came from outside and Herman didn't trust him. The crime was usually that they showed disrespect for the techniques or, even worse, came from some other silat teacher without first asking that person's permission. Once, for several months, I was relieved of my duty because a gentleman was showing up who regularly displayed these egregious tendencies. Herman decided that he didn't like him, and the demonstrations were excruciating to observe. He knew just how far to push the technique, until the breaking threshold was ever so close, and I'm sure you could hear that fellow's cries through the whole neighborhood. "Just like pullin' chickens apart," Herman would remark.

It should not go unmentioned that Herman was a traditional healer of unusual skill. He told of apprenticing to healers in Java for five or six years and worried that his skills would attract too much attention in the Indonesian community in Los Angeles. He certainly attended to the "accidents" in our practice sessions, although with peculiar and painful methods. He could make your legs work again after being so battered they ceased functioning. When my sparring partner dislocated his shoulder, Herman popped it back into place. Another student told me that Herman accidentally broke his arm during practice, and that Herman healed it in a miraculously short period of time, using massage and *balur cimande*. On one occasion he showed me a letter from a woman who had been told by her doctors that she would be in a wheel chair for more than a year. She praised Herman for having her up and walking in two weeks! He developed curious maladies of his own, as well. Once, when I arrived to pick him up for practice, he told of suffering several days of serious fever and continuous nightmares. In his youth, one of his teachers had inserted seven *susuk*, seven needles of gold under his skin at various points of his body to give him paranormal powers of perception. One of the charms had dislodged, traveling about in his body and causing the delirium, until it emerged from his foot. He placed my hand on his forehead and his arms so I could feel the other needles, still there under the skin, and told me that he was afraid to die without having them removed. I could only listen in wonder.

Herman finally got so upset over general misperceptions of silat in this country that he decided to set the record straight, once and for all. We would return to Java, this time armed with video cameras to document as much original silat as possible in one month. I immediately accepted his invitation to be second cameraman, knowing that I was in for certain high adventure. His plan was to follow the leitmotiv of the *kendang pencak* music, to document the settings of this instrumental ensemble consisting of drums, large gong, and the double reed *terompet*, which produces loud trance-like strains when blown in the upper octaves using circular breathing. This is the music that invariably provides the exciting background to the dynamic Sundanese martial arts. Herman was highly regarded as a silat dancer in West Java and loved this music deeply.

In August 1988, I arrived in Bandung, tired and dirty after a journey of some 40 hours. Herman was there already, and gave me an hour to nap before we dashed off to the train station again. In the parking square of the station, a large stage performance was already in full swing (fig. 8), with pencak silat artists from the region dancing and executing *demonstrasi* to live music and emcee, all amplified to deafening sound levels. Herman assured me that the best old guys always come after midnight, and we filmed away until the crack of dawn.

This was our pace for the next three weeks. Our cameras had no capability for recharging the batteries from a wall socket, so Herman had rigged up a tenuous connection to a car battery. On days with a great deal of filming,

Herman's brother Hery followed close behind the cameraman, carrying the battery. Our pursuit of *kendang pencak* performances took us to many unusual settings not accessible to the average tourist. First came the *adu bagong*, where a pack of dogs was set loose upon a huge bristly tusker of a wild boar inside a bamboo palisade, with a throng of onlookers placing bets. Amazingly, not a single animal was injured, since the owners sprang in as soon as the first dog sank its teeth into the poor beast for a couple of seconds, and pulled their dogs by the tail out of the fray. Similarly, we filmed the *adu dombak*, or ram fights (fig. 9). The concussion from their heads banging together dealt a solid blow to our own stomachs. When I advised Herman not to release this footage in the US, he was disappointed, but not discouraged. He had plenty more in store.

We filmed the scorpion oil seller, a fellow in shorts with large black scorpions crawling all over his body, all the while hawking his product from a little rack on the sidewalk. We filmed great silat masters at home. We filmed the *Ratu Pantai* festival, where a boar is sacrificed and the head is offered to the goddess of the beaches. We rented a hall, hired a *kendang pencak* band, catered a feast, and issued an open invitation to the old masters to bring their students and come over for a party, free and open to the public. The whole neighborhood danced to a cheering audience as we filmed children, old masters, and businessmen on their way home from the office who performed stunning knife dances in their office attire. We filmed the *kuda lumping* trance dancers, who, after many hours of dancing on hobbyhorses, come to believe that they really are horses and culminate the dance by eating horse fodder.

We traveled to Banten, known to be a center of magic, to seek out the masters of tiger style *harimau*, an exotic system of fighting low to the ground. We met a man who had just returned from three days and nights immersed up to his neck in the river, fasting and meditating to gain powers. He clearly felt that we were a threat, that we had come to challenge his silat. His eyes seemed to glow in the dark and he got into a heat, yelling at Herman while they exchanged *cimande* moves. Without warning, the thatched roof over his head burst into flames, as if ignited by his temper! After we departed, Herman confirmed what I thought I understood with my meager Indonesian–that the

two of them would meet tomorrow morning for a duel with goloks. "Don't forget the camera, Jim," he admonished. After a sleepless night and a hangman's breakfast, I was not looking forward to witnessing a horrible spectacle and Herman, undeterred, led us to the battleground. The challenger never showed up, and Herman assured me that guys like that always chicken out. At that point, I considered throttling him myself.

But Herman had saved a special spectacle for the end of the trip–all he would tell me was that I would experience *debus* (strong magic). When we arrived at a courtyard on the edge of town, the *kendang* band was warming up and a fellow was spending a great deal of time and care sharpening a pair of *golok* knives, which I was then allowed to test for their keen edge. After a parade of dancers, choreographed fights, and magicians, the main act was brought on. A very tough looking man began a slow dance to the *kendang*. Herman urged me to step in very close with the camera while he filmed from another angle. The man picked up the razor sharp *goloks* and continued dancing, as if in a trance, as I moved in. Just as I managed to get close to him, he stuck out his tongue and sawed away at it with the *golok* until blood ran down his naked chest. My heart stuck in my throat and I felt suddenly faint, but somehow managed to keep filming without wobbling too much. He then ate several double edged razor blades, fresh out of the package, followed by the glass stovepipe of an old fashioned kerosene lamp, after which his friend poured acid over him until the piece of sheet metal he was standing on smoked around his bare feet. With a flourish, he took the bottle and swallowed the remaining contents, then continued his dance with spikes the size of knitting needles pierced through his cheeks, jutting from his mouth. He wrapped up the show by lying on a bed of thorns while blocks of sidewalk concrete were broken on his chest with a sledgehammer. I was exhausted from the spectacle, but still had the energy to beat a hasty retreat when it was suggested I could learn these feats if I stuck around for three months.

By now, Herman figured I was ready to try the *potong besi* for the camera, breaking the iron pump handle with my forearm. Instead, I contracted a bad amoebic dysentery and, after a trip to the local hospital, spent my last few days in Bandung recuperating. Pak Uyuh paid a visit to wish me a safe return home and pressed a knife into my hand. "I've seen TV and the movies, Jim," he said. "I know you live in a dangerous place. If you have trouble there, this is the knife to use." A miniature golok, the sheath was wrapped with black cloth and the blade itself was black, etched with the image of a tiger and a mullah, with Arabic inscriptions. It was covered with an oily substance, which exuded a poisonous stench. "Don't cut yourself with that one," he joked.

Thinner by 25 pounds, I arrived back in the US with a load of wild tales and the videos to prove it. Herman edited our shots together to make the "documentary" videos, the first installments of his great series of Pencak Silat video releases. Not long after our return, Pak Uyuh passed away and Herman became the guru besar, inheriting the leadership of a large network of silat schools in West Java.

Our practice sessions continued in the back yard of one of Herman's students, a wrestling and judo coach in a high school. Herman continued teaching himself computer graphics and splicing his colorful creations into his silat videos. He made more frequent visits to Indonesia, engaging his family members in his filming, and worked hard to promote his family's art in the US. More and more, he longed to live in Indonesia and hoped to return there to start his own video production business, to write for television and document the vanishing old village styles of pencak silat. In August 1991, he certified several of his students to teach, and a few weeks later returned to live at home in Bandung. The Los Angeles group dissolved and went the way of the four winds. No one, not even Herman, knew that he would later return to the US and establish his new Jagabaya program over the next ten years. A deep repository of Indonesian culture and arcane silat practices, he had an untiring desire to share the beauty of his own traditions with those who had the open mind to step into his unusual world. It is no wonder that he became one of the greatest ambassadors of Indonesian Pencak Silat to the West.

Jim Wimmer

Chapter 23

My first meeting and training with Pak

During the late 1980's as a student of Guro Dan Inosanto, I was introduced to a certain Malaysian Seni Gayong Instructor named Cigku Sulaiman Sharif. Training in Pencak Silat on the hard concrete floor of an empty aircraft hangar near Los Angeles International Airport was my very first exposure to the Malaysian systems of Silat other than through Guru Inosanto whom I consider a walking encyclopedia of knowledge in the martial arts.

Sulaimen, as he preferred us to call him in those days, was very energetic and extremely traditional in his instruction. We were only a handful of private students but we did everything "by the book". This new type of training was very different from the Filipino Kali/ Eskrima/ Arnis that I had already been exposed to at the time training under other masters from the Philippines.

In those days, young and hard and putting in about 30 hours a week of training in a couple different disciplines, I considered my Silat Training to be "secret and special" because it was so very far off the beaten path of other "traditional" systems. Although it consisted of the usual rolling, breakfalls, joint-locks and conditioning as other arts, it had another element which is difficult to describe–that is the element of developing the mind to think outside the norm.

My teacher eventually introduced me to other private students and via this small group of devotees we all somehow ended up in the same room as Guru Inosanto and another master from Indonesia named "Pendekar Herman Suwanda."

When I first met Pak, it was like meeting your dad for the first time. He was too young to be your dad, but you could look in his eyes and see the wisdom of ages all stacked up on a couple of hard drives. He was hard, fast and could do things with his hands and feet at such speed and such amazing precision that you wouldn't believe it even if you saw it in a video. But, what was most impressive to me was how he thought and the things he could do with his mind.

After a few sessions with our small group, I politely and humble request of the Pendekar if I may train with him, he smiled and said "OK Stib, you see me on Monday..." and needless to say I had found my Pencak Silat Master. (fig. 1)

How it felt Training With Pak:

After my very first lesson with Pak I was hooked forever. Although firmly devoted to both Grandmaster Leo M. Giron (Stockton, CA) and Guru Dan Inosanto (LA) in the Filipino arts, I had found my home in the ancient arts of West Java through the tutelage of Pendekar Suwanda.

Training in different martial arts is a very JKD (Jeet Kune Do) concept—that is "take what is useful" as per Bruce Lee. But this mode of training doesn't go over very well with the old school teachers of the Philippines, Korea, China and Japan. If a master found out that you even walked by the house of another master you were banned forever from training with either one! Even after I began training with Punong Guro Edgar Sulite (founder of the LAMECO system of Eskrima) and still going back and forth to Stockton to train with Grandmaster Giron and also in LA at the Inosanto Academy under Guru Inosanto, I was VERY careful to not let another teachers technique or style "slip out" during training as I was fearful that one may find out about the other and ask me to take a walk.

However, Pak had a completely different mindset altogether. He ENCOURAGED me to train with other teachers! (fig. 2) As a matter of fact he not only encouraged me to train with other teachers, but when we trained together at his home in Indonesia he INTRODUCED me to a number of different instructors and also translated for them so that I could understand!!! Quite a different mindset from the norm in those days. Nowadays cross-training is the norm rather than the exception and most don't even think twice about studying with more than one master or instructor.

Unlike other masters that I had trained with over the decades, Pak truly got into your head. He wanted to see where you were coming from so that he could adjust his level of instruction to match your mindset and your perspective no matter what level you were at. As a matter of fact I would observe him employ this method of "tuning in " with other students and was amazed as it looked just like he was dialing in a radio station. Once he was tuned in (and it only took him about a fraction of a second to hone in on the right frequency) I could observe the level of communication increase tenfold.

My First Meeting and Training with Pak

Pak was a master not only in his art, but also in the art of communication. In those early days his English was a little rough, but no question about it you got what he was saying clear as a bell (fig. 3). Later on in my training, especially in Indonesia, I found out that Pak spoke numerous dialects and also completely different languages, but his greatest instructional attribute in my opinion was his ability to communicate clearly above and beyond the constraints of linguistic barriers–he taught from the heart and connected to you with his thoughts.

Toward our latter years together, he had a knack for "opening your eyes" as he'd used to say–that is develop your sense of perception to allow even greater flow of knowledge. It's really hard to describe, but it's like the old adage

"better to teach a man how to fish rather than just give him a fish." Pak was the consummate master level instructor and above and beyond all his amazing skills and wisdom, his greatest gift was to teach us how to fish.

How it felt being a Demo Guy at Seminars:

After numerous lessons with Pak, he asked me to be his crash dummy for seminars. It was a privilege and an honor to accept this offer as to feel Pak "put one on you" was the other half of the coin of learning how to do it. Later on, as the owner of an academy in Southern California, I asked if he would teach seminars at my academy.

He agreed and it was fun for all of my students to see me get thrown around like a rag doll (fig. 4) for a couple of days!

The level of control that Pak demonstrated in seminars was truly remarkable. As a dummy for his neck-snapping techniques (those of you who know what I'm talking about truly understand) one

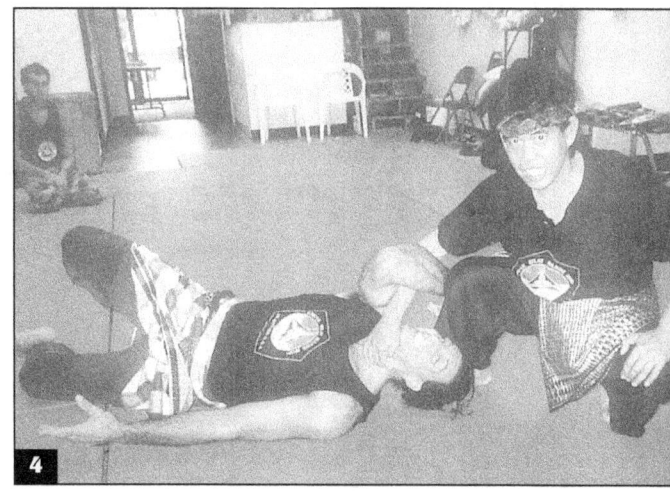

could feel that only another quarter of an inch movement and it would all be over–no more taxes, no more waiting in line at the bank and no need to save for retirement. His control was phenomenal. He could literally toss you across a room with his toes! (fig. 5)

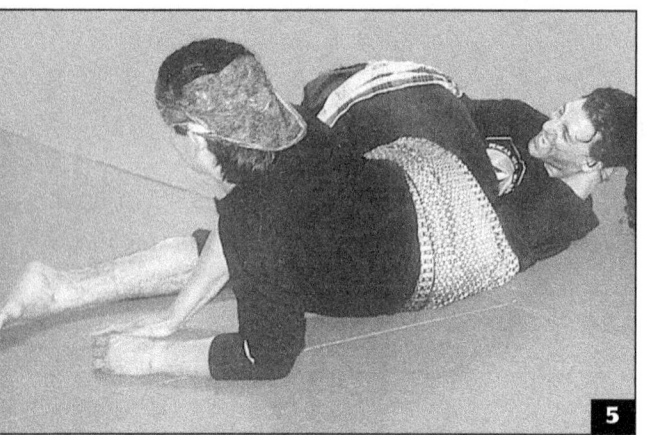

5

As amazing as he appeared, it was all for real. It was never once choreographed or rehearsed in any way. He could tie you up, throw you to the ground and get you to tap so fast it felt like you were caught in a washing machine stuck on spin cycle. But as hard as he hit and as tightly as he held you bound by sometimes even one toe—always the control. Unbelievable control. You could easily feel that he had done these techniques literally thousands of times before and that they were as routine

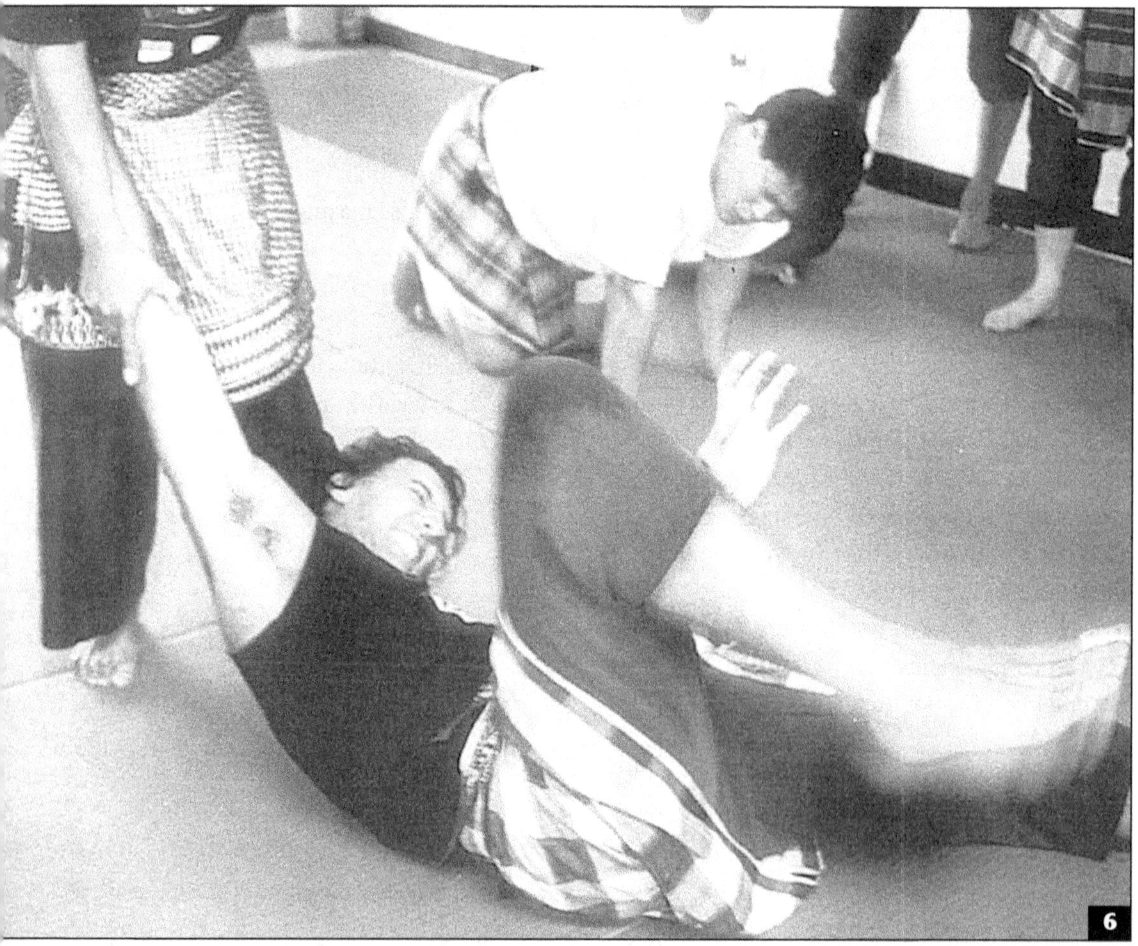

6

to him as tying your shoelace. A lot of times he would be addressing the students and his eyes would not be on me as his training dummy even at times when he was using a live blade! Even at that, the thought never occurred to me that I would be in any way harmed as skill and confidence radiated from his every move (fig. 6).

Sure it was a little bit uncomfortable being slammed to the floor (don't forget that this was in the pre-Brazilian Jiu Jitsu days when not every dojo was matted) but always was his masterful control. It felt almost like he was the puppeteer and your body was a puppet on strings. There's more than one picture of my face looking like it's stuck in a vice-grip between the floor and Pak's shin, knee or elbow!

All in all it was quite a memorable experience. He was strong and moved as quickly and stealthily as a big cat, but at the same time in total control. He could sometimes hit you with a strike that felt like a sledgehammer, but it was to your amazement only a single toe and you think "how the heck can somebody nail you that hard with only a toe??"

Pak was a one of a kind master–one of the few who could walk the walk and you could feel that it was real. By being his punching bag at seminars it was all just the other side of the coin of learning–reality and trust.

The Jagabaya Program and How I Started It:

Throughout the years training with Pak, I noticed a certain direction of training that he was taking me. Similar to my observations and experienced with my Filipino masters, Pak's teachings revolved on a primary focus.

Training with Punong Guro Sulite, an Eskrima master, I noticed that with some students he focused on the double sticks, some students with the single stick and still others with the knife (the area of my focus). Following this same training style, my focal point was both edged and impact weapons. Although the scope of application of the Mande Muda family system was far beyond that of impact and edged weapons, Pak knew that this was a prominent area of my interest as a practitioner (and he also knew that I was a long-time student of Eskrima under Gramndmaster Giron, Guro Inosanto and Punong Guro Edgar Sulite) and he focused upon those areas as such in his instruction–not the least of these being the Karambit.

However, one day he approached me with the concept of Jagabaya. Having been trained the old way ("Boy, you do like this..." from my Filipino masters), I had no interest in ranking whatsoever, but it was something that he strongly suggested I go through and I wasn't going to say no. As far as I was concerned in my mind I was a lifelong student of the arts (and still am) and rank meant very little or nothing to me (and still does). However, he was the master and if he said "go through this program" then I'm going through that program.

It was one of the happiest days of my martial arts life when I introduced Master Tony Somera of the Bahala Na System of Eskrima to Pak Herman. Master Somera, already an accomplished life-long high-ranking martial artist and Master of the Bahala Na System, immediately hit off with Pak and the two remained very close all the way until Pak's passing away (fig. 7). When it came time for testing for Jagabaya there's nobody else on the planet I could think of that I wanted as a testing partner than Master Tony.

The test was delivered (appropriately) at the Inosanto academy in Los Angeles by Pak himself and it was an even happier day when we both found out we had passed! There's a great picture of Pak, Master Tony and myself at the end of the test at the academy—hopefully it will end up in this book! (fig. 8)

Later on Pak pushed me to start training for higher levels of testing, but I was so side-tracked with my continued training that I did not devote the appropriate amount of time necessary to prepare for testing (which I'm not a real fan of anyway) and fell behind in ranking as I "wasted my time" learning more and more about other aspects of the art.

My travel and experience to the training camp in Indonesia:

Traffic was already worse than downtown LA at peak rush hour. The already narrow two-lane "freeway" (if you'd want to call it that) from Jakarta to Bandung had already turned into only one ragged, moonscape motorway. The scores of street children upon noticing the Americans rushed toward the bus when it was stopped in traffic. Thrusting their wares into the windows in hopes for exchanging them for Rupiah, the bus continues its tug and push through huddled masses of pedestrians, sheep and other vehicles.

The humidity was intense compared to the weather in LA from where most of our group originated. Asphalt pavement turned into compacted dust and concrete buildings melted into rows of tea trees as we climbed higher and higher up into the mountains.

Finally, arriving at the training compound located in a valley between two volcanoes—one which had already erupted some time ago and the other one expected to blast off any time soon, we began to unload the tired old bus. Beautiful farm terraces, lush open green fields and a deep humid fog hugged close to the ground gave the surrounding mountains an even more mystic feeling.

Waking up and training with Pak every morning was a truly joy. "Pagi-Pagi" smiled the street vendor's as they rolled out their sate carts. After stretching Pak would take us through various warm-up exercises and then into our training regimen.

The training day was pleasantly broken by a visit from one of Pak Herman's teachers. Today it was Pak Suherman. He spoke only seldom and Pak would translate. The day was replete with rich history of the art and the lineage of each style as demonstrated by my master's master. Pendekar Suherman showed us the stylized movement associated with which village and enlightened us on the how and why a particular move had come to be.

Throughout the training camp, Pak Herman introduced us to many such amazing masters from many different villages. On more than one occasion Pak would take us with him on a trip to some of these villages to meet those masters and experience total emersion of that particular village style and training methodology.

The best part about total immersion in a foreign culture is that it consumes you .

It consumes your senses, your mind and even your very soul as you feel the depth of the teachings from the masters from time immemorial. You are training in the ancient ways of the early villagers on the same patch of dirt that was treaded by the warriors of old. Late at night, when sitting around the camp listening to the exotic sounds of the tropical jungle, you can sometimes hear

drums across the timeless valley and the echo touches you through the humid night mist.

Learning my special skills with the Karambit from Pak:

As mentioned earlier, Pak focused on a different aspect of Mande Muda (the family system) with each of his students. Given my strong interest in the edged and impact weapons areas (as well as the philosophical aspects of the arts), Pak focused more and more upon me with the Karambit as well as the teaching of his indigenous religious philosophies (Agama Kuring).

It was very interesting to see that the two—one the physical and one the philosophical—ran parallel in their courses. When learning how to be direct and fight with positive energy the philosophy behind it exactly mirrored the movements and further even the thought process,

Much like the principals of Yin and Yang, there is the process of positive energy and negative energy and how there cannot be one without the other and further how one is dependent upon the other for its very existence. As this applies to edged-weapon application (specifically the Karambit) so does it apply to the philosophical aspect.

Pak shared with me the history and philosophy of the ancient knife and how it was used in combat in ancient times. Luckily I had foresight enough to write it all down. Years later I was invited by Unique Publications Inc. in the late nineties to write the very first book on the Karambit which was eventually published in 2002.

After a number of private lessons (as well as my journeys to Indonesia and training with Pak's brother who is an amazing practitioner of the Karambit) Pak began to share with me the similarities of straight edged training (such as from the Sabetan system) with curved edged training. There are many similarities but also some stark differences. Much of this information can be found in my book on the Karambit and is directly quoted from my lessons and interviews w/ Pak.

Back then, aside from a handful of obscure martial artists and even fewer students the Karambit was hardly known in the Western world. Now, you can't open a magazine or log onto the internet and not find a Karambit for sale.

My last private session with Pak was at his apartment in Walnut Creek California just around Christmas time. We just finished an amazing training session with the Karambit and it was the first time I really felt like I was finally getting the hang of it. We put down the blade and walked over to the kitchen table to drink some water. His usual bright smiled faded away and he told me that the next year was his time to go.

Recalling an earlier conversation in West Java, as he did mention this before how an elderly woman psychic had predicted his departure, it didn't make sense to me as he was a young man still under 50 years of age. But, he said something to me that sticks in my memory forever: "Steve, I'm not going to be around soon, I want you to keep this art alive in America".

How it felt to be around Pak when he was not teaching seminars

Regardless of where we were, be it in some hotel somewhere in the Midwest or out in LA at the Inosanto Academy or standing along side a volcano in West Java, Pak loved to train. We trained at night we trained during the day, after hours, before seminars, after seminars and any chance we could. When we weren't training, Pak would teach us about the history and the philosophy of the art and share with us the teachings of his father and other teachers who influenced his life.

Pak was profoundly deep however thoroughly enjoyed trying new things and having fun. Somewhere there's a picture of Pak, Scott Brady, Paul "Ted" Grybow, myself and a couple of other guys just coming out of a Native American style sweat lodge–something Pak always wanted to try. There's also another shot of us all goofing around with Pak clad in a leather jacket and posing with a shotgun! (like he needs a shotgun!!). Very playful, always quick with the one-liners and appreciates a good joke.

One time in Lembang (at night after a long day of hard training), Pak asked us what we wanted most while we were there training in the Indonesian heat. We about all cried out in unison "cold beer"! He laughed and actually went for a walk with us (a LONG walk—make that a hike) to where you'd never believe it but they sold cold beer!!! Later this became one of our favorite phrases in Bahasay Indonesian (the national language) "Bir Dingin"—cold beer!

Although his fun-loving personality shone through when he was also teaching (seminars, classes or private sessions) he was a dangerous mixture of light fun and games and deadly effective technique. On hell of a great balance in my opinion!

A Fun Story I would like to include about Pak:

One time when we were training by his home in West Java, I remember Pak telling us that we were going to visit Cimande village later on in that week. A couple days had gone by and some things happened where we couldn't go until the following week.

There were no phones and no cell phones and no radios, CBs or walkie-talkies where we were so there's no way in hell that a message could have gone from Pak's village to Cimande village (many miles away) other than by foot (word of mouth). So that next day for whatever reason Pak decides that now was the time to go to Cimande village. He finds Harry (the driver) and a bus to fit us all in and we hastily grab a few items and load the bus. Some of us went and some stayed behind—a random number of us sat on the bus and hung on for dear life.

The bus ride was something out of an Indiana Jones movie. First off the roads aren't really much other than a dirt path with pot holes the size of small craters. There were kids, goats and chickens running around all over the place and of course no speed limits and those dirt "roads" were the VERY edged of very tall cliffs in some places.

So the driver is flying in between wooden carts and farm animals dodging little kids and old ladies and squawking poultry. Pak is talking to us from up front next to the driver's seat. There's dust and rocks flying everywhere and you can barely hear Pak over the din of the road noise and the 1967 oil-belching motor pushing that old bus.

Looking through the front window you see chickens and other objects bouncing off the road and Pak continuing to smile and play tour guide. The bus suddenly veers into a larger truck coming straight at us head on at a high speed. Pak calmly leans over to Harry and says "you may want to avoid that truck", Harry nods and you couldn't have gotten a piece of paper between the molecular space that Harry missed the truck. We were all wide-eyed and trying to relocate our internal organs all the while Pak is still smiling–just another day at the office.

After our harrowing drive we dismounted and headed out into the open field at Cimande village. Amidst the wide-eyed gaze of the local villagers, we were definitely unexpected that day and Pak (speaking one of the unbelievable number of dialects he knows) strikes up a conversation with one of the kids. The kid goes running off and Pak beckons us to follow him.

Right around the corner, a family of Pak's relatives living in a grass wall hut had prepared the exact number of "plates" and "snacks" for us (how did they know we were even coming? And further how did they know how many?) Pak smiled his usual smile, introduced us to his relatives and welcomed us to Cimande Village!

What I remember when I heard about his parting:

Back in those days I owned and operated a martial arts training academy in Southern California. I remember training that day and getting a phone call from one of my students in Germany. He said I should be sitting down and he told me what happened.

At first I wasn't sitting down, but then my knees made that decision as he proceeded with the details.

It was not easy to accept at first, but then I remembered what he told us in Java and what again he mentioned only a couple of months earlier around Christmas that this was his last year and that it was his time to move on.

His last words to me were "Steve, keep the art alive in America" and so if you want to find out more you can contact me through this book, Grandmaster Somera, or even the internet as I'm a busy guy–keeping the art alive.

Steve Tarani

Epilogue

On March 22, 2000 while traveling in Europe conducting Pencak Silat Mande Muda seminars and on their way to Holland to conduct their next seminar, Herman Suwanda at the young age of 45 along with his wife Shannon age 30, along with Franziska Valena Holz, 25, Sang Min Chun, 31 and Carsten Domke, 31, were all killed instantly. The automobile accident occurred near the town of Pruem, Germany. Herman and Shannon Suwanda have been educating students all over the world about the history, culture, physical and spiritual teachings of Pencak Silat Mande Muda. Both of these great individuals were at the highlight of their careers. Pak Herman's dream for America was to have a silat academy in every state and to spread the art of his Indonesian homeland worldwide.

Pendekar Suwanda or "Pak" as he was known, assumed the leadership of his family art upon his father's death and took his system from the jungles and remote villages of Indonesia to the farthest reaches of the globe. He came to America during the 1980's and affected countless people in a positive way by creating a close knit, supportive family of martial artists and friends. He was a rare individual who was both a talented educator and a skillful, trained fighter. World-renowned Guro Dan Inosanto remarked, "Pak Herman is like the Bruce Lee of Indonesia."

His love of the art was equaled only by his love of life and his love for his students. He transcended his art to encompass a higher power that elevated everyone around him to a high physical, mental and spiritual plane. Many of his students loved not only Herman Suwanda the great martial artist, but also Herman Suwanda the wonderful human being. He hand the rare gift of being able to direct his students and friends into being productive martial artist in our fighting systems and better people to our friends and families.

Many times while executing a technique, he would stop to discuss his family before continuing to twist the student's arms and legs like a pretzel. He was never satisfied with any technique and always strove to 'take it to the next level." Although Pak possessed the ability to break your bones, choke you out, or tie you up in a knot, he had the touch, grace, and character to be your teacher on the mat and your dear friend off the mat. Pak was also a great provider. He and Shannon didn't drive a big car, or live in a fancy house or wear expensive clothes; they lived a simple and unselfish life. He was a simple man who provided his poor village with clothing, food and jobs. He and Shannon supported over 12 families and sent over 24 children to school and supported them financially. He mixed camaraderie and respect, happiness and passion, and wisdom and humor, with unimpeachable family values. This is how many people would explain Pak Herman to those of you that will never meet him. Pak Herman and Shannon taught us how to be good human beings and how his culture was not much different than ours. We will miss you both, but will share the knowledge you gave us to all of those that will never have the chance to play with you. God Bless you Herman and Shannon.

Antonio Somera

A Pictorial Memoir

A Pictorial Memoir

Indonesian Martial Arts: Pencak Silat

A Pictorial Memoir

325

A Pictorial Memoir

www.ingramcontent.com/pod-product-compliance
Lightning Source LLC
Chambersburg PA
CBHW081344080526
44588CB00016B/2368